CONCEIVED
in LIBERTY

American Individual
Rights Today

by **ELLIS SANDOZ**
East Texas State University

DUXBURY PRESS
North Scituate / Massachusetts

Library of Congress Cataloging in Publication Data

Sandoz, Ellis, 1931–
  Conceived in liberty.

  Includes index.
  1. Civil Rights—United States—Cases. I. Title
KF4748.S24   342'.73'085   77–18506
ISBN 0–87872–162–2

Duxbury Press
A Division of Wadsworth Publishing Company, Inc.

Conceived in Liberty: American Individual Rights Today was edited and
prepared for composition by Elaine Selle. Interior design was provided
by Dorothy Booth and the cover was designed by Oliver Kline.

L.C. Cat. Card No.: 77–18506
ISBN 0–87872–162–2
Printed in the United States of America

1 2 3 4 5 6 7 8 9 – 82 81 80 79 78

For my Wife, Alverne,
and our children:
Ellis III,
Lisa,
Erica,
Jonathan

CONTENTS

. . . we do, for Us, our Heirs, and Successors, Declare, by these Presents, that all and every the Persons being our Subjects, which shall dwell and inhabit within every or any of the said several Colonies and Plantations, and every of their children, which shall happen to be born within any of the Limits and Precincts of the said several Colonies and Plantations, shall have and enjoy all Liberties, Franchises, and Immunities, within any of our other Dominions, to all Intents and Purposes, as if they had been abiding and born, within this our Realm of England. . . .[1]

KING JAMES I, *First Charter of Virginia* (1606)

Our commitment to human rights must be absolute, our laws fair, our natural beauty preserved; the powerful must not persecute the weak, and human dignity must be enhanced.[2]

PRESIDENT JAMES EARL CARTER
(January 20, 1977)

PREFACE

From King James to President James Earl Carter is a long way. But a long tradition links them together. From the first colonial charter in our history to the latest presidential inaugural address, individual liberty as guaranteed by law has remained a constant priority. I have written this small book as one man's celebration of the American tradition of liberty. I confess that it is as much exhortation as information. For I am convinced that liberty and justice as they are pursued in America compose the crowning glory of government in our civilization. It is the grand tradition of liberty in specific detail, and its current state in this country, then, that is the subject of this book. I have here sought to make the subject vital and intelligible and to do so with brevity. Ideally, this book can be used for a number of courses in American government, constitutional law, and civil liberties offered in either political science or history programs.

Liberty in America is both a millennial theme and a living thing. From the dawn of civilization, people have divided into the slave and the free, and they remain so today. President Carter noted this division in speaking on human rights in the first several months of his administration. His statements caused alliances to be threatened and negotiations on important international issues to break down. Why? He had spoken on a subject that is taboo in most of the world—the fostering of human rights. Freedom of people is a philosophical principle contested and rejected by dictator and ideologue alike. Among the some 150 nations in the world today, barely two dozen enjoy free government. Far from living in the greatest age of liberty in human history, we might say that we live in the greatest age of calculated servitude since Israel's exodus from the Egyptian Empire three millennia ago.

Since liberty is a living thing, and fragile, it demands constant nurturing from its beneficiaries. The rhetoric of "human rights" is more in the tradition of the French Revolution than our own, the expansive language of the Declaration of Independence notwithstanding. Great and noble as the Declaration's self-evident truths are, Thomas Jefferson as their author knew that their self-evidence arose from the constitutional history of England. America was a living continuity of political experience and increasingly democratic institutions. The self-evident truths were actually operative principles of free government *only* in the concrete setting of the Anglo-American tradition. And there the decisive form was the protection of individual rights against government's abuse and abridgment. The specific protection of a person's particular rights under the law was the key.

Thus, in 1215 the Magna Carta set the pattern from which we have never departed. It took the form of protecting "any free man" (*liber homo*) from arbitrary and capricious rule. Rights and justice are transcendent, and they are secured to individual persons by the constitution and laws composing the "law of the land." The rights so protected, now so long ago, in the thirteenth century against an obstreperous King John, were as narrowly defined and specific as could be. They were politically as well as legally enforceable.

Human rights in America, then, is no fuzzy concept. Every individual person enjoys them under our Constitution. The "law of the land,"—a phrase from the middle of the thirteenth century—has become interchangeable with the phrase, "due process of law." The protection afforded individuals today still applies mainly, if not solely, against invasion of rights by governments and overzealous bureaucrats. As the Supreme Court remarked in 1972: "One might fairly say of the Bill of Rights in general, and the Due Process Clause in particular, that they were designed to protect the fragile values of a vulnerable citizenry from the overbearing concern for efficiency and efficacy that may characterize praiseworthy government officials no less, and perhaps more, than mediocre ones" (*Stanley* v. *Illinois*, 405 U.S. 645).

Every time the courts and legislatures—and especially the United States Supreme Court and the Congress—convene, they modify individual liberty and shape its configuration in new ways. This befits a living tradition. The main line betrays great continuity, however, as I have been suggesting.

The complexities and extent of American individual rights can only be sketched in the short space I have used. For fuller and more detailed information, the key sources are the Court's decisions themselves, collected as the *United States Reports* and as the *Supreme Court Reporter*. Several other valuable sources are the following: Bernard Schwartz, ed., *The Bill of Rights: A Documentary History* (2 vols.; New York: McGraw Hill, 1971); Bernard Schwartz, *The Great Rights of Mankind: A History of the American Bill of Rights* (New York: Oxford University Press, 1977); *The Constitution of the United States of America: Analysis and Interpretation* (Washington, D.C.: Government Printing Office, 1973), updated every two years with a *Supplement*, completely revised every ten years; Edward S. Corwin, *The Constitution and What It Means Today*, revised by Harold W. Chase and Craig R. Ducat (13th ed.; Princeton: Princeton University Press, 1974). A number of good casebooks are available, and there is an enormous literature on specialized questions.

It remains to acknowledge with thanks at least a few of those who have helped me in this work, without of course attributing to them its shortcomings. Professor Robert J. Harris, now of the University of Virginia, initiated me in an unforgettable way into the mysteries of constitutional law when I was a mere undergraduate student. The Earhart Foundation supported my work on this project with a fellowship. The editorial staff and academic consultants of Duxbury Press gave great assistance at each step of the way toward publication, and Bob Gormley, the publisher, never lost faith that something worthwhile would come of my efforts. My secretary Ms. Karen Harrison became convinced she should become a lawyer while typing the manuscript, so Ms. Susan E. Willbern picked-up the task and continued it in expert style through the final revision. To these and to many others, I am most grateful for assistance and encouragement.

*. . . our fathers brought forth on this continent
a new nation, conceived in liberty, and
dedicated to the proposition that all men are
created equal.*

ABRAHAM LINCOLN

Introduction

. . . the end of this kind of study is not
knowledge but action.[1]

ARISTOTLE (ca. 330 B.C.)

. . . the people of the Colonies [in America] are
descendants of Englishmen. England, sir, is a
nation, which I hope respects, and formerly
adored her freedom. The [Americans] . . . are . . .
not only devoted to liberty, but to liberty according
to English ideas and on English principles. . . .
As long as you have the wisdom to keep the
sovereign authority of this country as the
sanctuary of liberty, the sacred temple consecrated
to our common faith, wherever the . . . sons of
England worship freedom, they will turn their
faces toward you. . . . Slavery they can have
anywhere.[2]

EDMUND BURKE (1775)

W hen the aged Benjamin Franklin walked out of the State House in Philadelphia after adjournment of the Constitutional Convention on September 17, 1787, a Mrs. Powell stopped him to ask, "What have we got, a republic or a monarchy?" "A republic," Franklin replied, "if you can keep it!" [3]

Despite the difficulties of the following two centuries, the republic has been kept alive. The considerable effort required seems to me to have been eminently worthwhile. Yet if we are to keep the American republic alive and well through its third century, we must continue to practice the art of political maintenance that Franklin's response implied.

Framers of the Constitution in 1787 regularly described it as establishing "free government," pointing out that liberty lies at the heart of the American democratic republic. This book is about that liberty as it animates our living Constitution. The rallying cry for the nation coming-to-be was Patrick Henry's "Give me liberty or give me death!" It was the cry of one free man among others who would rather be free than merely exist at any price. Patrick Henry was neither a fanatic nor extraordinarily brave. But he—and they— knew that not to be free negates human existence.

The Americans who declared and fought for independence clearly believed they were seriously threatened with a kind of slavery by their British brothers, led by King George III and his ministers. Thomas Paine well understood the American preoccupation with liberty and fear of enslavement, and wrote pamphlet after pamphlet on these subjects. His earliest *Crisis* paper was first read to men gathered around campfires on Christmas Eve, 1776, in the deep gloom of retreat on the night before Washington's famed crossing of the Delaware. Paine said:

> Britain, with an army to enforce her tyranny, has declared that she has a right (not only to TAX) but "TO BIND us in ALL CASES WHATSOEVER," and if being bound in that manner, is not slavery, then is there not such a thing as slavery on earth. Even the expression [from Parliament's Declaratory Act of 1766] is impious; for so unlimited a power can belong only to God.[4]

During the War of Independence, all the new states adopted constitutions that explicitly protected individual rights; nine states adopted separate bills of rights while the other four (New Jersey, Georgia, New York, and South Carolina) incorporated protections into the body of their constitutions.[5] The first constitution for the whole country (the Articles of Confederation) so reflected touchiness about personal and state freedoms as to be unworkable as a general pattern of government for the nation. The American penchant for writing down, in constitutions and bills of rights, the powers of government and the liberties of persons is in no small part traceable to their devotion to liberty. Government's limits and people's rights are better secured by written documents.

The history of the United States is a biography of liberty. It is what the country is all about. Dedication to liberty fueled the Abolitionist movement in the second quarter of the nineteenth century and helped precipitate the Civil War in the 1860s. It also spurred the amendment of the Constitution, after Lee's surrender to Grant at Appomattox, to outlaw slavery and create powerful new protections for all citizens, regardless of race, creed, or color. It inspired the doctrine of Manifest Destiny as well as westward expansion to another ocean, which then became one more frontier. It was the nerve of policy decisions involving the nation in two great world wars in the twentieth century, one to "Make the World Safe for Democracy," the other to excise the cancer of totalitarianism. It formed a continuity with the old Abolitionist zeal to foster a new civil rights movement in the twentieth century.

Dedication to liberty prompted the rhetoric of political discourse in an era of hot and cold war in which the United States stood as a leader of the free world against expansive communism. It has repeatedly and in strange places exacted the price Patrick Henry claimed he would pay (but did not) from generations of our youth, at terrible cost in countless lives lost scarcely before they had begun. It is personified by a statue at the mouth of New York harbor to beckon the oppressed and despised of unfree lands to more hospitable shores. Dedication to liberty gave hope to humankind in a world of hopelessness. It inspired another statue of freedom which crowns the dome of the nation's Capitol, silently presiding over all our decisions of state. Liberty, as Lincoln well knew, is both the faith of the nation and a remorseless taskmaster.

But if liberty is as natural to America as air, it still is to constitutional provision that one must turn to learn line and verse of our individual rights. The scope of these rights will be surveyed here. We will see that these rights stress the sanctity of the individual. The most important of them are contained in the first ten Amendments to the Constitution, known as the Bill of Rights (*see* Appendix B).

Merely reading the Bill of Rights, however, is not enough to gain a grasp of the subject. One must turn to the writings of experts on the law who compose our judiciary for interpretations of its meaning. This is especially true since in America the courts are empowered to say what our Constitution means and therefore what the law is— short of changing the law through congressional enactment or constitutional amendment. However, our courts pronounce on the law on a case-by-case basis and (supposedly) only when they absolutely have to because of concrete grievances formally brought before them by individual persons. The courts do not give advisory opinions about legal questions [6] or proclaim the word about constitutional rights to the public by issuing press releases and manifestos.

I shall, then, give a summary sketch of what our individual liberties are today. These have been gradually defined, refined, and redefined, especially through decisions rendered by the Supreme Court of the United States since it began operating in 1790. The complex processes of revision and constant adaptation of abiding principles to changing needs of American society lie at the core of all this adjudication.

Why does the Bill of Rights appear as a series of amendments to the Constitution and not as part of the basic document itself? The question was raised from the beginning of the debate over ratification of the Constitution. The framers were suspected, because of the absence of a Bill of Rights, of being engaged in "a conspiracy against the liberties of the people," as Alexander Hamilton admitted in the final installment of *The Federalist* (No. 85).[7] The attacks were not ended by the several arguments offered in defense of the omission.

Hamilton pointed to the rights actually mentioned in the body of the Constitution as proof that basic liberties were, in fact, protected by the document: the writ of habeas corpus, jury trials, prohibitions against issuing titles of nobility, passing bills of attainder and *ex post facto* laws, the narrow definition of treason, vesting impeachment power in Congress. He argued that bills of rights are for protection against kings, gained "with sword in hand," and are out of place in a constitution "professedly founded upon the power of the people and executed by their immediate representatives and servants."

Such a bill of rights might even be dangerous, Hamilton thought, since the enumeration of rights could never be exhaustive and might lead to the possibility of invasion either by the very mention of the right or by its omission from the list. He hinted that the continuation in force of the ancient law of England, the common law and the statutes, under the new Constitution carried with it protection in America of all those rights previously secured by Englishmen. He asked, "Why ... should it be said that the liberty of the press shall not be restrained, when no power is given [in the Constitution] by which restrictions may be imposed?" Anyway, he said in good debating style, "the Constitution is itself ... A BILL OF RIGHTS"! [8]

Hamilton's arguments in *The Federalist* did not persuade the skeptical, however. Thomas Jefferson wrote from Paris to James Madison just before Christmas, 1787, to say what he liked and disliked about the proposed Constitution. What he most disliked was

> the omission of a bill of rights, providing clearly, and without the aid of sophism for freedom of religion, freedom of press, protection against standing armies, restriction of monopolies, the eternal and unremitting force of the habeas corpus laws, and trials by jury in all matters of fact triable by the laws of the land. ... Let me add that a bill of rights is what the people are entitled to against every government on earth, general or particular; and what no just government should refuse, or rest on inference. [9]

Similar complaints were heard everywhere in the country. Ratification of the Constitution was bargained for on the promise that a bill of rights would be drafted by the new Congress as priority business when it met under the new instrument of government. Madison

"It's agreed, then. You'll back us on Search and
Seizure. And we'll throw in the people's right to
keep and bear arms."
Source: © 1976 The Chicago Tribune-New York News
Syndicate.

himself was hard pressed by his antiFederalist opponent James Monroe in his campaign for election to the House of Representatives and so made a promise to lead the fight for a bill of rights in Congress if elected. By the time the first Congress under the Constitution assembled in Federal Hall in New York City on March 4, 1789, eight states had recommended some 210 amendments—containing 100 different provisions—for inclusion in a bill of rights. Madison made good on his campaign promise. Congress adopted a bill of rights as a series of twelve proposed constitutional amendments by September 1789. Ten of them were ratified by the necessary three-fourths of the states by December 1791, making our Bill of Rights part of the law of the land. The first two of the proposed twelve amendments—one dealing with apportionment of representatives in the House and the size of the House, the other with changing compensation of senators and representatives—failed to be ratified.

It remains for me to say a word about my approach to the subject matter in *Conceived in Liberty*. This book is a concise survey of individual rights as defined today. It is suitable as a textbook in college courses in American government, law enforcement, criminal justice, and constitutional law where a brief, self-contained interpretation of individual rights is wanted. It can be used in courses where a casebook is the primary text and the "discovery" method otherwise employed. Many cases are cited herein, and my interpretation of them can be matched with the interpretations arrived at by students and professors on the basis of their own reading of primary materials.

My bias runs to stressing two major dimensions of individual liberty. First, I think it is impossible to grasp the meaning of individual rights without being mindful of the historical tradition behind the liberties protected by our Constitution. No mere inventory will do. Rights did not grow up overnight like weeds. While this book is not a constitutional history, its approach must be historical: this is the way in which the rights emerged. It is the way in which the Supreme Court expounded and defined them; and it is what helped supply the settled quality of force of law through which liberty actually shaped and structured the American political and social order. Liberty is a living historical, theoretical, and legal process.

Second, I have stressed the ways in which the Supreme Court has defined individual liberty. This has two main consequences. One is to treat at some length the theoretical perspective of the Court which (taking a cue from Professor Edward S. Corwin) I call the "higher law" core of the subject.[10] I have dealt with this problem in chapters 1 and 2, especially by tracing the development of liberty through substantive due process. The other consequence is to rely heavily on the decisions and language of the Court itself in explaining the meaning of the various liberties. Whatever precision individual liberty has in this country is squarely dependent on the judges' definition of it. Since judges speak in the form of Court decisions, I rely on these. Accordingly, I must restrict my coverage of such significant factors as economic, sociological, and political developments in order to keep the treatment brief and focus on the subject of the law itself.

Conceived in Liberty covers the whole range of liberties protected today by the U.S. Constitution. I have tried to make it a reliable guide to the subject and at the same time add my own interpretations. You are invited to arrive at your own. Each of the chapters opens with quotations followed by a Supreme Court case, selected to show philosophical viewpoints and encounters with the law significant for the chapter's subject. The grandeur of liberty will often be seen to emerge from trivial or banal events. Such is the stuff of human existence. From such stuff even leading constitutional law decisions are sometimes made.

After staking out the terrain in the first two chapters and examining the large issues of due process and how the Court functions, I will discuss in chapter 3 the great First Amendment liberties of religion, speech, press, assembly, and petition. Chapter 4 traces the array of rights that come into play in the process of criminal justice, a large subject. Chapter 5 addresses the topic of civil rights in race relations, another large subject. In my Conclusion, I will briefly examine the privileges, meaning, and duties of American citizenship and reflect on the performance and promise of the system. Appendix A presents the Declaration of Independence, and Appendix B, the Constitution.

The extent and complexity of individual rights is such that discussion of any one of them—freedom of speech, trial by jury, due process of law—could easily fill a book. I have sought to be brief. More comprehensive treatments abound, some of them identified in the preface and footnotes. Whatever value this volume has lies simply in this: it supplies a concise statement of American individual rights today. When you finish reading it, you will have a pretty clear idea of what your rights are. If it does this in a way that stirs devotion to liberty, then my main purpose in writing this book will have been fulfilled.

CHAPTER ONE

Liberty, Law, and Due Process

. . . the laws of the land, administered by upright judges, would protect you from any exercise of power unauthorized by the Constitution of the United States.[1]

THOMAS JEFFERSON (1798)

The Constitution is either a superior paramount law, unchangeable by ordinary means, or it is on a level with ordinary legislative acts alterable when the legislature shall please to alter it. . . . It is emphatically the province and duty of the judicial department to say what the law is. . . . This is the very essence of judicial duty.[2]

JOHN MARSHALL (1803)

To consider the judges as the ultimate arbiters of all constitutional questions . . . would place us under the despotism of an oligarchy.[3]

THOMAS JEFFERSON (1820)

MARBURY v. MADISON

I T SEEMED ALL BUT CERTAIN that William Marbury would, at long last, receive his appointment as justice of the peace in the District of Columbia. It was February 1803, and the Supreme Court had convened for a new term. Marbury had waited for two years since President John Adams, during the final seventy-two hours of his administration, had tardily rushed Marbury's and forty-one other persons' names through the then heavily Federalist Senate for confirmation as justices of the peace. John Marshall, Adams's Secretary of State and himself the newly appointed Chief Justice of the United States, had in the last minute rush of the expiring term forgotten (or neglected) to send out the commissions to the new JP appointees. He left the commissions in sealed and addressed envelopes stacked on his desk when he vacated his old office to the new administration.

Thomas Jefferson's Republican administration was then sworn in, James Madison was named the new Secretary of State, and only twenty-five of the commissions were sent out. Marbury was one of the seventeen Federalist appointees Jefferson instructed Madison not to notify. Why should so many members of the defeated opposition party be awarded these federal positions, anyway?

Background of the Marbury Case

The positions themselves were of trifling importance. But, in December 1801, four of the slighted appointees (Marbury among them) brought suit against Madison and asked Marshall for relief. Marshall responded by ordering Secretary Madison to show cause at the next term of the Supreme Court why a writ of mandamus (a command from the Court to perform a specific duty) should not be awarded ordering him to deliver the commission to Marbury. Everyone anticipated that the case would be decided in Marbury's favor by the Federalist-controlled Supreme Court at its June 1802 term.

But the new Congress was dominated by Republicans, and the Federalist judiciary was under heavy attack by Jefferson and his followers. Above all, the Republicans feared that the Marshall-led Supreme Court would assert power to declare acts passed by Congress unconstitutional, thereby asserting the power of judicial review. To forestall the possibility they enacted a statute that abolished the Court's June term. Therefore, Marbury had to wait until 1803 to have his day in court. In effect, the Supreme Court itself had been abolished by Republican congressional majorities for fourteen months.

In addition, the Republicans were openly threatening impeachment and removal from office of Marshall and other Federalist judges who dared challenge Republican power, especially if the Marbury case turned out as they thought it would. The threat was no idle one. The Federalist judge from Pennsylvania, Alexander Addison, was swiftly impeached and removed from office in January 1803. Nine days later (February 4, 1803) Jefferson himself initiated the motion for impeachment and removal of Judge John Pickering from the U.S. District Court of New Hampshire. The United States House and Senate complied, and Pickering was impeached, convicted, and removed in March. Within an hour of the Senate's vote, Associate Justice Samuel Chase of the U.S. Supreme Court, a signer of the Declaration of Independence and an authentic hero of the American Revolution, was impeached by the House of Representatives. Were

Chase convicted, Marshall would surely be next. Senator William Branch Giles of Virginia had candidly announced the logic of Jefferson's attack: "Removal by impeachment was nothing more," he said, "than a declaration by Congress to this effect: You hold dangerous opinions, and if you are suffered to carry them into effect you will work the destruction of the Nation." [4]

A grave constitutional crisis clearly was brewing. States' Rights advocates were in ascendance, and their leading spokesman sat in the President's office. The burning issue was: Who had authority to declare a national law unconstitutional, hence null and void? The Constitution was silent on the subject. Virginia and Kentucky had asserted that any state might do so. That sentiment grew tremendously with the election of Virginia's favorite son, Jefferson, to the presidency in 1800. Congress, as representative of the people, claimed that it might do so. Jefferson himself held that each of the three branches of the federal government had that power, and as President he had already formally declared the Sedition Act unconstitutional in December 1801, and refused to enforce its provisions. Leading Federalists threatened secession in hot debates in the House and Senate over the issue of judicial review.

Against this turbulent background, Chief Justice Marshall took the trivial occasion of Marbury's now more than half-expired commission to address the burning issue of the day. Nobody outside the Court dreamed that he would do so. Marbury's case was argued by Charles Lee, the former U.S. Attorney General, on the basis of SECTION 13 of the JUDICIARY ACT OF 1789. That statute, enacted by Congress and already the basis of two previous cases decided by the Supreme Court, extended the Supreme Court's original jurisdiction beyond the parties explicitly mentioned in the body of the Constitution.

The Supreme Court Decision

On February 24, 1803, the decision was finally made in MAR-
BURY v. MADISON, with the Chief Justice speaking for a unanimous Court.[5] He began by pointing out the novelty and delicacy
of the issues before the Court. Marshall took 7000 words to reach
the issue of constitutionality. Along the way he affirmed that
Marbury had, indeed, been appointed to his office in the way
prescribed by the Constitution, and that he was entitled to it
since the commission itself was merely formal evidence of a
valid appointment. To bar him from that office by withholding
the commission was unwarranted and violated a vested legal
right. Marshall stressed that "the very essence of civil liberty
certainly consists in the right of every individual to claim protection of the laws, whenever he receives an injury. One of the
first duties of government is to afford that protection."

Marshall went on to say that ours has been "emphatically
termed a government of laws, and not of men. It will certainly
cease to deserve this high appellation, if the laws furnish no
remedy for the violation of a vested right. . . ." The delivery of
the commission moreover was commanded by statute: it was not
merely a political act, but a legal duty of the Executive, which
was ministerial, not admitting of discretion. Since it was the duty
of the courts to determine whether a right was vested by statute,
the question was a judicial one. The Court decided that Madison's refusal to deliver Marbury's commission was "a plain violation of that right, for which the laws of his country afford him
a remedy."

But was the correct remedy the writ of mandamus sought by
Marbury? Marshall saw nothing in the exalted station of the
Secretary of State that exempted him from "being compelled to
obey the judgment of the law." Mandamus was the correct

remedy specified by law. The remaining question, then, was whether the Supreme Court had the power to issue such a writ?

Marshall found that it did not. He believed that the power to issue such relief, not being granted to the Supreme Court by the Constitution itself, could not be subsequently granted to it simply by congressional enactment of a law. Hence, that congressional act (SEC. 13, JUDICIARY ACT OF 1789) was "not warranted by the Constitution." The Chief Justice, having by now expended 9000 words, came at last to the question of questions: Can "an act repugnant to the Constitution . . . become the law of the land"? Does the Supreme Court have the power to declare an act passed by Congress and signed by the President null and void because it was unconstitutional? In other words, does judicial power under the Constitution include the power of judicial review?

It does and it must, was Marshall's answer to the last question. The very purpose of our written Constitution, he explained, was to insure that we enforce the "fundamental" and "permanent" principles limiting the powers of the department of government. The Constitution is "a superior paramount law" that cannot be altered by Congress as though it were on the same level as ordinary legislative enactments. "The Constitution controls any legislative act repugnant to it." It is the "very essence of judicial duty" to determine whether a statute conflicts with the Constitution, and to prefer the Constitution whenever one does—unless the Court wishes to be in the absurd position of declaring "that an act which . . . is entirely void, is yet . . . completely obligatory" and that the Congress may do "what is expressly forbidden."

Marshall's conclusion, then, was: "A law repugnant to the Constitution is void; and . . . courts, as well as other departments, are bound by that instrument." SECTION 13 of the JUDICIARY

ACT OF 1789 was found unconstitutional. The Supreme Court could issue no writ of mandamus as a relief to William Marbury. He never received his appointment as justice of the peace after all.

Implications of the Marbury Case

This trivial occasion resulted in one of the greatest decisions ever rendered by the U.S. Supreme Court. It established once and for all the key doctrine of judicial review whereby our courts are empowered to say with finality what the Constitution means and declare invalid state and federal acts that conflict with its provisions. MARBURY v. MADISON was the first occasion in which a congressional enactment was declared unconstitutional. The next such declaration would not come for over half a century when, in 1857, the DRED SCOTT case was decided, which invalidated the Missouri Compromise, thereby judicially setting the stage for the Civil War.

John Marshall, for his part, had only just begun his great work as Chief Justice of the United States. Because Associate Justice Chase was acquitted in the Senate of the impeachment charges made against him, the purging of the Federalist judiciary by the Republican Congress subsided, and Marshall escaped impeachment. He rendered decision after decision of cardinal importance before retiring from the bench in 1835, but none more significant than that in Mr. Marbury's unlikely case.

The quotations from Jefferson and Marshall at the beginning of this chapter point toward the practical matter of establishing liberty under law. This core issue might be addressed by the following question: Since we have no angels to govern us, who shall say with finality what is law? The rising presidential star of Thomas Jefferson

in 1798 found him engaged in establishing the Democratic Party—
then called the "Republican Party" to everyone's confusion nowadays.
The judges, he said, will administer the laws and protect liberty from
unauthorized political actions. President Jefferson's viewpoint was
not supported by Chief Justice John Marshall, who rendered the
opinion in *Marbury* v. *Madison* (1803) that established once and
for all the proposition that the Constitution is superior in force to
Congress's enacted laws, which can be voided by the Supreme Court
in case of conflict. Nowhere did the Constitution clearly award such
a power to the Court, the power of "judicial review" or "judicial
supremacy." Jefferson did not, as we saw from the account just given,
like the decision when Marshall gave it. And he did not like it seventeen years later when he blasted the judiciary's assertion of final authority to declare what is, or what is not, the law of the land as the
"despotism of an oligarchy." The tensions illustrated here between
the demands of impartial justice and fairness on one side, and of
responsiveness to the will of the people in this democratic nation on
the other, continue to structure the American debate over the role
of the independent judiciary as one of the three coordinate branches of
the nation's government. Chief Justice Marshall clearly won his
cause, but Thomas Jefferson did not entirely lose his.

In the balance of this chapter we will sketch briefly the meaning of
certain key concepts of our constitutional system, including rule of
law, liberty, and judicial review. We will discuss the large subject of
due process, and the basic distinctions between procedural and substantive due process. We will clarify the meaning of "higher law"
as used herein, and show how it links together such varied developments as the "old" and "new" substantive due process, substantive
equal protection, the Court's elevation of certain protections of the
Bill of Rights into a "preferred position" and ultimately into a national application to all states by way of the Fourteenth Amendment.
We will then continue to sketch this extensive and core process of
constitutional development in chapter 2.

It is because of a single decision that our entire discussion of liberty in America is devoted to Court decisions. We turn now to it.

Rule of Law

As *Marbury* v. *Madison* stressed, law in America is paramount over governors and rulers as well as over ordinary citizens. This is the core principle of constitutional government itself. Indeed, the person who holds political power may be suspect on principle by this concept. His powers are limited. They can only be exercised according to established procedures. By implication, the reason of the law confronts the desire of the human governor. In the general context of our whole system of government, this assumed opposition is the very foundation of the "separation of powers" into legislative, executive, and judicial branches, an elaborate "system of checks and balances" woven into the Constitution. This opposition lies at the heart of the entire institutional pattern, and is the basis of the concurrent or dual sovereignty between the national and state governments within their respective spheres of the American federal system. In summary, the fact that the powers of government are limited by law, and that the limits are enforceable through established procedures, is the substance of constitutionalism itself. Ours is a government of laws, not of men. The law must be both reasonable and just, as Aristotle asserted over 2000 years ago in *Politics*:

> ... the rule of law ... is preferable to that of any man. ... [For] he who bids the law rule may be deemed to bid God and Reason alone rule, but he who bids man rule adds an element of the beast; for desire is a wild beast, and passion perverts the minds of rulers, even when they are the best of men. The law is reason unaffected by desire.[6]

Liberty

It is an ancient rule that liberty within society is defined by law. Cicero long ago said: "The laws are the foundation of the liberty which we enjoy; we all are the laws' slaves that we may be free."[7] The apparent paradox of Cicero's assertion dissolves when it is considered in the context of due process of law. Today due process of law (explicitly included in the Fifth and Fourteenth Amendments to our Constitution) has extraordinary importance. Due process is probably the provision in the Constitution that has resulted in the most cases and controversies. From the year 1215 A.D. when the Magna Carta was adopted by England's King John, it was intertwined with equal protection and treatment in the courts of justice. Due process requires legislatures to enact laws equally applicable to all persons. It protects the liberties of the citizenry to the fullest extent compatible with public well-being. It is because of the limits on the power of government, and the broad guarantees of due process, that the "scheme of ordered liberty" [8] and the freedom of thought, speech, and action indispensable to free government can even exist.

Doctrine of Judicial Review

Liberty in this country has largely been defined by decisions of the Supreme Court, a fact of central importance in understanding the subject of individual liberty. The reason is America's early acceptance (in 1803) of the doctrine of judicial review as part of American law when Marshall's Supreme Court decided the case of *Marbury* v. *Madison*. The results come down to this: apart from the recourse to political processes of legislation and constitutional amendment, the courts (and ultimately the Supreme Court) have final say in deciding (1) what the Constitution means; (2) whether any statute or action violates the limits imposed by the Constitution; and (3) whether any legislation or executive action conflicts with the Constitution and is thus "unconstitutional" (null and void). It is because of the doctrine of judicial review that "the Constitution means what the Supreme Court says it means." And it is because of the doctrine that persons frequently go to court whenever they believe their individual rights have been violated by the government or anyone else claiming to act legally.

Doctrine of Stare Decisis

The significance of judicial review is magnified by one further key factor. This is the general principle that once a decision has been made it will be incorporated into the law and will usually be relied on by the courts in resolving similar cases. This principle is called the doctrine of *stare decisis,* a Latin term meaning "stand by the decision" or "let the decision stand." Therefore, the Court constantly looks to previous decisions as precedents in resolving present controversies.

Stare decisis came into American law, as did almost all of our jurisprudence, directly from English judicial practice. In England the whole fabric of "common law" had been developed over a period of centuries out of case law. Judges applied the test of reasonableness to customary practices that (from the twelfth century onward) gradually were transformed into laws common to all of England—hence the name, "common law." This judge-made or (more cautiously) judge-pronounced law was built up slowly and methodically, one case at a time. The common law of England, thus developed, was brought to the American colonies by early settlers. It was understood to embody the reason and sense of justice of the nation. Today the common law continues to be enforced unless it has been superseded by statutes.

American courts, because of their reliance on the provisions of written constitutions (in contrast to English courts which have no written constitution to appeal to), have never placed quite the same stress on *stare decisis* as have the English. Still, that doctrine generally applies, and serves to make the constitutional interpretations of American courts more or less cumulative. For example, *Marbury* v. *Madison* remains the leading case and precedent of the Court's power of judicial review, even after 175 years. But breaks (as we shall see) occur. Previous court decisions can be overruled and abandoned for compelling reasons. Or the law itself can be changed by overt political means—statutory enactments or constitutional amendments. In recent decades the Supreme Court has sometimes reversed previous decisions, causing some citizens to assert that *stare decisis,* if not quite dead, is no more than a pretentious farce. One dissenting justice of the Supreme Court even compared Court decisions with railway tickets stamped "good for this date and passage only."

But that was hyperbole. Still generally correct is the eighteenth-century summary of *stare decisis* given by Sir William Blackstone in the *Commentaries* (I:60): "precedents and rules must be followed, unless flatly absurd or unjust; for though their reason be not obvious at first view, yet we owe such deference to former times as not to suppose that they acted wholly without consideration." [9] Subtract from this formulation a pound of judicial restraint and throw in two pounds of judicial activism blended with a compulsion to remedy the country's evils, and you then have about the right recipe for the Court's degree of reliance on *stare decisis* today.

Due Process of Law

In the American institutionalization of the rule of law, due process has assumed great prominence as the courts have proceeded from case to case to define the limits of governmental power and the extent and meaning of liberty. The Fifth Amendment (ratified as part of the original "Bill of Rights" in 1791) includes the words "No person shall . . . be deprived of life, liberty, or property, without due process of law." The Fourteenth Amendment (ratified after the Civil War in 1868) contains a parallel provision with specific applicability to the states. This amendment was necessitated by an 1833 ruling of the Marshall Court that "The Fifth Amendment must be understood as restraining the power of the general government, not as applicable to the states." [10] There are two kinds of due process, *procedural* and *substantive*.

Procedural Due Process

Procedural due process generally relates to the ways in which laws are enforced. It applies today not only to courtroom procedures but to many other kinds of governmental actions—ranging from disciplinary proceedings in prisons to the firing of school teachers and university professors. It limits the *manner* in which governmental power can be exercised against persons. At a minimum, procedural due process entails the requirements that adequate and specific notice be given; that opportunity to be heard is provided; that everything be done to guarantee the use of just and fair methods. Thus, excessive vagueness in a statute or regulation may be such that "men of common intelligence must necessarily guess at its meaning and differ as to its application." If so, it violates "the first essential of due process of law" [11] and will be declared unconstitutional by the courts. Impermissibly vague or broad statutory provisions also can violate procedural due process by, in effect, unconstitutionally delegating "basic policy matters to policemen, judges, and juries . . . on an *ad hoc* and subjective basis, with the attendant dangers of arbitrary and discriminatory application." A New Jersey statute was voided by the Supreme Court as impermissibly vague because it made it a crime to be a "gangster": the prohibited conduct was not defined with enough precision to satisfy due process requirements.[12]

The minimal demands of procedural due process—adequate notice, opportunity to be heard, specificity—can be illustrated in the Magna Carta (1215 A.D.). Due process requirements are not novelties of American law but continuing articulations of a great and enduring tradition of justice characteristic of Anglo-American civilization itself. Chapter 14 of the Magna Carta provided that convocation of the "Common counsel of the kingdom" for the purpose of considering a levy of new taxes must (with certain exceptions) follow this procedure:

> We [the King] will cause to be summoned, severally by Our letters, the archbishops, bishops, abbots, earls, and great barons; We will also cause to be summoned, generally, by Our sheriffs and bailiffs, all those who hold lands directly of Us, to meet on a fixed day, but with at least forty days' notice, and at a fixed place. In all letters of such summons We will explain the cause thereof. The summons being thus made, the business shall proceed on the day appointed, according to the advice of those who shall be present, even though not all the persons summoned have come.

It is unnecessary at this point in our discussion to illustrate the myriad ways in which procedural due process works to guard the personal liberties of life, liberty, and property against abuse by government officials. What is necessary, however, is to stress that careful—even strict—attentiveness to *fair* procedures in all their tedious detail is now, and always has been, of great significance in the preservation of all our liberties. It is this careful attention to procedures that procedural due process insists upon at every turn of the government's exercise of power and authority.

To simplify our discussion, procedural due process resolutely insists that "the end does not justify the means." An additional standard must be met: fairness, propriety, and justness must be employed in the means themselves. Correct procedure supplies the connective tissue of our constitutional government. It serves as the balance between personal liberty on the one hand and orderly government on the other. To an impatient age interested not in "details" but in "getting the job done," it may be irritating to prescribe scrupulous attention to the details of procedure. But Sir Henry Maine's great aphorism is indubitably true: The liberties we enjoy are "...secreted in the interstices of procedure...." [13] This adage can scarcely be better validated than by the Watergate crisis that brought President Richard M. Nixon's resignation from office in 1974. It was precisely Nixon's and

Endangered American Species
Source: from Herblock's State of the Union (Simon & Schuster, 1972).

his associates' addiction to expediency that cumulatively comprised a disproportionate abuse of power, thereby precipitating what probably has been our greatest constitutional crisis since the Civil War.

Due process of law acts as a blanket to protect the whole range of liberties (whether enumerated in the Bill of Rights or elsewhere in the Constitution) enjoyed by the American people. The Ninth Amendment underscores the existence of rights above and beyond those specifically mentioned in the Constitution, the theory being that no rights at all are conferred by the document but only are protected by it. This extended meaning of due process, together with the firm understanding that people hold natural liberties not enumerated in the Constitution, keeps our freedoms open to a higher law (see below) and provides the broadest theoretical and historical basis for doing so. This broad basis, I shall emphasize, has been utilized repeatedly in Supreme Court constructions of the meaning of various provisions of the Constitution. The due process clauses of the Fifth and Fourteenth Amendments have served as the cutting edge of the interpretations. Moreover, the due process clause of the Fourteenth Amendment has (in effect) made most provisions of the Bill of Rights applicable to the states as well as to the federal government. This is called "incorporation" and "nationalization" of the Bill of Rights (see chapter 2).

In summary, procedural due process assures the use of "fundamentally fair" means in attaining valid ends or purposes. Basic demands are for adequate notice, opportunity to be heard, and specific requirements. To be specific, a person is entitled by the "standards" or "tests" imposed by the courts in the name of procedural due process of law to at least three things: (1) to be given public and sufficient notification of a law's existence and content; (2) to be provided an opportunity to appear before an administrative or judicial body to be "heard" or to explain any circumstances that may affect compliance with whatever is demanded by law or regulation; and (3) to be told with sufficient clarity what the law really requires so that the meaning of specific demands can be comprehended in adequate detail.

If any requirement of procedural due process is omitted or slighted, then the procedure is defective. It can be nullified by a court of law as an unconstitutional denial of due process. This is true of state proceedings no less than federal, of administrative actions no less than judicial. Procedures must be correct in every significant detail.

Substantive Due Process

Substantive due process is rooted in the fact that the *objectives* of governmental action must be proper: within the power of the government in the first place, and not unjustly an invasion of the personal or property rights of individuals or corporations in the second place. This is but the tip of the iceberg, however.

The growth of substantive due process has been primarily through lawsuits brought by individuals or corporations against invasion of their rights by state laws and regulations. The Supreme Court has tended to slide back and forth occasionally in its decisions, from reliance on the due process clause to the privileges and immunities clause, and (more frequently) over to the equal protection clause. Therefore, all three clauses have to be kept in mind in considering the meaning of due process of law, procedural no less than substantive. This sliding back and forth can be illustrated from Court cases. For example, racial discrimination in the public schools of the District of Columbia was declared to be unconstitutional in 1954 in one of the original desegregation cases decided by the Supreme Court. Chief Justice Earl Warren said that the practice of segregation violated the due process clause of the Fifth Amendment. He explained the matter this way: [14]

> The Fifth Amendment [does] not contain an equal protection clause [as does the Fourteenth Amendment, applicable to the states. But] the concepts of equal protection and due process, both stemming from our American ideal of fairness, are not mutually exclusive. The "equal protection of the laws" is a more explicit safeguard of prohibited unfairness than "due process of law," and, therefore, we do not imply that the two are always interchangeable phrases. But ... discrimination may be so unjustifiable as to be violative of due process. ... In view of our decision that the Constitution prohibits the states from maintaining racially segregated public schools, it would be unthinkable that the same Constitution would impose a lesser duty on the Federal Government [which has direct responsibility for the schools of Washington, D.C.].

Similarly, a 1976 case arose after resident Chinese aliens who had been lawfully admitted to live in San Francisco were fired by the U.S. Civil Service because they were not citizens. The Civil Service Commission had acted unconstitutionally, the Court said, because the "federal sovereign, like the States, must govern impartially. The concept of equal justice under law is served by the Fifth Amendment's guarantee of due process, as well as by the Equal Protection Clause of the Fourteenth Amendment. . . . [Under certain circumstances] the Due Process Clause has . . . the same significance as the Equal Protection Clause." [15] The Court seems never to have seriously considered the possibility that the Fifth Amendment's due process clause might mean something different from the requirements imposed by the equal protection clause of the Fourteenth Amendment. An interesting blindspot, indeed.

Higher Law Background. The phrase, "our American ideal of fairness," quoted above from Chief Justice Warren's 1954 opinion, can be taken as a clue. It denotes the thread of natural or higher law that steadily runs through the entire discussion of individual rights to form the core of substantive due process and substantive equal protection in their many manifestations. I do not think our subject can be fully understood unless this unifying thread is borne in mind. The American ideal of fairness and liberty is strongly present in the mass of individual rights litigation handled each year by the courts; it has been pervasive from the time of the nation's founding. The ideal of fairness goes back to antecedents in England: to Blackstone's *Commentaries* in the eighteenth century,[16] to Coke's *Reports* and *Institutes* in the seventeenth century,[17] and eventually to the Magna Carta of the English barons and wicked old King John at Runnymede in the thirteenth century. Thomas Jefferson would trace it to the ancient Saxon or Gothic constitution that he believed emerged in the German forests of the fifth century. Sir Edward Coke, the oracle of common law, who effectively reaffirmed the Magna Carta early in the seventeenth century, suspected that the ancient constitution (of which the Great Charter was a restoration) had been brought to Britain by survivors of the Trojan War led by Brutus of Troy some time after the tenth century B.C.—a feat not chronicled by Homer or Vergil, to be sure. Coke spoke of established principles of justice and liberty of such antiquity in the actual conduct of English government that "the memory of man runneth not to the contrary." These principles took on all the qualities of the order of nature itself; and, added together, composed the "fundamental law" of the realm, the supreme "law of the land."

It is this assumption of the controlling reality of established and superior law that is meant when the phrase "higher law" is used. It may be conceived as merely historical and thereby traceable in numerous documents on earlier court decisions as legally prescriptive of the norms that govern society. Or it may also be conceived as the "law of nature," as did Blackstone in the *Commentaries* (1:41)—as old as mankind and "dictated by God Himself." Blackstone said on the eve of the American Revolution that higher law governs through superior obligation in all times and places. No laws can be valid that contradict the law of nature or the law of revelation. The obligations of all human laws flow from this higher law, for they are bound to articulate harmoniously the "Laws of Nature and of Nature's God," to borrow Jefferson's famous phrase from the Declaration of Independence.

It is unnecessary to debate whether it is more correct to take a legalistic-constitutional view of higher law or a philosophical one. Both approaches are amply represented in U.S. Supreme Court decisions, whatever the justices may say they are doing. For example, Justice Hugo L. Black repudiated the "natural law" approach but believed certain protections of the Bill of Rights were absolute and read all of the specific rights of Amendments 1 through 8 into the Fourteenth Amendment.[18] The Court, rather like Chief Justice Warren and his colleagues in *Bolling* v. *Sharpe* in 1954 (quoted above), generally has been able to find enough judicial elbow room to arrive at what it took to be just decisions in cases before it. Justices often have found their arguments wherever they could, as subsequent analysis of the Court's decisions will show. What is important to notice is that this higher law dimension has been in the minds of lawyers and judges and has played a key role in individual rights adjudication. Happily, the Magna Carta stands as a monument to the higher law acknowledged by everybody; it and its progeny constitute our fundamental law. The Constitution of the United States is a direct descendant of this body of laws.

To understand the development of substantive due process, it is helpful to refer to a key passage in the Magna Carta (chapter 39): "No free man shall be taken, imprisoned, desseised, outlawed, banished, or in any way destroyed, nor will We proceed against or prosecute him, except by the lawful judgment of his peers and by the law of the land." By the fourteenth century the phrase "law of the land" meant the same thing as "due process of law," Coke tells us. Blackstone later maintained that this provision of the Great Charter "protected every individual in the nation in the free enjoyment of his life, his liberty, and his property, unless declared to be forfeited by the judgment of his peers or the law of the land."

These are words echoed in our Fifth and Fourteenth Amendments. Moreover, the phrase "law of the land" is itself contained in the "Supremacy Clause" of the U.S. Constitution (ART. VI, SEC. 2):

> This Constitution, and the Laws of the United States which shall be made in Pursuance thereof; and all Treaties made, or which shall be made, under the authority of the United States, shall be the supreme Law of the Land; and the Judges in every State shall be bound thereby, any Thing in the Constitution or Laws of any State to the Contrary notwithstanding.

This provision directly affirms that the national Constitution and legal enactments following from it are supreme and compose our fundamental law. As has been seen, the early establishment of judicial review gave power to the federal judiciary to determine with finality the meaning of the fundamental law and to resolve any conflicts between statutory enactments (state or federal) and constitutional law.

Antecedents of Substantive Due Process. It is conventional to date the rise of substantive due process from cases decided by the Supreme Court in the 1890s, a development that we will consider shortly. Yet it is clear that the kind of higher law adjudication labelled "substantive due process" has been a staple of American constitutional law from its beginning. For present purposes, it is important to note that the same kind of judicial decision-making continued after the so-called heyday of substantive due process supposedly ended in the mid-1930s. But that is getting ahead of our story.

Whether they understood the common law as rights assured all people by the law of nature (in existence before the compact establishing society and government) or as rights guaranteed by continuity with the laws of England, our forefathers retained the common law largely intact in their postrevolutionary state and federal constitutions. The view was prominently held in the early days of the country that the Bill of Rights did not create rights but only protected pre-existing rights.

The 1798 case of *Calder* v. *Bull* [19] involved a Connecticut statute that served to affirm the legality of a will. Justice Samuel Chase—whom we met at the beginning of this chapter as a candidate for impeachment—stoutly maintained that property rights were protected by the higher law, even in the absence of any applicable provision in the state or federal constitutions. He said: "I cannot subscribe to the omnipotence of a State legislature, or that it is absolute and without control, although its authority should not be expressly restrained by the constitution or fundamental law of the State."

On the contrary, Justice Chase insisted that the powers of the state were limited due to the very fact that the people of the country had created government for the purposes of establishing justice, promoting the general welfare, securing the blessings of liberty, and protecting their persons and property from violence. This "fundamental principle" arises from the nature of free republican government itself. No one can be compelled to do what the laws do not require, or refrain from doing what the laws permit. Accordingly, certain acts lie beyond government's power. Justice Chase continued:

There are certain vital principles in our free republican governments, which will determine and overrule an apparent and flagrant abuse of legislative power; [such] as to authorize manifest injustice by positive law, or to take away that security for personal liberty or private property for the protection whereof the government was established. An ACT of the legislature (for I cannot call it a law), contrary to the first great principles of the social compact, cannot be considered a rightful exercise of legislative authority.... The legislature ... cannot change innocence into guilt, or punish innocence as a crime; or violate the right of an antecedent lawful contract, or the right of private property. To maintain that our Federal or State legislature possesses such powers, if they had not been expressly restrained, would in my opinion be a political heresy, altogether inadmissible in our free republican governments.

These ideas voiced by Justice Chase concerning natural law, social compact, and vested rights only sporadically appeared in court decisions during the next seventy-five years. But they did not completely disappear. Chief Justice John Marshall himself toyed with the notions in 1810 as an alternative basis for voiding Georgia's attempt to revoke a land grant by statute. Revocation would be illegal, Marshall said, "either by general principles which are common to our free institutions, or by the particular provisions of the Constitution of the United States." [20] The higher law was again invoked in 1819, and an enduring theme in individual rights decisions sounded, when Justice William Johnson summarized the intent of the Magna Carta as "to secure the individual from the arbitrary exercise of the powers of government, unrestrained by the established principles of private rights and distributive justice." [21]

Finally, the power of substantive due process to impose limits on Congress's power to legislate was hinted at in Chief Justice Roger B. Taney's decision in the controversial *Dred Scott* case. He declared that the Missouri Compromise of 1820 was unconstitutional because, by prohibiting the importation of slaves, it had violated liberty and property rights. "An Act of Congress," Taney said, "which deprives a citizen of the United States of his liberty or property, merely because he came himself or brought his property into a particular Territory of the United States and who had committed no offense against the laws, could hardly be dignified with the name of due process of law." [22]

Substantive Due Process as Economic Liberty. For a long time (roughly from 1890 until 1937) the application of substantive due process by the Supreme Court appeared to lie exclusively in the area of property rights. Only later did the term "liberty" (as anything other than economic liberty) in the phrase "life, liberty, and property" attract the Court's attention. This is today called the "old" substantive due process. What kinds of "property" have found protection? Let us review several cases below to see what property rights have been protected by substantive due process.

Wynehamer v. New York. The grandfather of all substantive due process cases, *Wynehamer* v. *New York*,[23] was decided by a state court in 1856. The "property" given protection in this case was that of a saloon keeper to pursue his livelihood by selling liquor, an activity infringed, the Court said, by New York's prohibition law. All the big guns of Anglo-American jurisprudence were rolled out on this noble occasion—fundamental principles of liberty, common reason, natural rights, and the fundamental law, among others. The New York Court of Appeals, after quoting the state constitution's due process clause, said:

> the power of the legislature is restricted, not only by the express provisions of the written constitution, but by limitations implied from the nature and form of our government; ... aside from all special restrictions, the right [of the state] to enact [prohibition] laws is not among the delegated powers of the legislature, [hence] the act in question is void, as against the fundamental principles of liberty, and against common reason and natural rights.... we cannot forget that the highest function intrusted to [the courts] is that of maintaining inflexible the fundamental law.

The Slaughterhouse Cases. It would be forty-one years before a majority of the justices of the Supreme Court of the United States would become equally indignant about the limits on the police power of the states in regulating capitalist free enterprise. The *Slaughterhouse* cases (1873) found only Justice Stephen J. Field (one of four dissenting justices) sufficiently excited about the subject to write a spirited dissenting opinion. He argued that a New Orleans butcher's professional calling is lawful employment pursued in a lawful manner, one protected through the Fourteenth Amendment against Louisiana's invasion by the "privileges and immunities ... which of right belong to the citizens of all free governments." [24] Justice Bradley dissented on due process grounds. But the majority of the Court disagreed and, largely on the basis of the privileges and immunities clause, it upheld the state's regulatory power. We should note that the issue was the legitimacy of the *objectives* of governmental action.

Munn v. Illinois. Similarly, the power of Illinois to regulate the rates farmers must pay grain elevator operators was upheld four years later in *Munn* v. *Illinois* (1877), when the Court found that the due process clause did not serve to restrain the state's regulatory power. The grain elevator business was found to be "affected with a public interest" and thereby (in accordance with the old common law rule) subject to regulation "for the common good." [25] If the legislature could regulate at all, the Court said, then the degree was a matter for its discretion: "for protection against abuses by legislatures the people must resort to the polls, not to the courts."

The doctrine of business "affected with a public interest" was applied by the Court down to 1934 when it was finally abandoned. The result, generally, was that the state's regulatory power could be channeled by judicially deciding whether rate setting and price fixing were justifiable in a business affected with a public interest or to be disallowed as unconstitutional deprivations of liberty and property without due process of law. In other words, with the eventual establishment of the "liberty of contract" dogma of substantive due process, the doctrine of business "affected with a public interest" became a major basis for the Court's allowing (or disallowing) state economic regulation under broad power to foster the general welfare. It was a two-edged sword, wielded by the Court, with which many rate-fixing statutes were upheld and many were voided.

Allgeyer v. Louisiana. That the Fourteenth Amendment restrained the power of the state to regulate business was first clearly held in 1897 in the landmark case of *Allgeyer* v. *Louisiana* when a majority of the Supreme Court first formally affirmed substantive due process.[26] Allgeyer, who represented a New York insurance company, had been convicted of violating a Louisiana statute prohibiting any person from acting to insure property in Louisiana with any firm not licensed to do business in that state. The Supreme Court reversed the conviction. It found that the statute infringed on the freedom of contract protected by the term "liberty" in the Fourteenth Amendment. The Constitution, the Court said, protected from state interference a person's liberty to be an insurance agent: the Fourteenth Amendment protects the rights of citizens to live and work where they will and to pursue any lawful calling. The Court went on to affirm that due process protects the citizen from physical incarceration or other restraints of person, protects the free enjoyment of all one's faculties and their use in all lawful ways, and the freedom to enter into contracts that may be "proper, necessary, and essential to his carrying out to a successful conclusion the purposes above mentioned."

Lochner v. New York. The whole *laissez faire* philosophy of American capitalism was embraced in 1905 in the case of *Lochner v. New York*, in which the Court found the "general right to make a contract" to be protected by the due process clause.[27] Lochner had been convicted and fined in Utica, New York, under a state labor law that prohibited employing bakery workers more than ten hours a day or sixty hours a week. The Supreme Court reversed the decision, citing *Allgeyer*, and declared the New York statute unconstitutional: "...the freedom of master and employee to contract with each other in relation to their employment ... cannot be prohibited or interfered with, without violating the Federal Constitution." The Court majority was unimpressed by a recitation of evidence showing the hazards of long hours of labor in overheated bakeshops, of little sleep, of chronic inflammation of the respiratory system that resulted from inhaling flour dust, of rheumatism, cramps, and swollen legs, or the evidence that bakers had shorter than average lifespans. They were also not persuaded that, because "nearly all of" the other states (and Congress itself) had recognized the justifiability of regulating hours of work, the judiciary should defer to such legislative judgments. Such matters of public policy, subject to majority will, were not within the proper scope of the states' police power to protect the general health and well-being of the citizenry. In fact, *Lochner* specifically held that New York's limitation on working hours had "reached and passed the limit of police power." In short, the Court had embarked on a course that eventually would lead it to be pilloried as a "super-legislature." But it had done so out of conviction and the best of motives.

What were those motives? The essence of the *Lochner* philosophy (as the Court applied it for a generation) was that statutes ought to be invalidated if their goals were illegitimate or if their means did not further some permissible end. More deeply, this philosophy gave expression to the Court majority's aversion to the "paternal theory of government," which it found to be "odious." It was convinced that the "utmost possible liberty to the individual, and the fullest possible protection to him and his property, is both the limitation and duty of government." [28]

Thanks to legal fiction, corporations already were understood to be "persons" within the meaning of the Constitution, and therefore subject to its protections. The Supreme Court ruled repeatedly on behalf of business because it believed that self-help by individuals is preferable to governmental paternalism and intervention in private affairs. The Court intervened to overturn legislation similar to that invalidated in *Lochner*, and to institute what labor critics termed "government by injunction." This period (1880–1920) marked the arrival of the industrial revolution in America. Unions began organizing as substantial portions of the population moved from the country to work in the city: 22.7 percent in 1880, 43.8 percent in 1920, and 49.1 percent by 1930. The conditions hinted at in the *Lochner* case were to be seen generally throughout American industry: long hours, low pay, exploitation of women and children, and degrading and unsanitary working conditions. There was a lack of effective labor legislation to combat the sweatshop evils, and a reluctance to recognize unions as bargaining agents. The hostility of the courts toward unions was evident even after useful legislation began to be enacted in the decades following 1900.[29]

Thus, substantive due process was used to strike down state and federal legislation prohibiting "yellow dog" (anti-union) contract clauses for workers, and it was used to nullify minimum wage laws. Regulation of the maximum number of hours one could be compelled to work, however, was received sooner with less hostility by the Court in cases decided in 1908 and 1917 that overturned *Lochner*. It should be noted that the Court's antilabor bias was for a while matched by that of Congress, which in 1890 passed the Sherman Anti-Trust Act outlawing secondary boycotts (the use of coercion to get customers and firms to withhold business from an employer experiencing labor troubles). Strikes were "unlawful restraints on trade," and injunctions continued to be used to prohibit them. Contempt citations were issued to punish defiant strikers, and triple damages were awarded companies for losses suffered through strikes. Relief from such Court interventions was only partial, even after adoption of the Clayton Act of 1914.

End of Substantive Due Process in Economic Matters. The end of substantive due process in economic matters came all at once in 1937. The Court's mindset was changed, not by logic, but by steadily mounting progressive public sentiment, the effects of the Great Depression of the 1930s, and the political power of President Franklin D. Roosevelt's "New Deal." Chief Justice Charles Evans Hughes, speaking for a new five-to-four majority of the Court, seemed astonished that anyone ever might have supposed "liberty of contract" to be protected by any provision of the U.S. Constitution.[30] This was the Supreme Court's "revolution" of 1937. The Court thereafter became generally "liberal" and pro-labor in its decisions on economic matters, exercising judicial "restraint" on such questions. It seemed content to let the "political" (legislative and executive) branches of state and especially of federal government have their way in nursing the American economy back to life from the depths of the Depression. It affirmed that the states have discretion to legislate health and safety measures and to insure "wholesome conditions of work and freedom from oppression." The clock on substantive due process was turned back to the old days of the *Slaughterhouse* cases.

What did this mean? Simply that, henceforth, the exercise of citizens' fundamental liberties in economic and property matters would be more readily subject to regulation by state and federal governments. The citation in *Slaughterhouse* by Justice Miller's majority opinion of a much earlier (1823) case illustrates the nature of the shift in Court doctrine after 1937. The shift was at once subtle and profound.

> ... what are the privileges and immunities of citizens of the several States? We feel no hesitation in confining these expressions to those ... which are *fundamental*; .... They may all ... be comprehended under the following general heads: protection by the government, with the right to acquire and possess property of every kind, and to pursue and obtain happiness and safety, subject, nevertheless, to such restraints as the government may prescribe for the general good of the whole.[31]

The "new" emphasis after 1937 in the area of economic liberty was the old one reflected in the decision of 1873 as expressed in the concluding phrase just quoted: "subject ... to such restraints as the government may prescribe for the general good of the whole." As in *Slaughterhouse*, the modern Court has declined to act as "a perpetual censor upon all legislation of the States," which restricts the "civil rights of their own citizens." It has declined to use its "authority to nullify such as it [does] not approve" or to fetter and degrade the state governments "in the exercise of powers heretofore universally conceded to them [as] of the most ordinary and fundamental character. . . ." [32]

Did application of the doctrine of substantive due process really end in 1937? For economic applications, the answer for a long time has seemed to be "yes." But in the area of civil liberties, the Court's day was only just beginning, as the next chapter will show. Even in economic matters there still remains a flicker of life in substantive due process if we take our cue from the dictum of Justice Potter Stewart in a 1972 decision: ". . . the dichotomy between personal liberties and property rights is a false one. Property does not have rights. People have rights. The right to enjoy property without unlawful deprivation, no less than the right to speak or the right to travel is, in truth, a personal right. . . ." [33]

Summary

In this chapter we have shown the way in which the Supreme Court came to be the authoritative interpreter of the Constitution by establishing early the doctrine of judicial review. This unique feature of the American political system was shown to make the judges, and especially the justices of the Court, the custodians of the rule of law. The independence of the judiciary, armed after 1803 with the power to declare legislative acts unconstitutional, has made it also the custodian of liberty in America. Judicial thinking was seen to be infused with a devotion to the higher law, a congeries of principles based on the conviction that justice must be served by government. This justice includes the array of rights protected by the Bill of Rights. The roots of these principles and rights were shown to lie in remote antiquity and to be conceived of as arising both from ancient practices and precedents and from a philosophical analysis of natural right forming a part of the order of human existence.

The principal means for diffusing these ideas into the law have been the Due Process of Law clauses of the Fifth and Fourteenth Amendments. Procedural due process relates to the fundamental fairness of the government's procedures and processes, its way of pursuing its objectives. Substantive due process relates to the legitimacy of the government's objectives, the substance of policy decisions by the political branches of the state and federal governments. Liberty is fostered and protected because of the limits imposed by the Constitution on both procedures and goals: if the government's actions were without these real limits, then the liberties of individuals would be without firm footing under settled law. Higher law took the form of substantive due process as we have so far surveyed it. During the period from 1897 to 1937, substantive due process was understood to apply especially to economic matters—the freedom of contract was nearly an absolute principle. It is usually this phase of substantive due process that is meant when the expression is used by lawyers. From 1937 to the present day, however, substantive due process has emerged as a surety for other personal liberties and its economic dimension has all but disappeared. Government regulation of the economy has expanded without much judicial hindrance since 1937. But government infringement of noneconomic liberties has become a major arena of judicial activism and intervention as the Court has brought the "new" substantive due process and other doctrines into play on behalf of individual liberties.

We shall discuss in chapter 2 how thinking on the higher law persists today, garbed in the jargon of a Court speaking of the new substantive due process, new equal protection, preferred position, absorption and selective incorporation of basic individual rights.

REVIEW QUESTIONS

1. What is the great significance of Marshall's decision in *Marbury* v. *Madison?* Explain the doctrine of judicial review.

2. How is the principle of rule of law related to the American conception of liberty?

3. What is the doctrine of *stare decisis*? Why is it important?

4. From the perspective of constitutional history, what is the relationship of the phrase "law of the land" in the Magna Carta and the same phrase in the U.S. Constitution? What does it mean to say that "due process of law" in the Fifth and Fourteenth Amendments is equivalent to the phrase "law of the land"?

5. Define and explain the meaning of *procedural* due process of law as that doctrine has been developed by the American courts.

6. What is *substantive* due process? Why is it important? Distinguish between "old" and "new" substantive due process.

7. What is meant by "higher law"? Explain its general importance for the interpretation of American liberty today.

8. What is the importance of the "*Lochner* philosophy"? When did it apply? Why was it abandoned?

9. Do you agree with the soundness of entrusting (short of constitutional amendment) final say about the meaning of the law to the Supreme Court? Why? What alternatives might be found to this kind of reliance on the courts?

CHAPTER TWO

A Scheme of
Ordered Liberty

Neither have Judges power to judge according to
that which they think to be fit, but that which out
of the laws they know to be right and
consonant to the law.[1]

SIR EDWARD COKE (1609)

For myself it would be most irksome to be ruled
by a bevy of Platonic Guardians, even if I knew
how to choose them, which I assuredly do not.[2]

LEARNED HAND (1958)

"How can you advocate breaking some laws and
obeying others?" The answer lies in the fact that
there are two types of laws: just and unjust. . . .
One has not only a legal but a moral responsibility
to obey just laws. Conversely, one has a moral
responsibility to disobey unjust laws. I would
agree with St. Augustine that "an unjust law is
no law at all." [3]

MARTIN LUTHER KING, JR. (1964)

GITLOW v. NEW YORK

*B*ENJAMIN GITLOW was a militant communist and lead-
ing member of the revolutionary Left-Wing Section of the
Socialist Party, which held a national meeting to organize in
June 1919 in New York City.

Gitlow was elected to the National Council of the Left-Wing
Section. The council adopted and published in its newspaper,
the REVOLUTIONARY AGE, a MANIFESTO and a COMMUNIST PRO-
GRAM, to which all members of the organization were required to
subscribe and which fervently advocated violent action, including the fomenting of industrial disturbances, mass strikes, the
overthrow of the American government, and other revolutionary
mass action. In the Manifesto's words, "The proletarian revolution and the Communist reconstruction of society—the struggle
for these—is now indispensable. . . . The Communist International calls the proletariat of the world to the final struggle."

There were 16,000 copies of the REVOLUTIONARY AGE published, paid for, distributed, and sold by Gitlow, the publication's
business manager. He went to different parts of New York to
address Socialist Party branches and urge them to adopt the principles and pursue the activities outlined in the paper. Although
there was no evidence that anything revolutionary resulted from
Gitlow's efforts, New York police arrested him (along with three
other members of his organization), and the Supreme Court of
New York indicted them for the statutory crime of criminal
anarchy. Gitlow was separately tried, convicted, and sentenced
to jail. After that judgment was affirmed by the Appellate Division and the Court of Appeals of New York State, the case of
GITLOW v. NEW YORK came before the United States Supreme
Court in 1925.

Background of the Gitlow Case

New York had enacted the statute under which Gitlow was convicted in 1902. This law made it a felony to advocate, either by word of mouth or in writing, that organized government should be overthrown by force or violence or by the assassination of the executive head or other officials of the government. Advocacy was so defined as to include advising or teaching the necessity or propriety of committing such actions. The statute also extended illegality to the printing, publishing, editing, circulation, selling, distributing, or displaying of any book, paper, document, or other written or printed material in any form advising or teaching that organized government ought to be overthrown by force, violence, or unlawful means.[4]

The Supreme Court Decision

The determination of guilt in the Gitlow case tried by the New York Supreme Court, and its subsequent affirmations by higher courts, was upheld by the U.S. Supreme Court. The Court based its decision in GITLOW on the premise that New York's statute was a proper exercise of its police power. The state might legislatively determine in advance of specific events "that utterances advocating the overthrow of organized government by force, violence, and unlawful means, are so inimical to the general welfare, and involve such danger of substantive evil, that they may be penalized.... That determination," continued Justice Sanford for a majority of the Court, "must be given great weight. Every presumption is to be indulged in favor of the validity of the statute."

This was so despite the Court's willingness to assert for the first time in history that the guaranties of free speech and press contained in the First Amendment applied to and limited state legislative powers: "... we may and do assume that freedom of speech and of the press—which are protected by the First Amendment from abridgment by Congress—are among the fundamental personal rights and 'liberties' protected by the due process clause of the Fourteenth Amendment from impairment by the States." [5]

The key to the Court's disposition of the case was that the New York statute made advocacy and incitement to violent acts tending to the overthrow of organized government by unlawful means a punishable crime. The statute did not restrict utterances or publications of a merely historical, philosophical, or expository kind, or limit the statement of abstract doctrines for discussion. Justice Sanford stated:

> The "Left-Wing Manifesto's" words imply urging to [criminal] action. Such utterances, by their nature, involve danger to the public peace and to the security of the state. They threaten breaches of the peace and ultimate revolution. And the immediate danger is none the less real and substantial because the effect of a given utterance cannot be accurately foreseen. The state cannot reasonably be required to measure the danger from every such utterance in the nice balance of a jeweler's scale.
>
> We cannot hold that the present statute is an arbitrary or unreasonable exercise of the police power of the state, unwarrantably infringing the freedom of speech or press; and we must and do sustain its constitutionality.

Associate Justices Oliver Wendell Holmes and Louis D. Brandeis dissented. The majority of the Court had rejected as inapplicable the defendant's argument (based on Holmes's opinion in the SCHENCK case [1919])[6] that "the question in every case is whether the words are used in such circumstances and are of such a nature as to create a clear and present danger that they will bring about the substantive evils that [the state] has a right to prevent." The dissenting associate justices urged that the clear and present danger test was the proper one to apply in GITLOW—and that by it he should be freed. This, they insisted, was so because "it is manifest that there was no present danger of an attempt to overthrow the government by force on the part of the admittedly small minority who shared the defendant's views."

Of course, they said:

> Eloquence may set fire to reason. But whatever may be thought of the redundant discourse before us, it had no chance of starting a present conflagration. If, in the long run, the beliefs expressed in proletarian dictatorship are destined to be accepted by the dominant forces of the community, the only meaning of free speech is that they should be given their chance and have their way.

Implications of the Gitlow Case

Notwithstanding the persuasiveness of Holmes and Brandeis, Benjamin Gitlow went back to prison. But, for the first time, the selective incorporation of the First Amendment's protections of speech and press into the Fourteenth Amendment's guaranty of liberty against invasion by state governments without due process of law had become part of American law. The consequences were to be tremendous.

Would Gitlow be convicted today? Would such a conviction be upheld by the Supreme Court? Almost certainly not. For although Gitlow has not been overruled by the Court, the conditions under which advocacy of violence can legitimately be regulated by state statute have narrowed considerably. In 1969 another Court, in deciding a criminal syndicalism case from Ohio, laid down:

> the principle that the constitutional guarantees of free speech and free press do not permit a State to forbid or proscribe advocacy of the use of force or of law violation except where such advocacy is directed to inciting or producing imminent lawless action and is likely to incite or produce such action.[7]

This restrictiveness approaches what Justice Sanford had termed weighing each utterance "in the nice balance of a jeweler's scale." His colleagues Holmes and Brandeis would have been delighted by the wisdom of the more recent Court's doctrine. They had felt that, since "[e]very idea is an incitement . . . only an emergency can justify repression," and that (in Brandeis's great words from the 1927 Whitney dissent): "If there be time to expose through discussion the falsehood and fallacies, to avert the evil by the process of education, the remedy to be applied is more speech, not enforced silence." [8]

The viewpoints expressed in the quotations at the beginning of this chapter show the range of approaches to law and liberty, which we will discuss in this chapter. All three men agree that the content of justice is not arbitrary. But how is one to find and fix standards of judgment? Coke profoundly believed, as did Martin Luther King, that the principles of right and justice partake of the absolute—that they are natural and sanctioned by God. But Coke also agreed with Judge Hand that a judge is bound by the law and is not entitled to judge merely according to abstract principles of justice or on the basis of his own prejudices and private opinions. The judicial role is to "speak" the law, not to "make" it, according to Coke and Hand. King's view is broader, for he readily appealed to private conscience as the criterion of the law itself; a duly enacted law that falls short of the standards of natural and eternal justice is no law at all and must be disobeyed as a matter of duty. One need not wait for judges and courts to determine that a statute is invalid because of unjustness. This was King's message from the Birmingham Jail.

Yet neither Coke nor Hand would disagree with King's principle in one respect: an unjust law is no law at all, as St. Augustine said long ago. The law is reason and justice itself, but to the judges (to paraphrase Chief Justice Marshall) the power of the laws and judicial power are one and the same and cannot be contradistinguished. If orderly society is to be preserved, the orderly pronouncement of the boundaries between law and liberty must come from the courts. And if a proper law, one which does not violate the Constitution, is thought to be undesirable, then it is the task of the legislature to enact new law. King's response to this proposition is contained in his book, *Why We Can't Wait* (1964), from which I have quoted.

We have begun this chapter with a discussion of the *Benjamin Gitlow* case, which deals with the protection of the First Amendment against invasion of rights by the state. We shall devote the balance of this chapter to the following issues: What is the new substantive due process? What is the logic of selective incorporation? What standards or tests are applied by the Court in deciding whether a state has exceeded its rightful police powers by unconstitutionally invading a person's rights? What is the scope of the police power itself? Finally, what is the character and drift of judicial activism as practiced by the modern Court?

Fundamental Rights

The means for securing the fundamental personal rights of individuals as Americans now enjoy them is substantive due process and equal protection (see chapter 5) as applied by an activist Supreme Court. Through "nationalization" of the liberties protected in the Bill of Rights by their "selective incorporation" into the Fourteenth Amendment, the modern Court now applies most of these protections against infringement by the states no less than by the federal government (see Table 2–1, p. 69). This means that we may include the basic personal rights of the first ten amendments in a definition of the word "liberty"—or of life or property when the occasion demands it—in the due process clause. This is the new substantive due process of personal liberties as contrasted to the old substantive due process of property rights (discussed in chapter 1).

Let us now go on to discuss the range and meaning of the new substantive due process as the Court has defined it in leading decisions since the 1920s.

The New Substantive Due Process

The cloud of legalistic jargon in which our subject is shrouded is best dispersed by bearing in mind a point in the preceding chapter: adherence to higher law goes far to explain the Court's willingness to interpret and apply fundamental liberties of Americans *as if* the Constitution embraced all of those liberties. Granted, there are exceptions and the matter is complex. To claim that judicial interpretation is often (if not always) rooted in this adherence is tricky, simply because the judges themselves rarely admit this. My argument remains that this reticence (or even outright denial) should not mislead the student of politics into supposing the higher law dimension of judicial review does not apply, as the silence of most commentaries would suggest. On the contrary, I argue that it is of central importance. The technical language used sometimes tends to obscure what actually is happening. The situation is similar to that in Andersen's fairy tale, "The Emperor's New Clothes," in which only the child blurts out that the Emperor is naked, while the ogling multitude oohs and ahs at the splendor of the Emperor's imaginary finery. The actual situation was sketched by a legal scholar, Thomas Grey, in 1975:

> The last generation has seen further development of constitutional rights clearly—and sometimes avowedly—not derived by textual interpretation [from the Constitution], notably the right of privacy, the right to vote, the right to travel, and generally the rights resulting from application of "equal protection of the laws" to the federal government. The intellectual framework against which these rights have developed is different from the natural-rights tradition of the founding fathers—its rhetorical reference points are the Anglo-American tradition and basic American ideals, rather than human nature, the social contract, or the rights of man. But it is the modern offspring, in a direct and traceable line of legitimate descent, of the natural-rights tradition that is so deeply embedded in our constitutional origins.[9]

Such titles (with their attached subject matter) as substantive due process, preferred position, incorporation, a scheme of ordered liberty, nationalization of the Bill of Rights, fundamental fairness in procedural due process, and much else go to compose the pieces that fall into place to form the higher law mosaic of today's constitutional law. Procedural due process relates to the ways in which valid policies are implemented, while substantive due process relates to the goals envisaged by the policies; that is, their very purposes.

A Judicial Discovery

So-called "new substantive due process" conventionally is identified with a constitutional doctrine that explicitly surfaced in 1965. I have argued that it appeared long before that time, but the case of *Griswold* v. *Connecticut* is of great significance.[10] There the Court, reversing the conviction and $100 fine of officials of a New Haven planned parenthood clinic, declared unconstitutional a Connecticut law forbidding the sale of contraceptives. It did so by asserting a newly discovered "right of privacy" which, not being mentioned anywhere in the Constitution, it claimed was one of a number of "peripheral liberties" implicit in those enumerated rights that spill over from them, radiating from "penumbras, formed by emanations from those guarantees that help give them life and substance." In the same decision, the Court was able to identify a series of earlier cases that it said showed the reality of the newly identified substantive liberty. In fact, however, only one of these cases had been decided without reference to some specific guaranty in the Bill of Rights.[11]

In *Griswold*, the Court pointedly declined to rely on *Lochner* and denied (by quoting Justice Oliver Wendell Holmes's *Lochner* dissent)[12] that it sits "as a super-legislature to determine the wisdom, need, and propriety of laws that touch economic problems, business affairs, or social conditions." But it is a different matter, the Court said, when a law "operates directly on an intimate relation of husband and wife and their physician's role in one aspect of that relation." Court critics, not taken in by this disclaimer, promptly asserted the revival of *Lochner*-like substantive due process in *Griswold*.

The continuity between *Griswold* and *Lochner* can be shown. No doubt a major shift in Court doctrine occurred in the abandonment of the "*Lochner* philosophy" in 1937. What was it? Between *Lochner* v. *New York* (1905) and its final collapse in *West Coast Hotel Co.* v. *Parrish* (1937),[13] the Supreme Court invalidated some 200 state laws aimed at regulating various aspects of economic activity, because it considered economic liberty and freedom of contract protected by the due process clause of the Fourteenth Amendment. Between 1937 and 1976 not a single statute directed toward economic regulation was voided on substantive due process grounds. Only one such statute (in 1957) was nullified on grounds of the equal protection of the laws clause during the same period—and that decision was abandoned in 1976 as "erroneous," and overruled.[14] Most such cases are dismissed in lower courts today for lack of a federal issue.

But the impression of a clear break is clouded by two considerations. First, the Court, itself, in *West Coast Hotel* was able to list an impressive inventory of regulatory laws that had been upheld during the heyday of *Lochner* (before 1937). These laws included limiting employment in mines and smelters to eight hours; requiring workmen's compensation; forbidding payment of seamen's wages in advance; making it unlawful to contract to pay miners employed at quantity rates on the basis of screened coal rather than on the basis of the coal as originally produced in the mine; and prohibiting contracts limiting liability for injuries to employees. In short, the Court's hostility to economic regulation through state legislation was not total even during the earlier period.

Second, the same philosophy of expansion of individual liberties through application of due process, which brought the liberty of contract to prominence after *Allgeyer* and *Lochner,* also yielded a series of cases affirming other aspects of personal liberty. And this is the decisive consideration that places *Griswold* and subsequent "new substantive due process" cases in line with *Lochner* as arising from a common tendency of the Court. That tendency is attributable to a steady and continuing adherence to higher law principle that, despite the absence of convenient pegs in the Constitution upon which to hang decisions, the Court has persisted in asserting by way of protecting individual liberties. Some of these important decisions must be briefly considered here.

Substantive Due Process and Personal Rights

Let us focus our attention at this point on several important cases that show how the revival of substantive due process was a major factor in personal rights decisions of the Supreme Court.

Meyer v. Nebraska. In 1923 the Court overruled Nebraska's conviction of a German teacher for teaching a foreign language to young children contrary to state law.[15] The teacher asserted a "property" right under the Fourteenth Amendment in the form of the occupation of teacher. The Court agreed, but it also affirmed that the liberty protected by that amendment included the rights of parents to have their children instructed in the German language. Of liberty the Court said on this occasion:

> it denotes . . . the right of the individual to contract, to engage in any of the common occupations of life, to acquire useful knowledge, to marry, establish a home and bring up children, to worship God according to the dictates of his own conscience, and generally to enjoy those privileges long recognized at common law as essential to the orderly pursuit of happiness by free men.

Nebraska's legislative interest in fostering "a homogeneous people with American ideals" was understandable, especially in light of the patriotic demands made on its people during the recently concluded World War I. But that interest was insufficiently compelling in a time of peace and absence of national emergency to justify the extreme means of imposing a law barring children from studying other languages, to their great harm and to the infringement of rights long enjoyed. "[T]he statute," said the Court, "as applied is arbitrary and without reasonable relation to any end within the competency of the State."

Pierce v. Society of Sisters. A 1925 decision soon after sustained an attack by parochial and private schools in Oregon on a statute requiring children between the ages of eight and sixteen to attend public schools.[16] In doing so the Court relied on *Meyer* (just cited). Again, property rights were protected in that the plaintiffs' business interests (the private schools) were threatened with destruction by the statute. But the Court took this opportunity to insist that the statute "unreasonably" interfered with "the liberty of parents and guardians to direct the upbringing and education of children under their control. . . . The child is not the mere creature of the State; those who nurture him and direct his destiny have the right, coupled with the high duty, to recognize and prepare him for additional obligations."

In subsequent years, assertions of liberty in the face of exercises of state powers on the grounds laid down in *Meyer* and *Pierce* generally were unsuccessful, although the Court's dicta continued to give broad definition to liberty as protected by the due process clause. Justice Brandeis remarked in a 1927 opinion that "... it is settled that the due process clause of the Fourteenth Amendment applies to matters of substantive law as well as to matters of procedure." [17]

Skinner v. Oklahoma. In a 1942 case (*Skinner* v. *Oklahoma*) the Court decided that marriage and procreation are among "the basic civil rights of man." [18] In a 1944 case (*Prince* v. *Massachusetts*) the Court found the nurture and care of children to be within "the private realm of family life which the state cannot enter." [19]

The *Skinner* case is of interest because it mixed equal protection claims with due process arguments, and therefore was a forerunner of the special protection subsequently given to "fundamental interests" by the Court under "new equal protection" decisions. The case was brought under a state law that required sterilization of criminals after conviction for three felonies. In 1927 Justice Holmes had, in a comparable case sustaining mandatory sterilization of mental defectives confined in institutions (and rejecting due process and equal protection arguments in doing so), proclaimed that "three generations of imbeciles are enough." [20] Justice Douglas in *Skinner*, on the other hand, thought three felony convictions not enough. He noted that sterilization of the criminal would "forever deprive [him] of a basic liberty." And he served notice that the Court would apply the rigorous test of *"strict scrutiny"* (rather than mere "reasonableness") in examining any statute that imposes "invidious discriminations ... against groups or types of individuals in violation of the constitutional guaranty of just and equal laws.... Sterilization of those who have thrice committed grand larceny, with immunity for those who are embezzlers, is a clear, pointed, unmistakable discrimination."

Aptheker v. Secretary of State. In 1964, the year before *Griswold*, the Court had invalidated a portion of a federal statute denying passports to Communist Party members because it "too broadly and indiscriminately restricts the right to travel and thereby abridges the liberty guaranteed by the Fifth Amendment." [21] That "liberty" was the "right to travel" asserted in a dictum by a 1958 case, one which the Court had said is not ascribed to any "particular constitutional provision." [22]

Poe v. Ullman. Justice Harlan's dissent to a 1961 Court decision [23] pointed toward more recent decisions in insisting that due process is "a discrete concept which subsists as an independent guaranty of liberty and procedural fairness, more general and inclusive than the specific prohibitions" of the Constitution. The liberty so protected, he said, "is a rational continuum which . . . includes a freedom from all substantial arbitrary impositions and purposeless restraints . . . and which also recognizes, what a reasonable and sensitive judgment must, that certain interests require particularly careful scrutiny of the state needs asserted to justify their abridgment." Due process and specific provisions of the First Amendment tended thereby to become indistinguishable. A kind of judicial shell game then ensued. For example, Justice Douglas reinterpreted *Meyer* and *Pierce* as based on the First Amendment in the 1965 *Griswold* decision.

Loving v. Virginia. Violation of due process was the basis for voiding a Virginia statute prohibiting miscegenation in a 1967 case.[24] There, marriage (including interracial marriage) was affirmed to be "one of the 'basic civil rights of man'" and a "fundamental freedom . . . one of the vital personal rights essential to the orderly pursuit of happiness by free men."

Roe v. Wade. *Griswold's* majority opinion affirming a "right to privacy" arising as we saw from "penumbras, formed by emanations" of specific constitutional guarantees had tacitly rejected direct reliance on substantive due process. A 1973 abortion case confirmed the impression that the rejection was merely semantic.[25] Privacy as a right protected *by* substantive due process was sweepingly affirmed, and Texas's abortion laws were ruled void in a suit brought by a pregnant single woman ("Jane Roe") and her physician, Dr. Hallford, who had been awarded declaratory relief by the three-judge district court under the Ninth Amendment. The Supreme Court cited in support of this right the whole array of cases just discussed, from *Griswold* back to *Meyer,* as follows:

> The Constitution does not explicitly mention any right of privacy. In a line of decisions, however . . . the Court has recognized that a right of personal privacy, or a guarantee of certain areas or zones of privacy, does exist under the Constitution. . . . These decisions make it clear that only personal rights that can be deemed "fundamental" or "implicit in the concept of ordered liberty" . . . are included in this guarantee of personal privacy. They also make it clear that the right has some extension to activities relating to marriage, procreation, contraception, family relationships, and child rearing and education. . . .

The Court went on to say that this right of privacy is founded on the Fourteenth Amendment's "concept of personal liberty and restrictions upon state action" and that it "is broad enough to encompass a woman's decision whether or not to terminate a pregnancy." This right is "fundamental" and, hence, to be *strictly* protected against state infringement. Only a "compelling state interest" expressed through narrowly drawn regulations or laws might be acceptable in limiting this fundamental personal right. Two such sufficiently compelling valid state interests identified by the Court were, first, "preserving and protecting the health of the pregnant woman . . . [and, second] . . . protecting the potentiality of human life. These interests are separate and distinct. Each grows in substantiality as the woman approaches term and, at a point during pregnancy, each becomes 'compelling.' "

Since the focus of our discussion is to show that the revival of substantive due process is one major strand in the recent Court's higher law mode of judicial review, the ramifications of the right of privacy need not be pursued at this point (see the discussion of privacy in chapter 3, however). Enough has been said to illustrate the thesis. Dissenters to the decisions of the Court in the privacy cases are exemplified by Justice Rehnquist, who wryly observed in *Roe v. Wade:*

> While the Court's opinion quotes from the dissent of Mr. Justice Holmes in [the *Lochner* case], the result is more closely

attuned to the majority opinion of Mr. Justice Peckham in that case. As in *Lochner* and similar cases applying substantive due process standards to economic and social welfare legislation, the adoption of the compelling state interest standard will inevitably require this Court to examine the legislative policies and pass on the wisdom of these policies in the very process of deciding whether a particular state interest put forward may or may not be "compelling." The decision here . . . partakes more of judicial legislation than it does of a determination of the intent of the drafters of the Fourteenth Amendment.[26]

Beyond Substantive Due Process

The extraconstitutional, higher law mode of judicial review is not confined to reviving substantive due process. Rather, the bulk of modern adjudication in the individual rights area adheres to the higher law principle. This principle underlies the broad interpretations of the equal protection clause of the Fourteenth Amendment, the identification of "preferred position" status for First Amendment rights, the nationalization of the Bill of Rights by a process of selective incorporation, and inclusion of the equal protection clause protections of the Fourteenth Amendment in the due process clause of the Fifth Amendment so as to apply them against federal action (in *Bolling* v. *Sharpe* [1954] [27] and afterward).

We see another side of this mode of judicial review when we consider that the test of reasonableness and the even more rigorous test of strict scrutiny, employed by the Court in reviewing legislation limiting the exercise of liberties, are themselves incapable of precise application. They lend themselves, rather, to a higher law understanding of constitutional protections (one that agrees with a majority opinion of the Court as to what is demanded by reason, justice, fairness, or "the tradition and conscience of our people" from case to case). Consider the word "liberty" in this light—into which the protections listed in the Bill of Rights have been set for Fourteenth Amendment application to the states. "Liberty" can only absorb the range of rights mentioned in (or emanating from) the Bill of Rights and Court decisions by also incorporating judicial reason, the mysterious judicial "right reason" of a bygone era. One scholar sees the linkage between the intentions of the Constitution and the procedural limitations imposed on states by the due process clause to be no more than "what is required by the conscience of mankind." [28] But this same "standard"—linking words and constitutional limitations—could as well be applied to the substantive limitations now imposed. And who will doubt that "reasonableness" and "the conscience of mankind" are higher law standards?

In a concurring opinion of the *Griswold* case, Justice Goldberg (joined by Chief Justice Warren and Justice Brennan) reminded the Court of the *conscience* standard:

> ... the Ninth Amendment shows a belief of the Constitution's authors that fundamental rights exist that are not expressly enumerated in the first eight amendments and an intent that the list included there not be exhaustive. As any student of this Court's opinions knows, this Court has held, often unanimously, that the Fifth and Fourteenth Amendments protect certain fundamental personal liberties from abridgment by the Federal Government or the States ... the ... Fourteenth Amendment prohibits the States ... from abridging fundamental personal liberties. [These are] now protected from state, as well as federal, infringement. In sum the Ninth Amendment simply lends strong support to the view that the "liberty" protected by the Federal Government or the States is not restricted to rights specifically mentioned in the first eight amendments. . . .
>
> In determining which rights are fundamental, judges are not left at large to decide cases in light of their personal and private notions. Rather, they must look to the "traditions and conscience of our people" to determine whether a principle is "so rooted [there] ... as to be ranked as fundamental." ... I agree fully with the Court that, applying these tests, the right of privacy is a fundamental personal right, "emanating from the totality of the constitutional scheme under which we live." [29]

If there was still a doubt that tacit higher law assumptions do in fact control judicial logic in matters of personal liberty, these words, together with those of the majority opinion in *Griswold*, are convincing evidence to the contrary. New frontiers of judicial discovery may yet lie before the Court, as Justice Douglas—doubtless the arch practitioner of higher law reasoning among recent justices—hinted in his remarkable concurring opinion in the 1973 abortion cases. He wrote:

The Ninth Amendment obviously does not create federally enforceable rights. It merely says, "The enumeration in the Constitution, of certain rights, shall not deny or disparage others retained by the people." But a catalogue of these rights includes customary, traditional, and time-honored rights, amenities, privileges, and immunities that come within the sweep of "the Blessings of Liberty" mentioned in the preamble to the Constitution. Many of them in my view come within the meaning of the term "liberty" as used in the Fourteenth Amendment.

First is the autonomous control over the development and expression of one's intellect, interests, tastes, and personality.

These are rights protected by the First Amendment and in my view they are absolute, permitting of no exceptions. . . .

Second is freedom of choice in the basic decisions of one's life respecting marriage, divorce, procreation, contraception, and the education and upbringing of children.

These ["fundamental"] rights, unlike those protected by the First Amendment, are subject to some control by the police power. . . .

Third is the freedom to care for one's health and person, freedom from bodily restraint or compulsion, freedom to walk, stroll, or loaf.

These rights, though fundamental, are likewise subject to regulation on a showing of "compelling state interest." [30]

Summary of Implications

Serious implications follow from the higher law mode of judicial review common to American courts. First, it is evident that the content of various rights protected under the Constitution is spelled out by judges on the basis of their own convictions about what is reasonable, just, fundamentally fair, and in accordance with American ideals, traditions, and conscience. Moreover, new rights regularly emerge out of the same convictions that have no basis in the words of the Constitution itself and are simply extraconstitutional products of higher law (the rights to education, procreation, marriage, travel, association, to attend desegregated schools, the extensive rights of privacy, and the right to have an abortion). The Ninth Amendment, the "Preamble" to the Constitution, and various historical theories concerning the origins of such key portions of the fundamental law

*"The opportunity to be fair and just is rewarding
—but what I especially like is taking the law into
my own hands."*
Source: Reproduced by special permission of Playboy
magazine; copyright 1974 by Playboy.

as the Fourteenth Amendment, in effect, serve to provide judges
with a license to enter into this wide-ranging activity.

That this judicial activity is itself strictly extraconstitutional (not
warranted by any words in the Constitution) seems past dispute. But
it cannot be deemed wrong, for it is as old as the judiciary system in
Anglo-American civilization itself. It stems from the higher law atti-
tude that gave rise to American independence originally, through
devotion to liberty under law. Judicial activity based on the higher
law has great merit in adapting the text of a 200-year-old document

to the changing needs of society, and in fostering a vital sensitivity to liberty and justice. It is our major means of protecting individual rights from the crushing effects of an aggressive, positive state that increasingly dominates our lives. In short, it invigorates the *living* Constitution.

Yet we should not minimize the difficulties attached to this role of the Courts. We may recognize that very little of the existing fabric of personal liberty would be in force today without this mode of judicial review, but we should also recognize that this mode requires the Court to act as a superlegislature. The Court imposes policy decisions and value judgments on the rest of the country in the name of the supreme law of the land, actions armed with the full power of the federal government itself. This is essentially authoritarianism. Whether it is baneful or benign does not affect the fact of the matter. Jefferson had this point in mind when in 1820 he spoke of the judiciary as potentially creating "the despotism of an oligarchy." [31]

Is this kind of authoritarianism indispensable to the satisfactory functioning of our supposedly "democratic" system? That is a hard conclusion for Americans to accept, since it overwhelmingly opposes the image we present to one another and to the world at large. We are a people ruled by the consent of the governed, a government of, by, and for the people—not of, by, and for the values dear to the hearts of the "nine old men" who happen to be justices of the U.S. Supreme Court. Yet it is plain that major social consequences follow from the kind of judicial review we have been discussing, whether the reprehensible implications of Chief Justice Taney's *Dred Scott* decision to abolitionists in 1857, or of Chief Justice Warren's *Brown* decision to segregationists in 1954, or of Justice Blackmun's *Roe* decision to the Roman Catholic bishops and "pro-lifers" generally in 1973. Strife, upheaval, and carnage sometimes follow in the wake of such Court decisions. It is commonly said to have taken our Civil War to reverse Taney. In the South for years Warren was a prime candidate for impeachment, if not lynching. Reverberations still echo from his decisions a quarter of a century later in such unlikely places as South Boston, Detroit, and Pasadena. The abortion decisions were a prominent theme in the 1976 presidential election and the subject of several constitutional amendments introduced in the U.S. House and Senate. Many other examples might be added to this list.

What the Supreme Court actually did in simultaneously abandoning substantive due process and expanding it after 1937 was simply to operate with a double standard in deciding due process cases. In the name of judicial deference to legislative judgments, the Court has dealt with economic regulations by asking only that they bear some "reasonable relation" to justifiable state interests under the police power. As was shown, this meant "hands off," with *one* state economic regulation voided on due process or equal protection grounds in four decades. When fundamental "personal" rights are at stake, however, and not "economic" rights, things are entirely different. Then the Court demands that the state demonstrate a "compelling interest" in limiting the exercise of the right, and it examines any such statute under the test of "strict scrutiny." Many statutes have been voided in this area.

The principal objection to the higher law mode of judicial review had been voiced as early as 1798 in *Calder* v. *Bull*. Justice James Iredell of North Carolina said:

> ... it has been the policy of all the *American* states ... and of the people of the *United States,* when they framed the Constitution, to define with precision the objects of the legislative power, and to restrain its exercise within marked and settled boundaries. If any act of Congress, or of the Legislature of a state, violates those constitutional provisions, it is unquestionably void. ... If, on the other hand, the Legislature of the Union ... shall pass a law, within the general scope of their constitutional power, the Court cannot pronounce it void, merely because it is, in their judgment, contrary to the principles of natural justice. The ideas of natural justice are regulated by no fixed standard: the ablest and the purest of men have differed upon the subject; and all that the Court could properly say, in such an event, would be that the Legislature (possessed of an equal right of opinion) had passed an act which, in the opinion of the judges, was inconsistent with the abstract principles of natural justice.[32]

Throughout his long tenure on the Court (1937–1971), Associate Justice Hugo L. Black constantly reminded his colleagues of the same objections voiced so long before by Justice Iredell. On the one hand (as he wrote in the *Adamson* dissent of 1947),[33] Black steadily repudiated the majority's evident view "that this Court is endowed by the Constitution with boundless power under 'natural law' periodically to expand and contract constitutional standards to conform to the Court's conception of what at a particular time constitutes 'civilized decency' and 'fundamental liberty and justice.'" He contended that "the 'natural law' formula which the Court [used in *Adamson*] to reach its conclusion . . . should be abandoned as an incongruous excrescence on our Constitution. . . ."

On the other hand, Justice Black tenaciously held to the view that legislative history proved "the original purpose of the Fourteenth Amendment [was] to extend to all the people of the nation the complete protection of the Bill of Rights." He disparaged what he called "the natural-law-due-process" philosophy of the Court as "entirely too speculative" because it substituted the concepts of natural law for those of the Bill of Rights; he drew what he believed was a crucial distinction:

> . . . to pass upon the constitutionality of statutes by looking to the particular standards enumerated in the Bill of Rights and other parts of the Constitution is one thing; to invalidate statutes because of application of "natural law" deemed to be above and undefined by the Constitution is another. "In the one instance, courts proceeding within clearly marked constitutional boundaries seek to execute policies written into the Constitution; in the other, they roam at will in the limitless area of their own beliefs as to reasonableness and actually select policies, a responsibility which the Constitution entrusts to the legislative representatives of the people."

Nearly two decades later, Justice Black dissented from the Court's decision in the *Griswold* case (1965) because he could find nothing in the Constitution that absolutely protected any "right of privacy" and because he, again, found the majority relying on the defective "premise that this Court is vested with power to invalidate all state laws that it considers to be arbitrary, capricious, unreasonable, or oppressive, or on this Court's belief that a particular state law under scrutiny has no 'rational or justifying' purpose, or is offensive to a 'sense of fairness and justice.'" Justice Black then went on:

If these formulas based on "natural justice," or others which mean the same thing [a footnote lists such "catchwords" at this point] are to prevail, they require judges to determine what is or is not constitutional on the basis of their own appraisal of what laws are unwise or unnecessary. The power to make such decisions is of course that of a legislative body. Surely it has to be admitted that no provision of the Constitution specifically gives such blanket power to courts to exercise such a supervisory veto. . . .[34]

Finally, Justice Black was able to concur in the Court's decision in the *Duncan* case (1968) that jury trials are required in state criminal proceedings because of his belief that "the Fourteenth Amendment, *as a whole*, makes the Bill of Rights applicable to the States. This would certainly include the language of the Privileges and Immunities Clause, as well as the Due Process Clause," he said in a footnote to his opinion. He continued in the text: "What more precious 'privilege' of American citizenship could there be than that privilege to claim the protections of our great Bill of Rights? I suggest that any reading of 'privileges and immunities of citizens of the United States' which excludes the Bill of Rights' safeguards renders the words of this section of the Fourteenth Amendment meaningless." [35]

Nationalizing the Bill of Rights

The present rationale of the Supreme Court in approaching the subject of individual liberties is that certain of these rights deserve to hold a "preferred position" in our constitutional system because they comprise "the very essence of a scheme of ordered liberty." [36] These preferred rights provide a "unifying principle" "fundamental" to the liberty and justice basic to "all our civil and political institutions." The rights protected by the First Amendment have always stood at the head of the list of these preferred and fundamental liberties. The modern Court has lengthened the list of fundamental rights to include almost all of the enumerated personal rights of the first eight amendments *and* the expansive indeterminate body of rights recognized by the Ninth Amendment, including the "right of privacy"— "customary, traditional, and time-honored rights, amenities, privileges, and immunities that come within the sweep of 'the Blessings of Liberty' mentioned in the preamble to the Constitution." [37]

Absorption and Selective Incorporation

The Court has adopted different language at different times to nationalize the Bill of Rights (that is, to make the provisions of the first eight amendments apply to the states, since they originally applied only to the federal government), with different justices taking different terms to designate one and the same general process. I will not attempt to distinguish among these terms or their rationales, for they are all aspects of a common trend in the Court. We have seen from the *Gitlow* case (1925) how the Court, for the first time, formally accepted the proposition that the freedom of speech and press protected by the First Amendment from abridgment by Congress "are among the fundamental personal rights and 'liberties' protected by the due process clause of the Fourteenth Amendment from impairment by the States."

To cite another example: in 1968, a Louisiana man, Gary Duncan, was convicted of a misdemeanor in a simple battery case, sentenced to serve sixty days in the parish jail, and to pay a $150 fine. Duncan appealed the decision to the Supreme Court, arguing that he was entitled to a jury trial under the Sixth and Fourteenth Amendments. Associate Justice Byron White agreed with Duncan's contention, and delivered the Court's opinion:

> Because we believe that trial by jury in criminal cases is fundamental to the American scheme of justice, we hold that the Fourteenth Amendment guarantees a right of jury trial in all criminal cases which—were they to be tried in federal court—would come within the Sixth Amendment's guarantee.

To support this conclusion, Justice White noticed the variety of ways in which the test for incorporation by the Fourteenth Amendment had been phrased by the Court. "The question has been asked whether a right is among those 'fundamental principles of liberty and justice which lie at the base of all our civil and political institutions,' ...; whether it is 'basic in our system of jurisprudence,' ...; and whether it is 'a fundamental right, essential to a fair trial,' ..." The claim to trial by jury in state criminal cases now had met the test, White concluded.[38]

The argument made here is that substantive due process, absorption, selective incorporation—the whole complex development of a nationalized Bill of Rights—is rooted in the Court's devotion to higher law principles of adjudication no less than in its devotion to the U.S. Constitution and the rule of law generally. "Selective incorporation" is, today, the official term for designating this process. It began, in fact, long before *Gitlow*. As early as 1897 the Court (without mentioning the "just compensation" clause of the Fifth Amendment) held that private property could not be taken by the City of Chicago for public purposes (the power of eminent domain) without just compensation under the Fourteenth Amendment requirement of due process.[39] A case decided in 1908 produced a dictum that some of the personal rights enumerated in the first eight amendments possibly were protected against state action because to deny them would infringe due process of law. But were this so, the Court went on, it would not be because the rights were enumerated in the federal Bill of Rights but because "they are of such a nature that they are included in the conception of due process of law." [40]

Palko v. Connecticut. Justice Benjamin Cardozo expressed the Court's thinking on this subject in opinions written in the mid-1930s. Some state procedures, he said, might be offensive to the due process clause of the Fourteenth Amendment because they violate "some principle of justice so rooted in the traditions and conscience of our people as to be ranked as fundamental," and that certain proscriptions are "implicit in the concept of ordered liberty." [41]

The latter comment was elicited from Cardozo in the Court's decision in a murder case, *Palko* v. *Connecticut*. Palko had been tried by a Connecticut jury and convicted of second degree murder. He was sentenced to life in prison. The State of Connecticut appealed to the State Supreme Court of Errors, which reversed the judgment because of errors of law and ordered a new trial. At the second trial, Palko objected that he was being placed twice in jeopardy for the same crime, contrary to the protection he claimed from the Fourteenth Amendment. The objection was overruled, and Palko again was convicted—this time for first degree murder, and sentenced to death. His appeal before the Supreme Court was unsuccessful, the Court declining to "select" the double jeopardy clause of the Fifth Amendment for incorporation—a step it took much later (in 1969).

But Justice Cardozo, on the way to this unfortunate result, did have this to say:

> We reach a different place of social and moral values when we pass to the privileges and immunities taken over from the earlier articles of the federal bill of rights and brought within the Fourteenth Amendment by a process of absorption.... [T]he process of absorption has had its source in the belief that neither liberty nor justice would exist if they were sacrificed.... This is true, for illustration, of freedom of thought, and speech. Of that freedom one may say that it is the matrix, the indispensable condition of nearly every other form of freedom. With rare aberrations a pervasive recognition of that truth can be traced in our history, political and legal. So it has come about that the domain of liberty, withdrawn by the Fourteenth Amendment from encroachment by the states, has been enlarged ... to include liberty of the mind as well as liberty of action.

Too bad for Palko! Liberty had not been enlarged to include double jeopardy protection, for the Court distinguished a "dividing line" to the disadvantage of the appellant. Does the kind of double jeopardy to which Palko was subjected, Justice Cardozo asked, impose "a hardship so acute and shocking that our polity will not endure it? Does it violate those 'fundamental principles of liberty and justice which lie at the base of all our civil and political institutions'? ... The answer surely must be 'no.'" Palko lived—and died— a generation before his time.[42]

The language of "absorption" still was used when, in 1958, a decision brought about the discovery of the new right of association. The Court then stated that it "is beyond debate that freedom to engage in association for the advancement of beliefs and ideas is an inseparable aspect of the 'liberty' assured by the Due Process Clause of the Fourteenth Amendment, which embraces freedom of speech...."[43]

But by the early 1960s the tag "selective incorporation" had supplanted "absorption." One by one, in case after case, the specific rights listed in the Bill of Rights were read into liberty in the due process clause of the Fourteenth Amendment. The preferred freedoms of the First Amendment (speech, press, and religion) were expanded to include the Fourth Amendment's prohibition of unreasonable searches and seizures and to exclude illegally seized evidence from criminal trials. The Fifth Amendment's guaranty against compelled self-incrimination was included, as were the Sixth Amendment's rights to counsel, to confrontation of opposing witnesses, to compulsory process for obtaining witnesses. Also read into liberty in the due process clause was the right that would have saved Palko from the death penalty: "[W]e today find that the double jeopardy prohibition of the Fifth Amendment represents a fundamental ideal in our constitutional heritage," said Justice Thurgood Marshall in 1969, "and that it should apply to the States through the Fourteenth Amendment." [44]

State v. Federal Absorption. The question remains as to whether the rights, once incorporated, apply against state violation to the same degree that they do against federal violation? Despite loud grumblings from the minority, the Court majority has consistently held that they do, and that the standards imposed on the states are identical to those on the federal government. The Court has emphatically rejected "the notion that the Fourteenth Amendment applies to the State [of Florida] only a 'watered-down, subjective version of the individual guarantees of the Bill of Rights.' " [45]

Despite these good words, however, these are signs that a "dual standard" may be emerging. Thus the guaranty of jury trial has been incorporated. But a jury need not have the traditional twelve members, the Court said, in finding a six-member Florida jury constitutional. The number twelve it viewed as merely a historical accident, a carryover from the English common law.[46] Another sign was the 1972 decision by which the Court (voting five to four) agreed that unanimous decisions by juries in the states are not necessary, and that the Fourteenth Amendment's demands incorporating jury trial are met by juries that reach their verdicts by a nine-to-three majority.[47] Would an eight-to-four majority suffice? What about a seven-to-five majority? The Court didn't say, but Justice Blackmun doubted that much below nine-to-three majorities could satisfy due process requirements.

As these examples suggest, each of the "rights" is highly complex, with the result that even when a right has been "incorporated," it may not have been completely incorporated in all aspects of application against state infringement. Hence, even if there are no "dual standards," there are meaningful degrees of incorporation. The federal prohibitions of incorporated rights are not necessarily identical to the prohibitions imposed by the same right on states. A number of other such instances will be encountered in our discussion of criminal justice later in chapter 4.

Results of Nationalization

Two consequences of nationalizing the Bill of Rights by applying the preferred position doctrine are: (1) the absorption or selected incorporation into the Fourteenth Amendment—one by one, especially between 1925 and 1969—of each of the personal rights listed and implied by the Bill of Rights so that they now apply to the states (see Table 2–1); and (2) the tightening of the standards applied by the Court against state actions that invade any of the preferred rights.

In general, the second point means that the preferred rights—most especially those rights protected by the First Amendment—are so sacred as to be placed beyond the reach of infringement by majorities. They verge on being absolute rights and "are susceptible of restriction only to prevent grave and immediate danger to interests which the State may lawfully protect." In fact, such modern justices as Hugo F. Black and William O. Douglas believed the freedoms of speech and press to be absolute rights, admitting of no exceptions whatever. For the entire Court, this is so strong a belief (again, especially in the First Amendment areas of freedom of thought, speech, press, and religion) that the Court usually presumes that a state statute is suspect against "the preferred place given in our scheme to the great, indispensable democratic freedoms secured by" the Bill of Rights. The Court's "priority gives these liberties a sanctity and a sanction not permitting dubious intrusions," [48] and it can abridge them only for "compelling state interests." We must now consider these state interests and their constitutional basis.

TABLE 2–1

The results of "Absorption" and "Selective Incorporation"
provisions of the "Bill of Rights" that apply to the states

Amendment:	What is incorporated:	What is not incorporated:

1	Speech:
	  Gitlow v. *New York*
	  (1925)
	  Fiske v. *Kansas* (1927)
	  Stromberg v. *California*
	  (1931)
	Press:
	  Near v. *Minnesota*
	  (1931)
	Free exercise of religion:
	  Hamilton v. *Regents*
	  (1934)
	  Cantwell v. *Connecti-*
	  cut (1941)
	No establishment of
	religion:
	  Everson v. *Board of*
	  Education (1947)
	  McCollum v. *Board of*
	  Education (1948)
	Peaceable assembly:
	  DeJonge v. *Oregon*
	  (1937)
	Right of petition:
	  DeJonge v. *Oregon*
	  (1937)
	  Bridges v. *California*
	  (1941)
	  Hague v. *CIO* (1939)	

2		Keep and bear arms:
		  U.S. v. *Cruickshank*
		  (1876)
		  Presser v. *Illinois*
		  (1886)

3		No quartering of soldiers in homes: No cases
4	Evidence admitted as re- sult of unreasonable search and seizure (exclusionary rule):	

TABLE 2–1 (*cont.*)

Amendment:	What is incorporated:	What is not incorporated:
	Wolf v. *Colorado* (1949) *Mapp* v. *Ohio* (1961) *United States* v. *Janis* (1976)	
5	Double jeopardy: *Benton* v. *Maryland* (1969) *Ashe* v. *Swenson* (1970) Due process of law (as per the 14th Amendment) Just compensation (eminent domain safeguards): *Chicago, B. & Q. Railroad* v. *City of Chicago* (1897) Self-incrimination: *Malloy* v. *Hogan* (1964) *Griffin* v. *California* (1965)	Grand jury indictment: *Hurtado* ˙v. *California* (1884)
6	Counsel in all criminal cases: Capital: *Powell* v. *Alabama* (1932) Non-capital: *Gideon* v. *Wainwright* (1963) Fair trial: *Powell* v. *Alabama* (1932) Public trial: *In re Oliver* (1948) Speedy trial: *Klopfer* v. *North* *Carolina* (1967) Jury trial: *Duncan* v. *Louisiana* (1968) Impartial jury: *Parker* v. *Gladden* (1967) Notice of charges:	

TABLE 2–1 (cont.)

Amendment:	What is incorporated:	What is not incorporated:
	In re Oliver (1948) Confrontation of accusers: *Pointer* v. *Texas* (1965) Compulsory process for appearance of witnesses: *Washington* v. *Texas* (1967)	
7	Fair trial: *Powell* v. *Alabama* (1932)	Jury trial in civil cases in which value of controversy exceeds $20: *Adamson* v. *California* (1947), J. Frankfurter concurring *Minn. & St. L. R. Co.* v. *Bombolis* (1916)
8	Cruel and unusual punishment: *Louisiana ex rel. Fran- cis* v. *Resweber* (1947) *Robinson* v. *California* (1962)	Excessive bail and fines: *Schilb* v. *Kuebel* (1971) *Tate* v. *Short* (1971), preventing automatic jailing of indigents

Source: The Constitution of the United States of America: Analysis and Interpretation, eds. Lester S. Jayson, *et al.*, Senate Document No. 92–82, 92d Congress, 2d Session (Washington, D.C.: U.S. Government Printing Office, 1973), 905–906. *See* the discussion in Henry J. Abraham, *Freedom and the Court: Civil Rights and Liberties in the United States* (3rd Ed.; New York: Oxford University Press, 1977), chap. 3, esp. pp. 56–105.

Police Power and Court Standards

Police Power

The inherent power of a state's government to legislate and take any action it deems necessary to secure the lives, safety, health, morals, welfare, and property of itself and its people is called "police power." This power is inherent in sovereignty and coextensive with the power of government itself. It will be seen that, with the rare exception of certain aspects of race relations (considered in chapter 5), almost all of the litigation surrounding the Bill of Rights has involved alleged violations of individual rights by governmental agents and laws. That you enjoy your rights within the bounds set by an ongoing social, political, and legal system is obvious enough. That a tension exists in principle between law and liberty is also obvious.

Thus, the states' general power to govern and regulate is their police power. But police power has little or nothing to do with the power of the police. The best way to understand it is to see it as an extensive body of power possessed by each state that is intended by the "Reserve Clause" of the Tenth Amendment, as follows: "The powers not delegated to the United States by the Constitution, nor prohibited by it to the States, are reserved to the States respectively, or to the people." Such a vast power cannot be defined precisely. It is distinguished from the national power, which rests on the Constitution, and also from the power of taxation, so that police and taxing powers together are understood to compose the whole power within its reserved sovereignty of a state "to govern men and things."

The root principle of police power is expressed in a common and civil law maxim: use whatever is your own in such a way that you do not injure the person and property of others. By this principle, each state has the power to define the ways in which everyone may use one's own liberty and property without injuring others, and to pre-scribe how the lives, health, property, and general well-being of per-sons within its jurisdiction will be protected. Any law that either limits personal rights beyond what is necessary for the general wel-fare, or seeks to abolish rights that do not infringe on the rights of others, transgresses the limits of the police power of government.[49] It is on this contested ground between asserted regulatory authority and claimed personal rights that the skirmishes and battles over liberties are fought in law courts.

A 1976 decision in the sensitive area of free expression illustrates the collision between liberty and regulation by state authority.[50] The Court upheld Detroit's zoning regulations. These required "adult movie" theaters to be at least 1000 feet apart, the same distance from other "regulated uses" (such as bars, adult book stores, and hotels), and 500 feet from a residential area. The city had a justifiable interest in preserving the character of neighborhoods to prevent mid-city blight and emergence of skid rows. The Court insisted that it was not its function to appraise the wisdom of the [Detroit City Council's] decision to require adult theaters to be separated rather than concentrated in the same areas. In either event, the city's interest in attempting to preserve the quality of urban life is one that must be accorded high respect . . . the city must be allowed a reasonable opportunity to experiment with solutions to admittedly serious problems.

By this rationale, the Court rejected claims by theater owners for protection of expression under the First Amendment as incorporated by the due process clause of the Fourteenth Amendment. Justice Stevens's majority opinion asserted that "reasonable regulations of time, place, and manner of protected speech" are permitted when necessary to further significant governmental interests. Even protected speech, he said, may be judged by the content of the speech, and the nature of the audience, to ascertain the degree of protection it is afforded by the Constitution—or whether it should be totally suppressed, as with obscenity or the communication of adult fare to juveniles. Total suppression was not at issue here. Justice John Paul Stevens said:

But few of us would march our sons and daughters off to war to preserve the citizen's right to see "Specified Sexual Activities" exhibited in the theaters of our choice. Even though the First Amendment protects communication in this area from total suppression, we hold that the State may legitimately use the content of these materials as the basis for placing them in a different classification from other motion pictures.

Nothing more was at stake, the Court concluded, "than a limitation on the place where adult films may be exhibited. . . ."

Court Standards

By what standards (or "tests") do the courts judge the limits of powers and the scope of rights? The question is of great importance in determining how individual rights are defined by the judiciary. But it is hard to answer in general terms because different courts at different times use different tests. Tests have varied not only from case to case and from right to right, but frequently have been determined by the specific facts of a case. The problems can be illustrated by considering the several tests applied from time to time especially in freedom of expression cases arising under the First Amendment: clear and present danger, bad tendency, clear and probable danger, weighing and balancing, fighting words, chilling effect, vagueness, over-breadth, and least restrictive means.

Clear and Present Danger. The best known of these tests is clear and present danger. As the Supreme Court defines it, it means that a person is not liable to punishment by the government for what he says, writes, or otherwise expresses unless, by its nature or the circumstances attending it, the expression creates a clear and present danger of substantive evil within the power of the government to prevent. For instance, said Justice Oliver Wendell Holmes (who invented the test) in a famous sentence: "The most stringent protection of free speech would not protect a man in falsely shouting fire in a theatre and causing a panic." [51] But Justice Holmes said this in a 1919 decision upholding a conviction for violation of the World War I Espionage Act, and it was twenty years before a majority of the Supreme Court ever applied the test in supporting freedom of expression against state invasion, although there was much talk about it in minority opinions.

Bad Tendency Test. The Court majorities have generally relied on the bad tendency test, which says that the states' police power is validly applied against any person who abuses the freedom of speech and press by uttering things injurious to the public welfare, tending to corrupt morals, inciting a crime, or disturbing the peace. The *Gitlow* decision illustrates this test, with the Court insisting "that the general provisions of the statute may be constitutionally applied to the specific utterance of the defendant if *its natural tendency and probable effect* was to bring about the substantive evil which the legislative body might prevent." [52] Roughly between 1940 and 1950, clear and present danger finally came to be applied in a number of cases by Court majorities, and it now was yoked with the preferred position doctrine in protection of our most prized liberties.

Terminiello v. *Chicago.* Perhaps the last application of the clear and present danger test was in a 1949 case that arose from a riot in Chicago. A defrocked Catholic priest, Father Terminiello, appeared at a mass meeting of anticommunists to be greeted outside the hall by rock and brick throwing picketers as part of "a surging, howling mob" shouting "God damned Fascists, Nazis, ought to hang the so and sos," among other epithets. About twenty-eight windows were broken. Terminiello spoke at length, addressing the audience as "Fellow Christians" but adding that "I suppose *some of the scum got in by mistake....*" He went on to speak of the "*slimy scum*" outside the hall who were attempting to "*destroy America by revolution.*" Terminiello identified the hostile crowd with the "murderous Russians" and spoke of the "fifty-seven varieties of pinks and reds and pastel shades in this country," all traceable to the New Deal. He said much else in a similar vein. The audience within the hall responded, not only with applause, but with statements including: "Jews, niggers and Catholics would have to be gotten rid of." "Yes, the Jews are all killers, murderers." "Kill the Jews," "Dirty kikes."

Terminiello was found guilty of disorderly conduct by a jury, in violation of a Chicago city ordinance, and fined. He claimed the protection of freedom of speech. The Supreme Court acknowledged that, while not an absolute right, one function of free speech in America is "to invite dispute." The Court continued: "It may indeed best serve its high purpose when it induces a condition of unrest, creates dissatisfaction with conditions as they are, or even stirs people to anger." Speech cannot be prohibited or penalized for such reasons. Rather it is "protected against censorship or punishment, unless shown likely to produce a clear and present danger of a serious substantive evil that arises far above public inconvenience, annoyance, or unrest." Terminiello's conviction was overturned.[53]

Clear and Probable Danger. Just when the country was trying to decide how to cope with the domestic dangers of communism, there emerged the clear and probable danger test, a modification of the clear and present danger test. The Supreme Court reasoned, under these circumstances, that in free speech cases it must ask itself "whether the gravity of the 'evil,' discounted by its improbability [of actually occurring], justifies such invasion of free speech as is necessary to avoid the danger." [54]

The Court is here quoted from a 1951 decision in which it sustained the Smith Act, a federal law that prohibited advocacy of the overthrow of the U.S. government by force and violence. At the same time, the clear and present danger doctrine was rewritten, and convictions of eleven leaders of the Communist Party of the United States were sustained on the basis of the revised test. The Court agreed with Congress's determination that "[o]verthrow of the Government by force and violence is certainly a substantial enough interest for the Government to limit speech." Congress need not wait until a revolution is about to occur to take action. The Court found the Communist Party's leadership devoted to advocating and intending precisely the kinds of actions prohibited by the Smith Act. It rejected the "contention that success or probability of success is the criterion" for deciding whether such advocacy is permissible. "If the Government is aware that a group aiming at its overthrow is attempting to indoctrinate its members and to commit them to a course whereby they will strike when the leaders feel the circumstances permit, action by the Government is required," the Court stated.

Balancing Public Interest Against Personal Rights. The further test of balancing (or weighing) has been widely used since 1950 and is still prominent today. Its rationale is to weigh the public's interest against personal rights in regulating particular kinds of conduct or utterances. If the result is a partial and conditional abridgment of some protected right (belief, expression, association), then it becomes the duty "of the courts to determine which of these two conflicting interests demands the greater protection under the particular circumstances presented." [55] The 1976 Detroit zoning case (discussed above, in connection with the exercise of police power) well illustrates the balancing test; for there the public interest of preserving a wholesome urban environment was balanced against the right of free expression through the public showing of "adult" motion pictures. The Court concluded that regulation of such expression, not amounting to suppression, was allowable because of the weight of the public interest at stake.

Fighting Words and Chilling Effect. A state was within its authority, according to the fighting words test, if it prevented or punished speech of a lewd, obscene, profane, libelous, or insulting kind—words whose "very utterance inflict injury or tend to incite an immediate breach of peace." This was said by the Court in 1942 in upholding the conviction of a man for calling a policeman "A God damned racketeer" and "a damned Fascist" where the state's interest was prevention of violence by curbing free speech.[56] The chilling effect test has been applied to a variety of governmental actions that tend to inhibit ("chill") the exercise of First Amendment liberties without being justified by compelling public interests.

Vagueness, Over-breadth, and Least Restrictive Means. These tests have been widely used to void statutes that are so imprecisely worded as to violate procedural due process or to delegate legislative authority to police or administrative officials. For example, the vagueness test was used to void the New Jersey statute previously noted because it too vaguely made it a crime simply to be a "gangster." [57] This was a procedural due process case, but the principle was the same in the area of the First Amendment.

While often linked together, vagueness and overbreadth are not synonymous. A statute that is quite specific can be voided because it is too broad or sweeping in its prohibition of action or speech. For example, a Georgia law was reversed on the basis of overbreadth because it provided that any person "who shall without provocation, use to or of another, and in his presence ... opprobrious words or abusive language, tending to cause a breach of the peace" was guilty of a misdemeanor. When a scuffle occurred between anti-war picketers and police at an Army building, one of the picketers told a policeman: "white son of a bitch, I'll kill you," "You son of a bitch, I'll choke you to death," and "You son of a bitch, if you ever put your hands on me again, I'll cut you all to pieces." By a four-to-three majority the Court found the statute overbroad on its face and freed the picketer.[58]

The least restrictive means test was used in determining that Arkansas school teachers could not be compelled to list all their memberships annually over a five-year period as a condition of employment in the public schools. The statute requiring this was held unconstitutional because it violated personal, academic, and association rights, and used an unjustifiably unrestricted means to accomplish the legitimate purpose of investigating the competence and fitness of teachers.[59]

These three tests underscore the necessity that statutes and regulations be narrowly and precisely drawn. They have been relied on by the Court in nullifying laws aimed at obscenity, public demonstrations, and requiring loyalty oaths. Specifically, they have been deployed so as to (1) presume on its face the unconstitutionality of legislation that abridges a preferred freedom, with the burden of proof lying on the government to prove otherwise; (2) require as proof that a clear, immediate, and actual danger to some substantive public interest is present in the exercise of the abridged freedom; and (3) require the government to show that the legislation in question is sufficiently narrow in scope so as to eradicate an immediate evil without endangering other protected liberties.

Conclusions

Use of these tests by an activist Court under Chief Justice Earl Warren (1953–1969) effected nothing less than a civil rights revolution by greatly expanding federal judicial and congressional authority in the sphere of individual rights and race relations. The revolution resulted in: (1) expanding Supreme Court review jurisdiction to cover local, state, as well as national actions when they collide with the claims of personal rights; (2) giving the Court authority to establish guidelines and standards in the sphere of personal rights for *all* governmental authorities; (3) expanding jurisdiction of federal district judges to respond to habeas corpus petitions based on claimed rights' violations by local and state officials; and (4) creating in fact (if not in theory) new authority for Congress to draft legislation as "necessary and proper" to implement the broadened scope of rights now incorporated and nationalized.[60]

The high-water mark in Court activism and liberalism was reached by 1969. Chief Justice Warren retired to be replaced through President Nixon's appointment of Warren E. Burger. While no counterrevolution has occurred to undo all of the enterprising things done by the Warren Court, the Burger Court now includes a solid majority of justices appointed by Republican Presidents Richard M. Nixon and Gerald R. Ford: Harry A. Blackmun, Lewis F. Powell, William

H. Rehnquist, and John Paul Stevens, in addition to the Chief Justice. The Court today is quite clearly less prone to judicial intervention, less activist, less libertarian. The general result is that there has been some narrowing of protections afforded individual rights. We have seen that Detroit, for example, was permitted to restrict expression by means of a zoning ordinance regulating the location of adult motion picture theaters. The impression given by a number of other decisions is that the Court has chipped away at the expansive reach of the federal judiciary in ways best seen in the context of the more detailed consideration of the specific liberties taken up in the next chapters.

The Burger Court is showing itself less eager to jump into controversies that the Warren Court would eagerly have entered. It has turned down major cases on the technical grounds that the appellants had no "standing" to sue (no real interests concretely at stake that the Court has power to protect). The Court defined "standing" as follows:

> The essence of the standing question, in its constitutional dimension, "is whether the plaintiff has 'alleged such a personal stake in the outcome of the controversy' as to warrant his invocation of federal-court jurisdiction and to justify exercise of the court's remedial powers on his behalf." [61]

The Court went on to quote a previous case to substantiate its position: "The plaintiff must show that he himself is injured by the challenged action of the defendant. The injury may be indirect . . . , but the complaint must indicate that the injury is indeed fairly traceable to the defendant's acts or omissions. . . . It has long been clear that economic injury is not the only kind of injury that can support a plaintiff's standing." [62]

These statements indicate that it will henceforth be tougher to get cases into the Supreme Court. The Court has tended, correspondingly, to give greater support to the states' judicial proceedings by cutting off the recent flood of habeas corpus appeals of persons convicted in state courts by restricting federal court jurisdiction in that area. It has narrowed the rights of individuals under investigation and arrest by rulings which: (1) relax the criteria of what kind of evidence is admissible in court, (2) modify the rights of criminal suspects during police interrogation, and (3) curb assertion of constitutional rights by prison inmates.

Counter to this general trend to narrow rights, however, were 1976 and 1977 decisions that expanded rights. They increased the protections afforded defendants in the courtroom; the reach of the First Amendment in cases involving door-to-door solicitation; freedom of speech and press to include "commercial speech" (by upholding pharmacists' rights to advertise drug prices and lawyers' rights to advertise fees).

In short, the current trend is toward: (1) narrowing individual rights, (2) supporting the integrity of state judicial and legislative decisions, and (3) retrenching federal judicial involvement in local affairs. But the Burger Court is far from being "conservative," much less monolithic and doctrinaire in its approach to individual rights cases. What may happen in the long run is hard to say. But it is worth mentioning that only with the appointment of Justice Stevens in December 1975 (to replace retired Justice William O. Douglas, a leading libertarian and activist) did the Nixon-Ford appointees finally achieve a majority on the nine-member Supreme Court.

Summary

In this chapter we have examined the formal emergence of the "new substantive due process" and shown its continuity with both the old version of substantive due process and the higher law strand of American legal thought. We have paid considerable attention, then, to the process of nationalizing the Bill of Rights. From the *Gitlow* decision, with which the nationalizing of the rights contained in the first eight amendments began, thereby making them applicable to the states, we have traced the extension of protections from 1925 through 1969. In that period, all rights contained in these amendments were absorbed or selectively incorporated into the due process clause of the Fourteenth Amendment, except five: (1) the Fifth Amendment's requirement of indictment by grand jury; (2) the Seventh Amendment's requirement of a jury trial in *civil* cases over controversies involving more than $20; (3) the Eighth Amendment's prohibition of "excessive bail . . . and fines"; (4) the Second Amendment's guaranty that ". . . the right of the people to keep and bear arms, shall not be infringed"; and (5) the most obscure of all the Bill of Rights, the Third Amendment which forbids involuntary and illegal quartering of troops in private homes. In addition to the explicitly mentioned rights, we saw that a number of other implied and peripheral rights were also incorporated, including the rights of association, travel, procreation, multiple rights of privacy, and abortion.

We also examined the meaning and extent of the police power of the states, and then surveyed the judicial standards or tests applied, especially in cases dealing with First Amendment rights. These tests are asserted to challenge various exercises of the police power. We ended with a view of the present outlook of the Supreme Court.

Chapter 3 continues to examine the First Amendment rights that hold a preferred position in our system. These fundamental rights are the freedoms of speech, press, thought, petition and assembly, and religion.

REVIEW QUESTIONS

1. Discuss the facts and significance of the *Gitlow* case.

2. What is meant by the "new substantive due process"? In what decision did it first formally arise? How is it related to "higher law"?

3. Relate the old and new substantive due process doctrines.

4. What is the "double standard" in substantive due process cases?

5. What is meant by the "right of privacy"?

6. What is meant by "nationalizing" the Bill of Rights?

7. Explain absorption and selective incorporation.

8. Discuss the *Palko* case. Is it still in effect?

9. What is "police power"? What is its significance in defining individual rights?

10. List and explain the principal standards or tests used by the U.S. Supreme Court in deciding cases brought under the First Amendment.

11. What is meant by an "activist" Court? What impact did the Warren Court generally have on the scope of individual rights?

12. From the present inconclusive evidence, how do trends of the Burger Court seem to compare with those of the Warren Court in the field of individual rights and in general judicial philosophy?

13. What is meant by "standing"?

CHAPTER THREE

A Preferred Position: First Amendment Liberties

Make up your minds that happiness depends on being free, and freedom depends on being courageous.[1]

PERICLES (430 B.C.)

The prescriptions in favor of liberty ought to be levelled against that quarter where the greatest danger lies, namely, that which possesses the highest prerogative of power.[2]

JAMES MADISON (1789)

The heart and life of a free Government is a free press; take away this and you take away its main support.[3]

JOHN NICHOLAS (1798)

NEAR v. MINNESOTA

*T*HE SATURDAY PRESS, a Minneapolis newspaper, was not your everyday run-of-the-mill weekly shopping guide. You could see this from "Facts Not Theories," an article its editor, Mr. J. M. Near, published in the November 19, 1927, issue. It was typical of his journal:

> "I am a bosom friend of Mr. Olson [the County Attorney]," snorted a gentleman of Yiddish blood, "and I want to protest against your article," and blah, blah, blah, ad infinitum, ad nauseum. . . .
>
> Practically every vendor of vile hooch, every owner of a moonshine still, every snake-faced gangster and embryonic yegg in the Twin Cities is a JEW.
>
> Having these examples before me, I feel that I am justified in my refusal to take orders from a Jew who boasts that he is a "bosom friend" of Mr. Olson. . . .
>
> I simply state a fact when I say that ninety per cent of the crimes committed against society in this city are committed by Jew gangsters. . . .
>
> It is Jew Jew, Jew, as long as one cares to comb over the records.
>
> I am launching no attack against the Jewish people AS A RACE. I am merely calling attention to a FACT. And if the people of that race and faith wish to rid themselves of the odium and stigma THE RODENTS OF THEIR OWN RACE HAVE BROUGHT UPON THEM, they need only to step to the front and help the decent citizens of Minneapolis rid the city of these criminal Jews.

Editor Near regaled the citizenry of the Twin Cities with this kind of choice fare for nine consecutive issues. His targets were the principal officials of local government, the Minneapolis JOURNAL and TRIBUNE, the Jewish race, and the Hennepin County grand jury. He took particular delight in pillorying the mayor, chief of police, and prosecuting attorneys. He claimed that the city and county governments were under the thumb of a Jewish gangster who controlled gambling, bootlegging, and racketeering in the Minneapolis area. Officials were charged by Near, throughout 327 pages reprinted in the trial court's record, with gross neglect of duty, illicit relations with gangsters, participation in graft. He redoubled his attacks when his associate, Mr. Guilford, was shot by gangsters soon after the series of articles began to appear.

Background of the Near Case

What could be done about obnoxious Editor Near and his scandal sheet? As it happened, Minnesota law included a statute that made it a "nuisance" (which Near no doubt was) to publish or distribute "an obscene, lewd, and lascivious newspaper, magazine, or other periodical" or "a malicious, scandalous and defamatory newspaper, magazine or other periodical."

By invoking the statute, Mr. Floyd B. Olson (the victimized County Attorney) entered a complaint and secured a temporary injunction from a state district court stopping publication of THE SATURDAY PRESS. Near challenged the order on freedom of the press and due process grounds and appealed the case to the Minnesota Supreme Court, which ruled against him. The case was then tried in district court, which issued a permanent injunction against further publication. Violation of the injunction was punishable under contempt of court proceedings by a fine of $1000 or imprisonment in the county jail for up to twelve months. The trial court found that Near had engaged in regularly publishing and circulating "a malicious, scandalous and defamatory newspaper," which was declared to be a "public nuisance" under state law. Near again appealed to the State Supreme Court, which upheld the conviction and denied that the statute violated the state's constitution or the federal "Bill of Rights."

The Supreme Court Decision

Undaunted, Editor Near took his case to the U.S. Supreme Court. There, in 1931, four years after all this started, a decision was rendered in the case of NEAR v. MINNESOTA EX REL. OLSON (1931).[4] The Court was closely divided on the case. Associate Justice Pierce Butler, himself a Minnesotan, spoke for the four-member minority in agreeing that Editor Near had got just what he deserved. The state statute was sound and ought to be upheld as a valid exercise of the police power to protect the general welfare of the community. THE SATURDAY PRESS, and Near with it, was, indeed, a nuisance as defined by the statute and "offensive to morals, order and good government. . . ." Near was in the "regular business of malicious defamation," Justice Butler said.

Chief Justice Charles Evans Hughes and the rest of the five-member majority took a contrary view. The case was unusual, perhaps unique, they thought. It raised issues "of grave importance transcending the local interests involved in the particular action." How so? Near had unquestionably made some serious accusations, Chief Justice Hughes admitted. But for the first time in its history, the Court's majority laid down this rule:

> It is no longer open to doubt that the liberty of the press and of speech is within the liberty safeguarded by the due process clause of the Fourteenth Amendment from invasion by state action. [Freedom of speech and press must be considered an] essential personal liberty of the citizen [protected] by the general guaranty of fundamental rights of person and property.

Chief Justice Hughes's analysis of the Minnesota statute led to the conclusion that it "not only operates to suppress the offending newspaper or periodical but to put the publisher under an effective censorship." If you cut through the details of procedure, the Chief Justice continued, that fact becomes plain. The statute allows public authorities to bring a newspaper publisher or editor before a judge on the charge of publishing "scandalous and defamatory matter" consisting of charges of official dereliction on the part of these same authorities. Then, unless the editor or publisher can prove to the judge "that the charges are true and are published with good motives and for justifiable ends, his newspaper . . . is suppressed and further publication is made punishable as a contempt. This is the essence of censorship."

Can a statute that so operates be constitutional? Is it "consistent with the conception of the liberty of the press as historically conceived and guaranteed"? The answer was no. And why not? Because, Chief Justice Hughes said:

> . . . liberty of the press, historically considered and taken up by the Federal Constitution, has meant, principally, although not exclusively, immunity from previous restraints or censorship. . . . That liberty was [during the Colonial period] especially cherished for the immunity it afforded from previous restraint of the publication of censure of public officers and charges of official misconduct. . . .

Both sides of the Court appealed to history. Justice Butler thought the English view, as represented in Blackstone's COMMENTARIES, could not sustain the majority's version of previous restraint. There the issue was prior restraint by requiring a license from administrative officials. But there was no administrative or licensing activity in advance of publication at issue in the NEAR case. Rather, there was a legislative determination that identified ways in which the "abuse of the right of free press" could occur. The statute "denounces the things done as a nuisance" on the good grounds "that they threaten morals, peace and good order. There is no question of the power of the State to denounce such transgressions."

Not so, retorted the Chief Justice. The absence of any administrative intervention in the NEAR case was brushed aside as a mere technicality. Chief Justice Hughes quoted James Madison in support.[5] "The great and essential rights of the people," Madison had written, "are secured against legislative as well as against executive ambition. They are secured . . . by constitutions paramount to laws. This security of the freedom of the press requires that it should be exempt not only from previous restraint by the executive, as in Great Britain, but from legislative restraint also. . . ."

The issue of "the permissibility of subsequent punishment" for publication of libelous material was not a question here, the Chief Justice observed, and Minnesota law provided for both public and private redress in its libel laws for any wrongs Near may have committed.

True, even the guaranty of freedom from prior restraint of publication is "not absolutely unlimited," Hughes acknowledged, "But the limitation has been recognized only in exceptional cases." The exceptions are: (1) when the nation is at war, certain utterances (such as those involving military secrets) protected during times of peace may be prohibited; (2) primary requirements of decency may be enforced by the states against obscene matter; (3) the security of the community may be protected against advocacy and incitement to violent acts tending to the overthrow of orderly government by force; and (4) the Constitution does not protect a person's speech in which his "words . . . may have all the effect of force."

None of these categories fit the NEAR case; however. The mere fact of scandal and discomfit of public officials was not sufficient ground to justify previous restraint of publication. The question of the "truth of the charges contained in the periodical" was of no account here. "Charges of reprehensible conduct, and in particular of official malfeasance, unquestionably create a public scandal, but the theory of the constitutional guaranty is that even a more serious public evil would be caused by authority to prevent publication. . . ."

Justice Butler vehemently disagreed. He thought that such logic, depriving officials of any means to curb "false and malicious assaults," exposed the "peace and good order of every community" to the dangers of having public officials vulnerable to schemes "for oppression, blackmail, or extortion" by unscrupulous and insolvent publishers. The State Supreme Court's judgment ought to be affirmed!

The majority of the justices advocated "a vigilant and courageous press, especially in great cities" as a vital means of protecting the public from the great "opportunities for malfeasance and corruption . . . by unfaithful officials" through criminal alliance and official neglect. The mere fact that "liberty of the press may be abused by miscreant purveyors of scandal does not make any the less necessary the immunity of the press from previous restraint in dealing with official conduct. Subsequent punishment," Chief Justice Hughes added, "for such abuses as may exist is the appropriate remedy, consistent with constitutional privilege."

The Minnesota statute was declared unconstitutional. The State Supreme Court's judgment was reversed. Editor Near was free to resume publication of THE SATURDAY PRESS and renew his crusade.

Implications of the Near Case

NEAR v. MINNESOTA is a landmark decision and the leading case in the area of freedom of the press. It was the first case to declare a state law unconstitutional for conflicting with the freedom of the press clause of the First Amendment; and it was the first case *to incorporate that clause into the due process of law protections of the Fourteenth Amendment.*

———————

At the core of American liberty lies the freedoms protected by the First Amendment, the freedom of conscience, speech, and thought. From the dim horizon of antiquity, Pericles long ago proclaimed the essential dependence of happiness upon liberty and of liberty, in turn, upon courage. A sense of priority and hierarchy is reflected in the formula, for to the old Greeks (as to the Americans of Madison's generation) the highest good attainable by action was happiness—by which was meant a life of no regrets, lived to the fullness of each person's human potential.

Liberty is indispensable to this kind of life, both our founders and Pericles believed, and it demands courage and perseverance if it is to be achieved and preserved. Pericles addressed soldiers and the survivors of soldiers' families in the midst of war. Madison spoke to the House of Representatives in urging adoption of our Bill of Rights, thereby fulfilling a campaign promise to his Virginia constituents to introduce one in the first Congress to convene after ratification of the Constitution of 1787, made when he ran for election to the House in that Congress. What does he mean by protecting liberty from "that quarter where the greatest danger lies . . . that which possesses the highest prerogative of power"? He means that liberty is most endangered by the majority of the people in the community trampling the rights of the minority; and in the second place, he means that liberty must be protected against invasion by government, especially by the legislative branch. The rights of the First Amendment he intends to put beyond the reach of majorities, whether of the community or of the legislatures.

Madison's effort was largely successful but, within less than a decade after his speech, Congress enacted the "Sedition Act of 1798," which made it a criminal offense (seditious libel) to criticize the government or its officials. It is from a portion of the debate over that bill, then in the House for consideration, that the obscure congressman from Virginia, John Nicholas, is quoted at the beginning of this chapter. Nicholas sounded the theme that became a permanent principle in our scheme of rights—even though he lost the debate on the floor of the House. The right to know, fostered throughout the country in a resourceful and persistent way by the free press, is the mainstay of free government itself. Nicholas, too, understood that the courage demanded by liberty is not only that of soldiers on the battlefield but includes the quiet courage of those who speak and write the truth as they see it, regardless of pretended official orthodoxies.

This chapter has first dealt with the leading case in the field of freedom of the press, *Near* v. *Minnesota*, in which you quickly saw the degree to which even outrageous utterances enjoy constitutional protection. We now go on to explore various aspects of the rights protected by the First Amendment, with emphasis on thought and expression, and conclude with a consideration of the rights of petition, assembly, and religion. Herein lies the heart of our preferred freedoms and fundamental rights.

Freedom of Thought and Expression

For centuries before the Supreme Court coined the phrase "preferred position," it had been a conviction that freedom of thought and speech "is the matrix, the indispensable condition, of nearly every other freedom." [6] Regarded as a sacred right essential to the existence and preservation of free government, freedom of thought and expression is protected by provisions in every state constitution in the country. Its inclusion within the protection given liberty against state encroachment under the Fourteenth Amendment began the process of incorporation and nationalization of individual rights through a decision in 1925.[7] In 1931 the first state statutes were declared unconstitutional for violating the free speech and free press guaranties of the First Amendment.[8] This was one further indication of the general conviction of the country—and not just of the Court—that freedom of thought and expression is sacrosanct, not lightly to be tampered with.

Background Principles

The basic thinking about free expression from its beginning in English and American law, as was seen in the discussion of *Near v. Minnesota*, has revolved around two considerations: (1) prior restraint of utterances; and (2) punishment for seditious or libelous statements. The concepts still are central to any understanding of what the right of free expression is.

John Milton's celebrated *Areopagitica* (1644), the classic defense of freedom of the press, was directed against the prior restraint of the "patriarchal licenser." The licenser system had been established by British Parliament in 1643 to censor publications by requiring prior licensing of all books published in England. This practice was finally ended in 1694. It had continued the older Court of Star Chamber censorship.

In 1769, Blackstone, then the oracle of the common law and influential with our founding fathers, stressed that liberty of the press is indispensable to a free state. It preeminently consists, Blackstone said, in "laying no *previous* restraints upon publications [but] not in freedom from censure for criminal matter when published." It is not justifiable either to censor or license publications. But it *is* justifiable to demand that anyone who publishes improper, mischievous, or illegal matter take the consequences of his own brashness or irresponsibility. "A man," Blackstone said, "may be allowed to keep poisons in his closet, but not publicly to vend them as cordials." [9]

Alexander Hamilton, in *Croswell's Trial* of 1805, a New York sedition case, gave an enduring definition: "The liberty of the press consists in publishing the truth, from good motives and for justifiable ends, though it reflects on government or on magistrates." [10] This (with certain expansions) is substantially the modern view.

Present Scope

The doctrine of prohibiting prior restraint has tremendous vitality and remains the core of the Court's position today. The doctrine, as spelled out in *Near*, for example, was the touchstone in the Court's important 1976 decision rejecting the power of a state judge to enforce a gag order on pretrial publicity by the communications media in a lurid multiple murder-sexual assault case in Nebraska. [11] Chief

Justice Burger's opinion for the Court stated that, if "it can be said that a threat of criminal or civil sanctions after publication 'chills' speech, prior restraint 'freezes' it at least for the time." Also of importance in this case was the application of the test of "clear and probable danger" in establishing the invalidity of the gag order. Justice Burger stated it this way: "We turn now to the record in this case to determine whether . . . 'the gravity of the "evil" discounted by its improbability,' justifies such invasion of free speech as is necessary to avoid the danger." The "danger" alluded to the state's case by way of jeopardizing the defendant's right under the Sixth Amendment to a fair and impartial trial. Nebraska's Judge Stuart had issued a gag

New Hand In the News Room
Source: from Herblock's State of the Union (Simon & Schuster, 1972).

order against publicity in the case until the jury was impanelled so as to prevent prejudicing their minds with advance information about the gory crimes committed by the defendant, Erwin Charles Simants. (Simants was later convicted and sentenced to death.)

Liability for illegal expression has now nearly vanished through the refined standards applied under recent Court decisions. Protection of expression covers a wide spectrum. It includes not only speech, press, and thought, but extends also to conscience, association, flow of information, academic freedom, speech-plus (demonstrating, marching, distributing leaflets), symbolic speech, lobbying, and picketing. Here, surely, lies what is noblest and best in American government. The Court repeatedly and fervently has underscored the sanctity of the liberties protected, speaking of "a profound national commitment to the principle that debate on public issues should be uninhibited, robust, and wide-open, and that it may well include vehement, caustic, and sometimes unpleasantly sharp attacks on government and public officials." [12]

Defining these most basic rights has proceeded by formulating various "rules" delineating the outer perimeter of constitutionally protected expression. One of the most important is the *Brandenburg* rule, which was applied to reverse conviction of a Ku Klux Klan leader under an Ohio criminal syndicalism statute that made mere advocacy of violence a crime.[13] According to *Brandenburg*, the Constitution's protection of expression does not permit a state to forbid or punish the mere *advocacy* "of the use of force or of law violation except where such advocacy is directed to inciting or producing imminent lawless action, and is likely to incite or produce such action." The law was declared to be in conflict with the First and Fourteenth Amendments and, hence, unconstitutional.

Obscene, seditious, and libelous expressions *per se* are not protected by constitutional guaranties. But the definitions of what these several classes of unprotected expression actually are have been so narrowed that punishment for them today is almost a novelty.

Sedition

The offense of sedition is little known to American law and only consists in attempting by word, deed, or writing to promote public disorder, induce a riot, rebellion, or civil war. If such attempts result in overt acts against the U.S. government and meet the Constitution's definition otherwise, they could constitute *treason* (Art. III, Sec. 3). It is plainly a rock-bottom function of government to preserve the security of its people from foreign and domestic enemies. Safety is at all times and places the primary justification for the very existence of government. How is this safety to be maintained along with free expression? Where does protection of mere expression end? Where does expression become overt action? These and related questions have structured the debate about free speech in America, and the various judicial standards I have listed have been used to help answer them in the courts.

The prominence in America since the early 1960s of terrorism, political assassination, attempted assassination (twice against President Gerald R. Ford), urban gang warfare, and violent protest makes the questions relevant today. Illustrations are not hard to find. A single Saturday edition of a city newspaper that headlined the "Big Event," the 1976 Texas-Oklahoma football game at which President Ford would toss the coin, also carried three stories related to political assassination.[14] The first item (page 9A) was about James Earl Ray, convicted and sentenced to serve life in prison for the assassination of Martin Luther King, Jr., in Memphis, Tennessee, in 1968. Ray was appealing to the U.S. Supreme Court for review of the case, "charging he was 'set up to take the rap' for a crime he didn't commit."

The second item (page 11A) concerned a 33-year-old Des Moines, Iowa, man who had been arrested and charged with threatening to kill President Ford. He said: "I know how to save the country, . . . by killing Ford." The man was being held in Polk County Jail in lieu of $25,000 bond. Steps were being taken by the U.S. Attorney's office for the man to receive psychiatric evaluation at the Springfield, Missouri, federal medical facility.

The third item (page 19A) stated that the FBI was searching for thirty-four-year-old Franklin Kirk, who had escaped from the Fort Worth Federal Correctional Institute where he was serving a five-year sentence for threatening former President Richard M. Nixon. The warden thought the October escape by Kirk "odd," since the man had an excellent record and was due for parole in December.

The escape came one day before President Ford was to be in town to open the Texas State Fair and Texas-OU football game.

That domestic terrorism has been a part of the past in this country is well known. That it also will be in the future was forecast in a 661-page report issued by the Task Force on Disorders and Terrorism in Washington, D.C., on March 1, 1977.[15] That report predicted a new round of disturbances of the kind experienced in the 1960s, saying that the more recent orderliness of American society was "a false calm, and we must see in the current social situation an accumulation of trouble for the future." By March 9 the prediction had come true. A handful of religious fanatics identified as the predominantly black Hanafi Moslem sect invaded Washington's City Hall, the headquarters of a Jewish organization (B'nai B'rith), and a Moslem religious center—all in the heart of the nation's capital—killing one man, injuring another dozen, and holding some 135 hostages. The leader, Khalifa Hamaas Abdul Khaalis, demanded that authorities deliver to him for revenge five members of the rival Black Muslim sect who had been convicted in 1973 for killing six members of Khaalis's family. He further demanded that leaders of the Black Muslims, Muhammed Wallace, Muhammed Herbert, and heavyweight boxing champion Muhammad Ali (Cassius Clay), also be delivered. He also ordered the movie, "Mohammad: Messenger of God," to be withdrawn from American theaters. By March 11, the terrorists had surrendered, releasing their hostages without further harm. On July 24, the twelve terrorists were convicted of an assortment of crimes, including second degree murder, assault with intent to kill, and conspiracy to commit armed kidnapping, at the end of an eight-week trial by jury before the District of Columbia Superior Court.[16]

A great range of state legislation exists to curb violent and criminal actions. Its major rationale is protection of the public peace, safety, and general welfare. Federal legislation aimed at protecting security began with the notorious Sedition Act of 1798, enacted under President John Adams and repealed under Jefferson, which punished anyone who would "write, print, utter, or publish ... any false, scandalous and malicious writing or writings against the government of the United States ... with the intent to defame...." [17] Prosecutions were conducted in the 1920s and early 1930s under federal espionage laws and state sedition and criminal syndicalism laws. The *Gitlow* case of 1925 (which we discussed in chapter 2) involving the Communist Party program of violent revolution, was an example of these laws' operation in New York.

Politics of Containment. Attempts of the United States to cope with the unprecedented internal and external threats of international communism resulted in national legislation in the 1940s and 1950s aimed at persons and organizations believed to be plotting both to *advocate* the overthrow of our government and actually to *accomplish* it. The threats of internal subversion and fear of the "Red menace" were then at their height. Stalin's Russia had filled the power vacuum left after World War II in Eastern and Central Europe by occupying it with the Red Army. British Prime Minister Winston Churchill condemned this action as erecting an Iron Curtain around formerly free peoples and nations. But Great Britain herself was left exhausted and nearly bankrupt by the war.

By 1948, President Truman knew that the accelerating Soviet imperialism could only be restrained if the United States took on the responsibilities previously shouldered by Britain. The Cold War began in deadly earnest. With it came the elaborate foreign policies of the Atlantic Alliance, creation of NATO, the Marshall Plan to rebuild Western Europe economically and militarily and, thereby, prevent the disastrous accession of those countries by the Soviet Union. The doctrine of "containment" then went into force as the keystone of U.S. policy; in simple terms it meant "this far but no farther." It was first implemented to frustrate the Soviet's designs on Greece and Turkey. The policy was implemented militarily by the United States, which entered the Korean War in 1950 against North Korea and Red China, a year after Mao Tse-tung and his communist troops had driven the Chinese Nationalist Government off the Asian mainland to the island of Taiwan (Formosa).

The McCarthy Era. In Washington, these cold war developments were accompanied by strong action to prevent penetration and subversion of the government and nation. During 1953 and 1954, the unscrupulous and fanatical few, including most notoriously Senator Joseph R. McCarthy (R.-Wis.), made political hay out of the country's difficult situation. McCarthy, chairman of the Government Operations Committee, tirelessly looked for communists under every rock, relying on senatorial immunity to irresponsibly accuse persons of spying for the Russians. He and the members of his committee conducted "witch hunts," public hearings, and exhaustive background checks on responsible officials in the federal service. They destroyed by slur and innuendo the reputations and careers of innocent citizens. McCarthy was finally condemned by the Senate in December 1954, when he was officially censured by a vote of sixty-seven to twenty-two. This came after a six-month investigation during which McCarthy accused his opponents in the Senate of holding a "lynch party" and "lynch bee" for him and called the Select Committee investigating him "unwitting handmaidens" and agents of the Communist Party. After censure, and the election of a new Congress controlled by the Democratic Party, McCarthy fell to obscurity. He died of a liver ailment in 1957. By that time, too, the Red scare had subsided in the United States, even if communist ambitions to establish worldwide domination through force and fraud had not.

Convictions under a number of the statutes enacted in this period were achieved and sustained by the Supreme Court in cases to which it applied the various tests discussed previously. The most prominent of these was the *Dennis* case in 1951 (which we reviewed in chapter 2), in which eleven leaders of the Communist Party were convicted and sent to prison under terms of the Smith Act. This marked the first application of the "clear and probable danger" test.

How do things stand today? In general, restrictions on all forms of expression are much more relaxed. The *Brandenburg* rule appears to be in keeping with the older "clear and present danger test" and requires seditious speech to be more than mere advocacy of political violence. Violent or otherwise illegal action must be immediately in view and likely to result in fact, if the expression is to be punishable.

The Pentagon Papers Case. Sedition was not committed, for example, in the so-called Pentagon Papers case,[18] when the New York *Times* in June 1971, during the Vietnam War, published "top secret-sensitive" Department of Defense documents which they had obtained surreptitiously. According to the U.S. Government, the *Times* had harmed vital national security interests. "Harm" was defined (in one of the Court's dissenting opinions) as "the death of soldiers, the destruction of alliances, the greatly increased difficulty of negotiation with our enemies, the inability of our diplomats to negotiate. . . ." The Court ruled that even these weighty considerations (as urged on this occasion by the government's lawyers, at any rate) did not suffice to meet the test of the "very heavy burden" of proof needed to overcome the presumed unconstitutionality of any demand for prior restraint of publication of information by the press.

While there was no majority opinion in this case, that *burden* was phrased by Justice Stewart as being this: disclosure through publication must "surely result in direct, immediate, and irreparable damage to our Nation and its people." Or, in Justice Brennan's language: the requisite burden of proof is only met when there is "governmental allegation and proof that publication must inevitably, directly, and immediately cause" a major catastrophe to the country; ". . . in no event may mere conclusions be sufficient."

Instead of punishment for sedition, what resulted from the *Pentagon Papers* affair? The admitted supplier of the documents, Dr. Daniel Ellsberg, became something of a national hero, although subsequently twice indicted on up to twelve criminal charges. The New York *Times* for publishing the stolen documents was awarded the Pulitzer Prize in 1972 for its excellence in journalism.

The denouement came in May 1973, when after eighty-nine days of the trial of Dr. Ellsberg and his associate, Anthony J. Russo, federal district court Judge William M. Byrne abruptly dismissed all government charges of espionage, theft, and conspiracy against them. The decision precluded a retrial. The government's evidence was tainted. A Justice Department memorandum released by Judge Byrne showed that the same two principal operatives who engineered the June 1972 break-in at the Democratic National Committee Headquarters which precipitated the "Watergate Crisis," Gordon Liddy and E. Howard Hunt, also had broken into the office of Ellsberg's psychiatrist in an attempt to steal medical records. In dropping the charges against Ellsberg, Judge Byrne also released Hunt's secret testimony before the federal grand jury. There Hunt had stated that the Nixon "White House" had conceived the whole plot, supervised it, and paid him for the break-in! It was a matter of national security, he said.

Libel

What constitutes libel apparently depends on whether the subject of the offensive statements is a private or public person or group. The old rule formulated by Hamilton (on the basis of the common law definition of libel) remains generally intact with regard to private persons: to be protected, a statement must not only be true but also published with good motives and for justifiable ends. Whenever any of these features is absent, the First Amendment does not protect expression—whether the statement is aimed at individuals or classes.[19] Mere truth is not enough. But even an erroneous statement is protected under certain circumstances, especially if the subject of the statement happens to be a public official. This major shift in the understanding of libel is premised on the importance attached by a democratic society to free and open debate about public issues and to leaving open all possible avenues for criticism and scrutiny of public officials. By the "New York *Times* rule," as it is called, neither truth nor good motive is essential. The only requisite is that a statement (even if false) not be made with *actual malice*, that is, with the *knowledge* that it is false *or* with reckless disregard of whether it is false or not.[20] The case of *Ashton* v. *Kentucky* [21] illustrates the use of the New York *Times* rule in suits for libel.

Ashton v. Kentucky. Ashton came to Hazard, Kentucky, in 1963 during a bitter labor dispute between miners and coal mine owners and proceeded to publish a pamphlet. In it he made accusations against the chief of police, the sheriff, and the publisher of the local newspaper, all of whom were on the owners' side in the strike. The three victims brought charges, and Ashton was convicted of libel, sentenced to six months in jail, and fined $3000. Among other things, Ashton charged Police Chief Luttrell with involvement in a plot to kill a pro-strike member of his own police force and of firing the officer when the plot failed. He accused Sheriff Combs of attempting to bribe a boy with $75,000 not to go to court against the sheriff for intentionally blinding the boy with tear gas while he was being held a prisoner; and then of probably bribing the trial jury of the court which, as a result, merely fined the sheriff for the offense. The publisher of the paper, Mrs. Nolan, was accused of misdirecting most of

$14,000 in cash and several truckloads of food and clothing contributed through the paper to aid the striking miners as a result of a CBS-TV show just before Christmas, and, because she was "vehemently against labor," of either giving the money and goods to local merchants and scabs or simply withholding it. The police chief, sheriff, and publisher all were public figures.

The U.S. Supreme Court reviewed the case in 1966 and applied the *Times* rule, requiring proof of "actual malice" *or* of "knowing reckless disregard for the truth" when libel liability is claimed by a public figure. It struck down Kentucky's common law definition of criminal libel: "any writing calculated to create disturbances of the peace, corrupt the public morals or lead to any act, which, when done, is indictable." The Court also held the old common law definition *too vague* to be a constitutionally satisfactory basis for a libel prosecution. It cited, as well, the *Terminiello* decision: "The right to speak freely and to promote diversity of ideas and programs is ... one of the chief distinctions that sets us apart from totalitarian regimes." [22] Ashton's conviction was reversed.

The *Times* rule does not fully apply to libelous and defamatory statements about *private* persons, it should be stressed. The rationale is that private individuals are more vulnerable to injury and hence more deserving of the states' protection than public figures. Public figures voluntarily expose themselves to increased risk of injury to reputation and, also, have available "self-help" remedies by easier access to the media than do private persons. Some falsehood must be allowed the media so as to protect free speech in a meaningful way and avoid intolerable self-censorship to the detriment of "the public interest in a free press." Still, there is an impact on private libel and defamation law which Justice Byron R. White condemned in the *Gertz* case as "eviscerating" and "scuttling the libel laws of the States in [a] wholesale fashion." [23]

The Gertz Case. The *Gertz* case (1974) dealt with the question: *Who is a public figure?* It was decided in that instance that Elmer Gertz, a prominent Chicago lawyer who had been attacked as a "Communist fronter" among other things by the John Birch Society's publication *American Opinion*, was not a public figure—hence the rigorous *Times'* test need not be met. Gertz collected $50,000 from the magazine. What is the test in private libel actions? The *Gertz* rule leaves the question to the states. Within limits, each state is free to impose any standard of liability short of "liability without fault" upon a publisher or a broadcaster of defamatory falsehood injurious to a private person.

In 1976 the Court applied the *Gertz* view to a suit against *Time* magazine by the divorced wife of a member of the Firestone family of Firestone Tire and Rubber Company.[24] *Time* had misinterpreted the divorce decree, given after a sensational trial in Florida, and erroneously reported that it had been granted on the basis of adultery as well as extreme cruelty. The Court decided that the strict rule of the New York *Times* decision need not apply here, since the former Mrs. Firestone was no "public figure." This was so because she had no public prominence other than in society. She had not "voluntarily exposed [herself] to increased risk of injury from defamatory falsehoods"—the test of being a "public figure." The exposure that the trial itself brought her could not be considered to change her status to that of a "public figure." The Court, however, did not agree to award a libel judgment to the plaintiff, since the lower court had failed adequately to determine whether *Time* had been sufficiently negligent in its reporting to be guilty of libel. The case was sent back to Florida for further determination of the matter.

Seditious libel of government officials—whether a local city council member or the President of the United States—which was prohibited by the old Sedition Act and was still in effect through the common law and statutory laws of the states, for all practical purposes, vanished from American law.

Today, freedom of speech, so long as it does not become illegal overt action or immediately ignite such action, is thoroughly protected under the Constitution. *Hess* v. *Indiana*, involving campus demonstrations against the Vietnam War, is an example. In this 1973 case, demonstrators were moved by police from blocking the street, when their leader shouted from the curb: "We'll take the fucking street later." The Supreme Court eventually decided that the *Brandenburg* rule protected this verbal incitement to further lawless action. "At best," the Court said, the "statement could be taken as a counsel for present moderation; at worst, it amounted to nothing more than advocacy of illegal action at some indefinite future time."

Imminent disorder was unlikely, and only the kind of speech producing that result is illegal.[25]

In another case testing freedom of speech, the Court unanimously held that the Georgia legislature could not deny Julian Bond the right to take the oath of allegiance to the Constitution of the United States, as required to hold state office, because earlier he had been speaking out against the draft and the government's policy in Vietnam generally. Excluding him as a newly elected legislator from taking the oath and thereby from office violated his First Amendment rights as protected by the Constitution.[26]

A verbal threat against the life of the President of the United States by a resentful draftee critical of American policy in Vietnam was found by the Court to be merely crude and exaggerated rhetoric, not illegal in a society that values robust debate on public issues and vigorous criticism of its public officials.[27]

Speech-Plus and Symbolic Speech

Such overt actions as burning flags and draft cards may be another matter, however, where these acts are prohibited by statute. Here the distinctions between speech and conduct obviously blur. As early as 1931 the Court declared unconstitutional a California statute that made display of a red flag illegal, as a sign or symbol of opposition to organized government. It decided the case on the basis of the law's excessive vagueness and, therefore, violation of the right of free speech ("symbolic speech"), which it therewith incorporated into the liberty protected by the Fourteenth Amendment.

Somewhat later it ruled that school children could not constitutionally be compelled to salute the American flag contrary to their religious scruples.[28] The burning of a draft card contrary to federal statute was not, however, a protected form of expression.[29] Whether the burning of an American flag on a public thoroughfare contrary to state law is protected expression remains uncertain, but the wearing of a replica of the flag sewn to the seat of one's pants, and the display of the flag upside down with peace symbols affixed to it, all have been given constitutional protection as exercises of free expression.[30] It was found to be "horse-play," however, rather than protected symbolic expression, when a conviction under a state flag desecration statute was upheld against a man who blew his nose on the flag, simulated masturbation on it, and finally burned it.[31] This leads into a consideration of obscenity.

Obscenity

The "fighting words" test that we mentioned in chapter 2, which was propounded in the *Chaplinsky* decision [32] of 1942, easily linked together lewd, obscene, profane, libelous, and insulting speech as kinds of expression that can be prohibited by law because, by their very utterance, they inflict injury and incite immediate breach of the peace. The Court has come a long way since then in dissolving that easy linkage.

It also has dissolved the "fighting words" test itself in the process, it would seem. Minds and sensibilities have evidently become so blunted in the years since *Chaplinsky* that combinations of words that constitute "scurrilous language calculated to offend the sensibilities of an unwilling audience" [33] may now simply surpass the reach of human language. Thus, wearing a jacket in a public place with the words "Fuck the Draft" emblazoned across the back was found blameless by the Court. It mused that, "while the particular four-letter-word being litigated here is perhaps more distasteful than most others of its genre, it is nevertheless often true that one man's vulgarity is another's lyric." [34]

The foul language soon became too "lyrical" to be printable in the Court record, however, even while that august body sanctioned its use under the protections afforded expression against overbroad and vague state statutes. Solemn litigation thereby partook of farce. Indeed, it was within protected free speech to address an audience of 150 people at a school board meeting and, as written in the record, use "the adjective 'm – – – – – f – – – – –' on four occasions, to describe the teachers, the school board, the town and [the] country." And it was acceptable even though not repeatable expression for an irate mother to call police officers arresting her son "g – – d – – – m – – – – – f – – – – –," and for another plaintiff to punctuate his remarks in the university chapel by railing at policemen as "m – – – – – f – – – – – – fascist pig cops" and at one particular officer as a "black m – – – – – f – – – – – pig." [35]

The ludicrous situation was noted by Chief Justice Warren Burger when he pointed out the "anomaly of the Court's holding [as] suggested by its use of the now familiar 'code' abbreviation for the petitioner's foul language." [36] The Court exonerated a witness giving testimony in open court who referred to an alleged assailant as "chicken shit" and reversed a lower court conviction for "insolent behavior." It said: "This single isolated usage of street vernacular, not directed at the judge or any officer of the court, cannot constitutionally support the conviction of criminal contempt." [37]

Since 1957 when the first decisions squarely dealt with the subject, obscenity has been a particularly tricky area for the Court. The issues brought in dozens of cases embraced many forms of questionable expression other than verbal. The whole lurid story cannot be told here. But the enormous increase in public nudity and in ready accessibility to "adult" movies, massage parlors, topless and bottomless bars, and newsstands bulging with lavishly illustrated magazines and paperbacks confirms that legal restrictions on obscenity and pornography are not what they used to be.

There scarcely exists either an acceptable definition of obscenity or a clear statement of the states' interests that justify its regulation, so far as the Supreme Court is concerned. There is only a consensus of sorts—now that Justices Black and Douglas are off the bench—that obscenity exists, that it is bad, and that the states are within their rights to control it. The Court's groping in the area of "hard core" pornography is illustrated in Justice Potter Stewart's remark in 1964 concerning the French film, "The Lovers": ". . . I know it when I see it, and the motion picture involved in this case is not that." [38]

Ginzburg v. United States. Two years later, the Supreme Court sent Ralph Ginzburg to prison for five years for using the mails in violation of federal law (18 U.S.C. Sec. 1461) to distribute the magazine *Eros*, the bi-weekly newsletter *Liaison*, and a short book entitled *The Housewife's Handbook on Selective Promiscuity*. In his dissenting opinion, Justice Stewart tried to explain more plainly just what he meant. He said:

Obscene materials include photographs, both still and motion picture, with no pretense of artistic value, graphically depicting acts of sexual intercourse, including various acts of sodomy and sadism, and sometimes involving several participants in scenes of orgy-like character. They also include strips of drawings in comic-book format grossly depicting similar activities in an exaggerated fashion. There are, in addition, pamphlets and booklets, sometimes with photographic illustrations, verbally describing such activities in a bizarre manner with no attempt whatsoever to afford portrayals of character or situation and with no pretense of literary value.[39]

Roth v. United States. The same federal obscenity statute relied on in the *Ginzburg* case had been at issue in the leading case in this field, *Roth* v. *United States*, in 1957. This law prohibited as "unmailable" every "obscene, lewd, lascivious, or filthy book, pamphlet, picture ... or other publication of an indecent character" *or* any "advertisement, or notice of any kind giving information ... where, or how, or from whom ... any such mentioned matters, articles, or things may be obtained." Violation carried penalties of up to five years in prison and a maximum fine of $5000. *Roth*, a New York case, was decided by a Court divided six to three, together with another similar case, *Alberts* v. *California*, which tested a state law making it a misdemeanor to traffic in obscene materials.[40] The Supreme Court upheld both convictions: *Roth*, by finding the federal statute not in conflict with the First Amendment; *Alberts*, by upholding the California statute as not in conflict with freedom of speech and press as applied to the states by the Fourteenth Amendment.

Roth had been convicted in a New York district court on four counts of a twenty-six-count indictment charging him with mailing obscene circulars and an obscene book, thereby violating federal law. The "dispositive question," the Supreme Court said in considering Roth's appeal, "is whether obscenity is utterance within the area of protected speech and press." The answer is *no*. Those liberties are not absolute, and are "not intended to protect every utterance": "implicit in the history of the First Amendment is the rejection of obscenity as utterly without redeeming social importance." The Court said that obscenity was classified with libel and profanity as falling outside the pale of protected speech.

Justice Brennan, speaking for the Court here, went on to say that all ideas with "even the slightest redeeming social importance—unorthodox ideas, controversial ideas, even ideas hateful to the prevailing climate of opinion—have the full protection of the First Amendment guaranties, unless excludable because they encroach upon the limited area of more important interests." But he pointed to the "universal judgment that obscenity should be restrained," as shown by an international agreement to that effect entered into by fifty nations, by obscenity laws in effect in every state of the nation, and by the twenty obscenity laws enacted by the Congress between 1842 and 1956.

But what is obscenity? Justice Brennan stated that "sex and obscenity are not synonymous. Obscene material is material which deals with sex in a manner appealing to prurient interest." Justice Brennan here inserted a footnote: "I.e., material having a tendency to excite lustful thoughts. Webster's [definition of *prurient* is, in part], as follows: '...Itching; longing; uneasy with desire or longing; of persons, having itching, morbid, or lascivious longings; of desire, curiosity, or propensity, lewd....' [T]he definition of the A.L.I., Model Penal Code [accords with the case law on the meaning of obscenity], *viz.*: '...A thing is obscene if, considered as a whole, its predominant appeal is to prurient interest, i.e., a shameful or morbid interest in nudity, sex, or excretion, and if it goes substantially beyond customary limits of candor in description or representation of such matters....'" On that basis, the Court concluded, "Both trial courts below sufficiently followed the proper standard. Both courts used the proper definition of obscenity."

Thus, the trial judge charged the jury in *Roth* as follows: "The test in each case is the effect of the book, picture or publication considered as a whole ... upon all those whom it is likely to reach. In other words, you [i.e., the jury] determine its impact upon the average person in the community.... You may ask yourselves does it offend the common conscience of the community by present-day standards.... [Y]ou and you alone are the exclusive judges of what the common conscience of the community is, and [you should] consider the community as a whole, young and old, educated and uneducated, the religious and the irreligious—men, women and children."

Associate Justices Harlan, Douglas, and Black dissented. The latter two joined in countering the majority's opinion with this, among other things:

I do not think that the problem can be resolved by the Court's statement that "obscenity is not expression protected by the First Amendment." With the exception of [only one libel case] ... none of our cases has resolved problems of free speech and free press by placing any form of expression beyond the pale of the absolute prohibition of the First Amendment. . . .

Freedom of expression can be suppressed [only] if, and to the extent that, it is so closely brigaded with illegal action as to be an inseparable part of it . . . [*citation* omitted]. As a people, we cannot afford to relax that standard. For the test that suppresses a cheap tract today can suppress a literary gem tomorrow. All it need do is to incite a lascivious thought or arouse a lustful desire. The list of books that judges or juries can place in that category is endless.

In the absence of a more widely acceptable definition of obscenity, numerous state and local laws have been voided by the vagueness test applied by the Court. The states generally have exercised their legislative power to curb obscenity out of their interests to protect society's moral standards, to avoid corrupting individual morals and character, to improve and protect the quality of life, and to maintain a decent society. These laws sometimes collide with individual rights "to receive information and ideas [which] . . . regardless of their social worth, are fundamental to our free society" and guaranties that bar "infringement of the individual's right to read or observe what he pleases." [41]

Miller v. California. The Court in 1973 again struggled to find an acceptable definition of obscene expression and to establish the general terms of its regulation in *Miller* v. *California*. But only a bare five-to-four majority was possible. Miller had been convicted of a misdemeanor under California law for knowingly distributing obscene matter, by conducting a mass mailing campaign to advertise the sale of illustrated "adult" books. The campaign included five brochures sent through the mail that primarily consisted of "pictures and drawings," as Chief Justice Burger recited the facts for the Court, "very explicitly depicting men and women in groups of two or more engaging in a variety of sexual activities, with genitals often prominently displayed." The Court vacated the state court's conviction of Miller and remanded it for reconsideration.

In doing so, the Court reaffirmed *Roth* but also modified its requirements. It was "categorically settled" that obscene material is not protected by the First Amendment. But the Court also said this:

State statutes designed to regulate obscene materials must be carefully limited. As a result, we now confine the permissible scope of such regulation to works which depict or describe sexual conduct. That conduct must be specifically defined by the applicable state law. . . . A state offense must also be limited to works which, taken as a whole, appeal to the prurient interest in sex, which portray sexual conduct in a patently offensive way, and which, taken as a whole, do not have serious literary, artistic, political, or scientific value.

The Court then specified "guidelines" to be followed in judging whether matter is obscene: (1) Does it appeal to "prurient interest" in the judgment of the average person, applying [local] community standards, and considering the work as a whole? (2) Does it depict sexual conduct as described in the state's law in a "patently offensive way"? (3) Does the work, when considered as a whole, lack "serious literary, artistic, political or scientific value"? Chief Justice Burger then (for one of three times) specifically discarded as a constitutional standard *Roth's* demand that, to be obscene, a work must be *"utterly* without redeeming social value." The stress given by the Court to *utterly* in 1966 had cinched the case that *Fanny Hill* was no obscene book (*Memoirs* v. *Massachusetts*).[42]

Anxious to be helpful, Chief Justice Burger went on to explain just exactly what was meant by the phrase, "depicting sex in a patently offensive way." He listed the following: "(a) Patently offensive representations or descriptions of ultimate sexual acts, normal or perverted, actual or simulated. (b) Patently offensive representations or descriptions of masturbation, excretory functions, and lewd exhibition of the genitals." Two sentences later, however, Chief Justice Burger said this: "At a minimum, prurient, patently offensive depiction or description of sexual conduct must have serious literary, artistic, political or scientific value to merit First Amendment protection." He pointed to medical textbook illustrations as a pertinent example of the sort of thing he meant. "Under the holding announced today," the Chief Justice stressed, "no one will be subject to prosecution for the sale or exposure of obscene materials unless these materials depict or describe patently offensive 'hard core' sexual conduct specifically defined by the regulating state law, as written or construed."

The majority in *Miller* claimed that, for the first time since *Roth* had been decided sixteen years before, the Court finally had agreed on concrete guidelines with which "to isolate 'hard core' pornography from expression protected by the First Amendment." The Court was pleased not to take the easy way out by declaring the rights of speech and press to be "absolute"—and thereby adopt the "anything goes" approach to those liberties generally followed by Justices Black and Douglas. Dissenting Justices Brennan, Stewart, Marshall, and Douglas responded by sounding the "alarm of repression." Douglas thought it a sad thing to put people in jail for trafficking in "obscenity"—a "hodge-podge" he said, "which even we cannot define with precision." Since no one knows exactly what it is, Douglas indicated, all statutes attempting to regulate obscenity are vulnerable to the "time honored void-for-vagueness test."

State police power may especially be exercised within the defined area to protect juveniles and unconsenting adult audiences from offensive material. Who is to decide what is so offensive as to be obscene? The community, through judgment rendered by juries, may decide, within limits. That "community" need not be the national community, nor the state-wide community, but may be the local community, provided the locally prescribed standards of what is patently offensive conform to the Court-approved criteria laid down in *Miller*. Juries do not have "unbridled discretion in determining what is 'patently offensive,' " the Court stated in reversing a Georgia conviction of the distributor of the movie "Carnal Knowledge." [43]

The Right of Privacy

Privacy was discussed at some length in chapter 2, where we linked it with the emergence of "new" substantive due process. It was first formally recognized by the Court in 1961, but only fully developed in *Griswold* v. *Connecticut* (1965),[44] a birth control case. The right to privacy has been invoked in obscenity controversies to justify the personal possession for private use of obscene materials in the privacy of one's home and to affirm that a person is entitled to receive for his personal use whatever information and ideas he desires under the constitutional "right to be free, except in very limited circumstances, from unwanted governmental intrusions into [his] privacy." The right of privacy, however, does not extend constitutional protection to the totally unlimited play of free will or to "the proposition that conduct involving consenting adults is always beyond state regulation.... The States [to the contrary] have the power to make a ... judgment that public exhibition of obscene material, or commerce in such material, has a tendency to injure the community as a whole, to endanger the public safety" and can, on these grounds, prohibit the exhibition of pornographic movies *even* when the audience consists only of consenting adults.[45]

The Court also summarily dismissed an appeal asserting the right of privacy as the basis for voiding Virginia's sodomy law. The 1976 case was appealed to the Court on the basis that a male homosexual's "active and regular homosexual relations with another adult male, consensually and in private," were protected by the right of privacy. This claim had been rejected by a majority of the federal district court, which distinguished the precedents cited by the challengers as applying to interferences with "the privacy of the incidents of marriage," "the sanctity of the home," or with "the nurture of family life." Homosexuality, on the other hand, "is obviously no portion of marriage, home or family life." It can be prohibited by the state "even when committed in the home" as an appropriate exercise of the police power directed toward "promotion of morality and decency." Thus, the district court concluded, Virginia's sodomy law "has a rational basis of State interest demonstrably legitimate and mirrored in the cited decisional law of the Supreme Court." The U.S. Supreme Court evidently concurred with these conclusions by affirming judgment and denying appeal.[46]

The scope of the right of privacy extends far beyond the sphere of obscenity. We have seen that its importance is great and promises to become even greater. The *Griswold* decision pulled together a variety of personal liberties not expressly protected by provisions of the Bill of Rights and gave them protection under the individual's right to privacy. These implied liberties arise as "penumbras, formed by emanations from those guarantees that help give them life and substance." Privacy is a right deriving from several sources: the First Amendment protections; the Third Amendment prohibition against quartering soldiers "in any house" without the owner's consent; the Fourth Amendment's protection of the people's security "in their persons, houses, papers, and effects, against unreasonable searches and seizures"; the Fifth Amendment's protection against self-incrimination, and the Ninth Amendment's protection of that presumably extensive body of unalienable natural rights possessed by the people before the Constitution came into effect and not specifically mentioned by it.

Privacy now is numbered among the fundamental rights rooted in the traditions and conscience of Americans which cannot be invaded except to preserve "compelling state interests." It requires legislative enactments to be narrowly drawn so as to express only the legitimate state interests at stake. The right of privacy so construed protects the freedom of association and privacy in one's association; the right to educate a child in a school of the parents' choice, and the right to study particular subjects as aspects of child-rearing and education; the personal intimacies of the home including such aspects of marital privacy as procreation, use of contraceptives, family relationships, motherhood, and the decision to have an abortion.[47]

The right to abortion, as a dimension of privacy, was expounded and broadened in Missouri and Massachusetts cases decided in 1976 by the Court. One Missouri case was a class action suit brought by physicians practicing in that state, who challenged various provisions of state law bearing on abortion surgery. The Court ruled that, among other things, an unmarried woman under eighteen years need not necessarily obtain the permission of a parent or guardian in order to have an abortion performed. It further ruled that the Missouri law was void because it was unconstitutional to require a married woman to obtain her husband's consent before having an abortion. As Justice Blackmun explained in the Court's majority opinion, it is the woman who "is more directly and immediately affected by the pregnancy"; consequently, he said, "as between the two, the balance weighs in her favor." [48]

Academic Freedom

Despite the disclaimers of the Court itself, we have seen that *Griswold* and related right-of-privacy cases revitalized personal rights by reviving substantive due process. Academic freedom as the precondition of the search for truth has also become more clearly established through the Court's tendency to extend constitutional protection to include rights not explicitly mentioned in the Bill of Rights.

Most of what has been said by the Supreme Court on this topic, however, comes in the form of "dicta"—statements of the Court not central to a decision directly dealing with the specific issue of the freedom of students and professors in the activities of study, research, and teaching. Nor is it, necessarily, desirable to separate "academic" freedom from the protections provided otherwise under the First and Fourteenth Amendments. Thus the Court has recently stressed that colleges and universities "are not enclaves immune from the sweep of the First Amendment." The faculty member there has the undisputed right to decide what and how to teach. The essentiality of freedom in universities "is almost self-evident," and no straitjacket can be imposed upon our intellectual leaders in the universities without imperiling the future of the nation. The First Amendment, the Court said in 1973, leaves "no room for the operations of a dual standard in the academic community with respect to the content of speech." [49]

The first case in which a majority of the Court specifically acknowledged the existence of academic freedom was in 1957. It resulted in the overturning of a professor's conviction for contempt. He had refused to answer questions put to him by the New Hampshire State Attorney General about the content of the lectures he had delivered in a university classroom. There was no majority opinion, but six justices concurred in the result. It is noteworthy that Justice Frankfurter, in his concurring opinion, argued on the basis of balancing substantive liberty protected by the Fourteenth Amendment against state interests in abridging that liberty; he thought state interests would have to be "compelling" if the statute were to stand. And he anticipated formal discovery of the right of privacy by saying this:

[T]he inviolability of privacy belonging to a citizen's political loyalties has so overwhelming an importance to the well-being of our kind of society that it cannot be constitutionally encroached upon on the basis of so meagre a countervailing interest of the State as may be argumentatively found in the remote, shadowy threat to the security of New Hampshire allegedly presented in the ... Progressive Party and in [Professor Sweezy's] relation to [it].[50]

Ten years later the Court in a case brought by SUNY-Buffalo professors struck down the elaborate loyalty oath statute (the Feinburg Law) of the State of New York as unconstitutional. The Court determined that a professor could not be dismissed for any associational activities for which he could not also be criminally prosecuted. Justice Brennan spoke for the Court and gave this glimpse of the justices' academic freedom philosophy:

> Our Nation is deeply committed to safeguarding academic freedom, which is of transcendent value to all of us and not merely to the teachers concerned. That freedom is therefore a special concern of the First Amendment, which does not tolerate laws that cast a pall of orthodoxy over the classroom.[51]

The public schools too, the Court has said, "may not be enclaves of totalitarianism" where officials possess absolute authority over the students. "It can hardly be argued that either students or teachers shed their constitutional rights to freedom of speech or expression at the schoolhouse gate." [52]

We have thus far in this chapter sketched the meaning of the freedoms of speech and press as defined by the Court. In addition we have discussed the right of privacy. We now turn to consider the remaining First Amendment liberties: the right of the people to assemble peacefully and to petition the government to redress grievances; and freedom of religion.

Freedoms of Petition, Assembly, and Religion

Petition and Assembly

The rights to petition government for redress of grievances and to assemble lie at the root of the whole tendency embodied in free government and its institutions whereby consent is given laws and policies, either by the people directly (as in elections) or by their elected representatives (as in state legislatures or the Congress). Yet concern for these rights has not provoked the welter of Court litigation noticed in our discussion of other First Amendment liberties. These rights go back to the creation of Parliament, beginning in the thirteenth century, and hence of representative institutions in England and America. The right of petition is logically prior to that of peaceable assembly. The sense of the liberties, therefore, is to protect "the right of the people peaceably to assemble" *so as* "to petition the government for a redress of grievances." [53]

The right to assemble is today linked with the rights of free expression and association and is equally fundamental to our "scheme of ordered liberty." It cannot be denied without violating those fundamental principles of liberty and justice basic to all our civil and political institutions. Neither the federal nor the states' governments can proscribe the "holding of meetings for peaceable political action." [54] The right to petition includes the right of individuals and groups to approach the administrative agencies that are the arms of both the legislative and executive branches no less than to petition the courts (the third branch of government) for redress of grievances. The right to petition extends access to all departments of government.[55]

Cox v. Louisiana. Freedom of peaceable assembly gained new importance in the 1960s when the black civil rights movement "took to the streets." The problems that then arose were well illustrated by 1961 events that occurred on two successive days in Baton Rouge, Louisiana, and led to two Supreme Court decisions rendered on the same day four years later. On December 14, 1961, twenty-three students from overwhelmingly black Southern University were arrested in downtown Baton Rouge for picketing stores that maintained segregated lunch counters. This activity was part of a general protest movement against racial segregation organized by the local chapter of CORE (Congress of Racial Equality). The arrests were based on Louisiana's "disturbing the peace" statute which requires crowds blocking public thoroughfares or sidewalks to disperse when ordered to do so by police.

On the next day, a CORE field secretary, the Rev. Mr. B. Elton Cox, with permission of the police chief, led a demonstration of 2000 students from Southern into downtown Baton Rouge to protest the arrests. They assembled across the street from the courthouse where their friends were being held in locked cells on the top floor of the building. They were standing five deep on the sidewalk, filling a city block. They sang "We Shall Overcome" and other hymns, repeated a prayer or two, and sang "God Bless America." The jailed picketers from the day before heard the commotion and joined in the singing. Cox gave a speech protesting the illegality of the arrests of the other students. He concluded his speech with: "All right. It's lunch time. Let's go eat." And he indicated that the 2000 should go to the segregated lunch counters to do so.

This was construed as "inflammatory" by the sheriff who, along with some seventy-five other officers, was present throughout. State witnesses said: "violence was about to erupt." The police warned Cox and his followers through a bullhorn that the "peaceful demonstration" was over now and to disperse, and within two to five minutes fired tear gas into the crowd, which fled the area. No further arrests were made at that time. But on the following day, the Rev. Cox was arrested and charged with four offenses under Louisiana law: criminal conspiracy, disturbing the peace, obstructing public passages, and picketing near a courthouse. He was subsequently convicted on three of these charges but acquitted on the conspiracy charge. He was sentenced to pay a $200 fine and serve four months in jail for disturbing the peace, to pay a $500 fine and serve five months in jail for obstructing public passages, and to pay a $5000 fine and serve one year in jail for picketing near a courthouse. The prison sentences were consecutive, not concurrent.

The Supreme Court decided the cases on appeal in 1965 as *Cox I* and *Cox II*. In *Cox I*,[56] it overturned the convictions of breach of peace and obstructing passages. Speaking for the Court, Justice Goldberg found that the breach of peace statute was unconstitutional because of vagueness and over-breadth. Cox's constitutional rights to free speech and peaceable assembly had been violated by Louisiana. The Court's own review of the facts of the case rejected claims that a riot and violence were threatened. The demonstration had been peaceful throughout, the evidence showed. People in this country may not be punished "merely for peacefully expressing un-popular views," Justice Goldberg said, citing *Terminiello* among other precedents.

The conviction for obstructing public passages met a similar fate. It was true, Justice Goldberg said, that the Fourteenth Amendment does not afford the same kind of freedom to communicate ideas by such conduct as marching, patrolling, and picketing on streets and highways as it does to communicate ideas through pure speech. While the

> rights of free speech and assembly [are] fundamental in our demo-cratic society, [they] still do not mean that everyone with opinions or beliefs to express may address a group at any public place and at any time. The constitutional guarantee of liberty implies the existence of an organized society maintaining public order, with-out which liberty itself would be lost in the excesses of anarchy.

It is, for example, said Justice Goldberg, clearly not within the scope of protected liberty to ignore

> the familiar red light because [doing so] was thought to be a means of social protest. Nor could one, contrary to traffic regula-tions, insist upon a street meeting in the middle of Times Square at the rush hour as a form of freedom of speech or assembly. Government authorities have the duty and responsibility to keep their streets open and available to movement. A group of demon-strators could not insist upon the right to cordon off a street, or entrance to a public or private building, and allow no one to pass who did not agree to listen to their exhortations. . . .

But none of this really applied to the Cox situation, Justice Gold-berg and his brothers decided. The trouble with Cox's conviction for obstructing public passages lay in the fact that the statute supplied no standards of application. It thereby allowed the police "uncon-trolled discretion" in deciding which assemblies to permit and which to prohibit, which expression of views to allow and which to sup-press, contrary to due process requirements. Such a pervasive restraint on discussion by the actual practice of state and local authorities in-fringes on protected liberties. It fosters the kind of "invidious dis-crimination" reflected in the treatment given Cox and the students by Louisiana authorities. Cox's conviction was reversed.

Cox II [57] was more troublesome to the Court, but a bare majority managed to reverse that conviction, too. The statute itself was a sound one, modeled on the federal law pertaining to the judiciary, prohibiting such conduct as picketing, parading, or demonstrating "in or near" a courthouse with the intent of interfering with or obstructing the administration of justice. The law itself was valid, said Justice Goldberg. The question was how near must "near" be in order to be illegal? Arguing that Cox and his demonstrators were across the street, and were there by permission of the local police chief, the majority concluded that *then* to arrest them for demonstrating there was a form of "entrapment." While Cox's reliance on the "clear and present danger" test was firmly rejected by the Court, it agreed that the conviction should be reversed on due process grounds because of faulty application of a sound statute under the particular circumstances. Justice Goldberg added the cautionary word, however, that nothing decided in either case should lead anyone to suppose the Court is "sanctioning riotous conduct in any form of demonstrations," and he recalled "the repeated decisions of the Court that there is no place for violence in a democratic society dedicated to liberty under law. . . ."

Mere "rhetoric," protested Justices Harlan and White, in dissent. And Justice Black, in dissenting, made it even stronger:

Those who encourage minority groups to believe that the United States Constitution and federal laws give them a right to patrol and picket in the streets whenever they choose, in order to advance what they think to be a just and noble end, do no service to those minority groups, their cause, or their country. I am confident from this record that this appellant violated the Louisiana statute because of a mistaken belief that he and his followers had a constitutional right to do so, because of what they believed were just grievances. But the history of the past 25 years if it shows nothing else shows that his group's constitutional and statutory rights have to be protected by the courts, which must be kept free from intimidation and coercive pressures of any kind.

Thus we see that the right "peaceably to assemble" is protected even when its exercise involves substantial disruption of a city's usual activities, and borders on threatened violence. So long as the threat does not become actual, the assembly is lawful.

Freedom of Religion

The very first clauses of the First Amendment extend protection to religious liberty. This reflects the primacy accorded religious liberty by the founders of our country. The Constitution prohibits government (Congress in the first instance, the states since incorporation by the Fourteenth Amendment in the 1940s) from acting either to establish a religious orthodoxy or to prohibit the free exercise of religion.

Potential conflict obviously exists between these two aspects of liberty. Consider, for example, that free exercise of religion produces congregations with church buildings and financial assets, denominations with schools and colleges, creeds with teachings about morality touching on observing Sunday as the day of rest, not paying devotion to symbols of state power, not attending public schools—or if you attend them having opportunities for religious instruction during the day—not committing acts of violence or taking another person's life. Insofar as each of these dimensions of the people's free exercise of religion impinges on the state and secular society it tends to involve some establishment of the religious belief by the state.

Consider, in this light such facts as these: churches enjoy exemption from paying taxes on their property and income to the state and federal government. Parochial schools receive substantial direct and indirect financial and material assistance from the states (books and buses, for instance, in some places). Sunday closing laws are based on Christian doctrine—if not, why not Tuesday closing laws? Children with various denominational beliefs may be authorized not to attend public school or even any school at all; not to say the Pledge of Allegiance to the flag or to salute it. Periods during the school day may be designated for religious instruction at locations off public property through "released time" programs. Religious or conscientious objectors may be exempted from serving their country in combat. To the degree that all of these practices may actually involve establishment of religion, does not that establishment inevitably infringe on the free exercise of religion (or of no religion) by others? These are some of the tensions and conflicts to be considered in examining religious liberty. Hence, the two aspects of *establishment* and of *free exercise* are relied on to define the scope of the liberty under the Constitution.

The most famous assertion ever made about the scope of religious liberty was by Thomas Jefferson in 1802. Addressing a gathering of Baptists in Danbury, Connecticut, Jefferson claimed that the First Amendment erected "a wall of separation between Church and State." This became a shibboleth eventually endorsed by the Court as an "almost authoritative declaration of the scope and effect of the amendment." [58]

Americans are so accustomed to the separation of church and state that it is sometimes difficult to grasp the revolutionary quality of that arrangement. Jefferson's Statute of Virginia for Religious Freedom, adopted in 1779, was the first of its kind. Previously, most of Western history was dominated by the spirit expressed in the decree of intolerance of Emperor Theodosis I in 380 A.D., who professed Catholic Christianity for himself and subjects and branded "all the senseless followers of other religions by the infamous name of heretics, and [forbade] their conventicles to assume the name of churches." Even after the Reformation the situation did not at once appreciably improve. The principle most often in force was that "the religion of the ruler is the religion of the state." The Anglican was and remains the established Church of England.

Each American colony had an official church, with one or two exceptions. The Congregational Church was established and tax-supported throughout New England, with the sole exception of Rhode Island. The Anglican Church was in a comparable position in Maryland (after 1693), in Virginia and the Carolinas, and in Georgia (after 1752). The Dutch colony of New Netherlands (New York and New Jersey) formally allowed only the Reformed Church from 1640 onward, although the Anglican Church was established there after 1664 when the Dutch surrendered to the British. Maryland's famed Toleration Act of 1649 effectively excluded Jews, Unitarians, and free-thinkers. Pennsylvania's religious tolerance was similarly limited: William Penn's Frame of Government (1682) required all magistrates and members of the governing council to "profess faith in Jesus Christ" and guaranteed complete liberty to all "who confess and acknowledge the one Almighty and Eternal God to be the Creator, Upholder and Ruler of the World." Atheists and deists were forbidden to enter Pennsylvania. Only Rhode Island from 1641 onward enjoyed full liberty of conscience.

American religious liberty was, then, most especially the liberty to be religious, with various churches tending to enforce their orthodoxies within the several colonial boundaries. Virginia's Statute for Religious Freedom was not immediately applauded elsewhere, nor was her example followed. Adoption of a law establishing religious liberty in Vermont in 1807 was widely deplored as proof of the pernicious consequences of the levelling spirit of democracy. Connecticut supported the Congregational Church with taxes until 1818; Massachusetts in the early days adhered to Puritan or Congregational tenets, and supported the Congregational Church from public funds as late as 1833. Religious tests were required to hold public office in many states long after independence was declared in 1776.[59]

The modern Supreme Court has, in fact, done much to modify the "wall of separation" view so often cited in some of its cases and so dear to Jefferson. Thus, in 1952 it said this: "We are a religious people whose institutions presuppose a Supreme Being", the state follows the "best of our traditions" in respecting "the religious nature of our people [by] accommodat[ing] public service to their spiritual needs." [60] The wall metaphor itself has been shunted aside by the contemporary Court, which finds that "the line of separation, far from being a 'wall,' is a blurred, indistinct and variable barrier depending on all the circumstances of a particular relationship." [61]

Three "tests" have been recently applied by the Court to freedom of religion cases: (1) What is the purpose of the governmental action? (2) What is the primary effect of the action? and (3) Does the action involve excessive entanglement of government with religious matters?

The prohibition against establishment never has blocked all aid and assistance to religious institutions so long as state sponsorship, financial support, and active involvement in religious work are avoided. The Constitution commands governmental neutrality in religious matters. Among other things, this means that the government cannot set up a church, aid one religion over another, influence anyone either to go to church or stay away from one, profess or not profess a belief, support through taxes any religious activities, institutions, or organizations. Nonetheless, government aid to hospitals owned and operated by churches is permissible. Also permitted are public health services, school lunches, loan of state-owned textbooks, and bus transportation of parochial school children on the basis of the "child benefit" theory: that is, transportation and loan of books benefit the child, just as do highways, fire protection, and the policeman at the intersection.[62] Contribution of construction-grant public funds to church-related colleges and universities is permissible if the structures are to be used for strictly secular (not sectarian) purposes. The "social welfare" aspect of church property exempts it from taxation. "Released time" from public school instruction may be allowed so as to permit students to have religious instruction, providing this is not done on public property.

"What Do They Expect Us to Do—Listen to the Kids Pray at Home?"
Source: from Straight Herblock (Simon & Schuster, 1964).

A state has been prohibited from requiring its public schools to teach the account of creation given in Genesis so as to balance instruction given pupils about the origin and development of life according to the theory of evolution. Prohibited also by the establishment clause is either state-mandated Bible reading or the use of a voluntary, nondenominational prayer by public school pupils. Various schemes of direct and indirect tuition subsidy for parochial school students' instruction (and schemes of tax rebate to their parents) have failed to satisfy the "primary effect" test applied by the Court, which demands that state-derived aid be used exclusively for "secular, neutral, and nonideological purposes." [63]

Wolman v. Walter. In an important 1977 decision originating in Ohio, the Court applied the three-prong establishment test in broadly supporting state support of parochial public schools by supplying textbooks, health services, standardized tests, therapeutic guidance, and remedial services to them. Because of a technicality in Ohio's statute, the Court disapproved state provision of transportation of field trips for pupils in such schools.[64]

Roemer v. Maryland. A 1976 Maryland case [65] showed the court continuing to have less difficulty approving state aid to church-sponsored colleges than to parochial schools. It viewed the colleges as less permeated with religious purpose and therefore more secular. Maryland's plan provided noncategorical annual grants to eligible colleges, the only restriction being that the funds not be used for sectarian purposes. One-third of the money expended went to church-related institutions. The "three-prong test" used in establishment cases—purpose, effect, and entanglement—was applied by the Court. The legislature's "purpose" clearly was to support private higher education generally, thereby providing an alternative to a wholly public system: the purpose was clearly secular, therefore. The "primary effect test," namely, that state funds can go only to the "secular side" of colleges, was met perfunctorily by noting the Maryland law's stipulation against sectarian use. What about "excessive entanglement"? Procedures for a one-time-only construction grant had been approved in an earlier case, the state government having had only a single administrative involvement with the sectarian institutions for each grant awarded. But the Maryland case involved more or less constant involvement because of the annual renewability feature of the support program. This, too, was not regarded as excessive entanglement. The so-called "political divisiveness" aspect of entanglement was alleviated because two-thirds of the grants and funds expended went to private colleges that were not church-affiliated.

Hence, despite the lower court's finding that many of the supported institutions offer "compulsory theology courses ... devoted to deepening religious experiences in the particular faith rather than teaching theology as an academic discipline," the Court validated the Maryland program. Justice Blackmun's opinion for the Court remarked that "a hermetic separation between" church and state is impossible. "The Court never has held that religious activities must be discriminated against. . . . Neutrality is what is required." Justice White's concurring opinion concluded: "As long as there is a secular legislative purpose, and as long as the primary effect of the legislation is neither to advance nor inhibit religion, I see no reason [to] take the constitutional inquiry further."

Justice Stevens dissented because he believed there was excessive entanglement. That entanglement was as damaging to the church as to the state, he thought: ". . . I would add emphasis to the pernicious tendency of a state subsidy to tempt religious schools to compromise their religious mission without wholly abandoning it. The disease of entanglement may infect a law discouraging wholesome religious activity as well as a law encouraging the propagation of a given faith."

McGown v. Maryland. Despite attack under the establishment clause, Sunday closing laws were upheld by the Court in *McGown* v. *Maryland*,[66] under the rationale that these state requirements are not significantly related to religion. Such laws or ordinances may have had religious origins, but today they merely provide a common and traditional day of rest for the community. A day of rest is within the state's police power to legislate in order to promote public well-being.

Free Exercise Clause. The free exercise clause has been defined through application of two concepts, freedom of *belief* and freedom of *action:* the first is absolute but the second is not. Consequently, Mormons might not be restrained for their belief in polygamy, but their advocacy (at least in the past) and practice of it could be prohibited and punished by the state in consonance with "the laws of all civilized and Christian countries."

Protection of the free exercise clause has been claimed more successfully by Jehovah's Witnesses. It has resulted in decisions condoning preaching in public streets and parks, proselytizing through distribution of leaflets house-to-house, sale of books, and solicitation of contributions. Refusal to salute the American flag during school ceremonies was at first condemned, but then sustained, by Court decisions. Compulsory school attendance by Amish children was avoided on religious exercise grounds, the Court declaring that "only those interests of the highest order ... can over-balance legitimate claims to the free exercise of religion."

Conscientious objection to military service is a complex issue. Such objection has been protected on unclear grounds, the decisions turning on whether the objection was based on genuine or fraudulent claims to ethical, moral, or religious convictions of the objector. Draft evasion was a major and disconcerting issue during the period of the Vietnam conflict. President Jimmy Carter's first official act—as promised during his election campaign—was to issue Executive Order No. 1 proclaiming the pardon of such evaders, although the pardon did not extend to evaders who used force to stay out of uniform nor to deserters or service personnel who received less than honorable discharges during the Vietnam period. The Court has generally expressed willingness for the Congress to provide exemption from military service for conscientious objectors by requiring alternative types of service of them which it has declined to find to be either "involuntary servitude" or an invasion of religious liberty. The Military Service Act of 1967 provides exemption from military service for anyone "who, by reason of religious training and belief, is conscientiously opposed to participation in war in any form."

Who can qualify for this exemption? The Court found that Black Muslim former heavyweight boxing champion Muhammad Ali could in a 1971 decision and on that occasion listed three tests which had to be met: "He must show that he is conscientiously opposed to war in any form. He must show that this opposition is based upon religious training and belief, as the term has been construed in our decisions. And he must show that this objection is sincere." While these statements are clear in themselves, the application of these tests by the Court is muddied by the considerable latitude retained by administrative agencies in deciding whether an objector is conscientious and by the expansive reading of "religious" so as to embrace almost any humanitarian conviction against participation in wars of any kind. This position, among other things, leaves unresolved the questions which arise from objection to some wars as "unjust" or "immoral" but not to others. The urgency of these and related issues subsided for the time being after the ending of the military draft in early 1973.[67]

Conclusions

The majesty and meaning of liberty in America was summarized in simple but powerful language by Justice Robert H. Jackson in the *Barnette* case (1943).[68] He held that children had no state-enforceable duty to salute the flag of the United States, if to do so violated their religious beliefs or conscience. Thus, he eloquently said:

> The very purpose of the Bill of Rights was to withdraw certain subjects from the vicissitudes of political controversy, to place them beyond the reach of majorities and officials and to establish them as legal principles to be applied by the courts. One's right to life, liberty, and property, to free speech, a free press, freedom of worship and assembly, and other fundamental rights may not be submitted to vote, they depend on the outcome of no elections. . . . If there is any fixed star in our constitutional constellation, it is that no official, high or petty, can prescribe what shall be orthodox in politics, nationalism, religion, or other matters of opinion or force citizens to confess by word or act their faith therein. If there are any circumstances which permit an exception, they do not now occur to us.

Summary

We have examined in this chapter the First Amendment rights and the right of privacy, which stand at the pinnacle of the "preferred position" in our constitutional scheme. From the protection of the obnoxious rantings of editor Near with which we began our discussion of freedom of expression to the protection of the religious sensibilities of Black Muslim Muhammad Ali as the basis of exemption from the draft, we have seen that a wide spectrum of liberty has been constitutionally assured to every American. Freedom of speech and press guarantied in the amendment is seen to embrace all but the most indefensibly seditious, libelous, and obscene forms of expression. The theory is that if modes of expression that border on the outrageous are protected, then more usual expression is doubly assured of constitutional support. Hence, we have reviewed the Court decisions dealing with cases on the knife-edge of legal and social tolerance.

None of the freedoms protected by the Constitution, including its First Amendment, is absolute; but limits have clearly been stretched to great latitudes by the Court since 1925 when nationalization of rights formally began. As the claim on individuals' lives and conduct has been steadily expanded by governments, so also has the judicial system steadily stiffened its assertion that constitutional rights are not subject to the whims and will of majorities, either in the states or in the nation as a whole. Gaps in the specific list of rights given in the Constitution have been filled by the Court through the discovery of the potentially vast reservoir of peripheral rights emanating from the explicit ones and, also, from rights noticed in the Ninth Amendment: privacy, travel, association, contraception, abortion, procreation, academic freedom, and others. As the *Barnette* case summarizes at the conclusion of this chapter, the stress on individual liberty implies that we are a nation without an official orthodoxy—unless liberty is itself the American orthodoxy. But in 1977 the Court negated even that possibility. For it extended *Barnette* in the New Hampshire license plate case by holding that religious scruples against displaying the slogan "Live Free or Die" on the license tags of one's automobile were protected by the First Amendment. As Chief Justice Burger tersely stated the proposition: "... where the State's interest is to disseminate an ideology, no matter how acceptable to some, such interest cannot outweigh an individual's First Amendment right to avoid becoming the courier for such message." [69]

We turn now to consider the range of protections afforded those who fall afoul of criminal laws. In chapter 4 we shall confront the "law" as a policeman on his beat or in a desperate moment of violence and possible bloodshed when lives are on the line. It is then that the rights of criminal procedure are triggered.

REVIEW QUESTIONS

1. What are the issues raised and resolved in *Near* v. *Minnesota?*

2. By what reasoning has the Court accorded a "preferred position" to the freedom of thought and speech? Do you find it sound?

3. Define and discuss the concepts "prior restraint" and "punishment" in free speech and press contexts.

4. What is sedition? State the *Brandenburg* rule and explain its protection of advocacy of violence. Compare this with the *Gitlow* doctrine.

5. What conditions gave rise to the Smith Act, the *Dennis* convictions, and the Court's reliance on the "clear and *probable* danger" test?

6. What issues were involved in the *Pentagon Papers* case? Do you agree with the Court's decision and reasoning?

7. May a judge issue a gag rule against pretrial publicity in a sensational murder trial? Why or why not? Why might he wish to do so?

8. What is meant by libel? Why are private individuals more fully protected by law against libel than public figures?

9. What is the New York *Times* rule? How does it differ from the

common law definition of libel? Illustrate it with reference to the *Ashton, Gertz,* and *Firestone* cases.

10. What kinds of expression are protected speech-plus and symbolic speech?

11. Compare and contrast the Court's approach to obscenity in the *Roth* and *Miller* cases. In what direction is the Court moving in this area? What did Justice Douglas think about this subject? What do you think?

12. What is the right of privacy? What are its constitutional sources? What limitations to it can you name? Does it have any bearing on academic freedom?

13. What is the freedom of petition and assembly? How does that protection differ from protection given pure speech? Do you agree with the Court's reasoning there? Why or why not? Discuss *Cox I* and *Cox II*.

14. What is the scope of religious liberty? Is there a "wall of separation" between church and state? What kinds of conflicts arise between *free exercise* and *establishment?* What problems and justifications do you see in (say) taking tax money paid by citizens who are Methodists and using it to buy books for use in Catholic parochial schools?

15. What is the "three-prong test" used in *establishment cases?* How was it applied in the 1976 Maryland case (*Roemer*)? Comment on Justice Stevens's observation in dissent.

CHAPTER FOUR

In the Dock: Rights of Criminal Procedure

A free man shall be punished for a small fault
only according to the measure thereof, and for a
great crime according to its magnitude. . . . None
of these punishments shall be imposed except by
the oath of honest men of the neighborhood.
No free man shall be taken, imprisoned,
dispossessed, outlawed, banished, or in any
way destroyed, nor will We proceed against or
prosecute him, except by the lawful judgment
of his peers and by the law of the land.
To no one will We sell, to none will We deny
or delay right or justice.[1]

THE MAGNA CARTA (1215)

. . . it is a bad policy to represent a political
system as having no charm but for robbers and
assassins. . . .[2]

SAMUEL TAYLOR COLERIDGE
on Edmund Burke (1809)

Most ov the happiness in this world konsists
in possessing what others kant git.[3]

JOSH BILLINGS (1876)

SCENE:	*Office of FBI.*
	A few straight chairs, a desk, at which is seated an investigator for the FBI.
	ENTER: A hillbilly backwoodsman.
HILLBILLY:	Is this the FBI?
INVESTIGATOR:	Yes. Is there anything I can do for you?
HB:	Yes, sir. I've killed a revenooer and I want to confess.
FBI:	Wait a minute. I'll have to hunt you an upholstered and plush-covered chair. A man can't confess unless he is comfortable. It's been so held by the court.
HB:	But I'm only uncomfortable in mind. I don't keer to set.
FBI:	You surely must not have read the ruling of Judge Frankfurter in which he held that you could not have a man uncomfortable who is about to confess to murder.
HB:	Shore nuff?
FBI:	Where are your kin folks?
HB:	I ain't got none lessen you think my mother-in-law's kin.
FBI:	You can't confess unless you brought your relatives along.
HB:	Well, me and her ain't a speakin' and she won't help me none.
FBI:	Did you graduate from college?
HB:	Did I what?
FBI:	How far did you get in school?
HB:	To the 4th grade.
FBI:	I'm afraid you can't qualify. The Supreme Court has

held that confessions by men who had not passed the 4th grade were no good. You've got to be educated to confess.

HB: But that's agin the Preacher and the Good Book. They say confess yer sins, and they don't say nothin' about schoolin' and kin folks.

FBI: But it's the law, brother. Furthermore, I haven't seen your lawyer. Where's he?

HB: Mister, you don't seem to understand. I want to tell the truth—not to git around it. I don't have to hire a lawyer before I can tell the truth, do I?

FBI: I'm sorry, but your notions are old-fashioned. It used to be the law that a criminal could confess, provided he was advised and warned of his rights, and provided no force or violence was used, and provided no promise or reward was made to him, and provided he was not put in fear or duress. Lots of them used to confess when they found we had the proof on them, but that was horse and buggy law. Now a criminal must have his kin folks with him, must be comfortable, must have a lawyer, whether he asks for one or not, must have been educated past the 4th grade, and must have traveled at least further than Jasper. By the way, how far have you traveled away from home?

HB: I ain't ever been out of the state in my life. I never run away. I jus' decided I'd stay and take my medicine.

FBI: Hell, that lets you out. You haven't got a single characteristic of a qualified confessor.

HB: But mister, I killed a man. . . .

FBI: Stop! I've been talking to you now nearly an hour, and that alone would disqualify you.

HB:	But the parson says that an honest confession is good for the soul.
FBI:	I sympathize with you, brother, but there are only two courses left open to you: One is to bear your troubles in silence; the other is to go back to school, then travel abroad, marry you some kin folks, hire you a lawyer, and bring them down here with you. In the meantime, I'll try to get this office air-conditioned, and also have a nice overstuffed chair for you. Then I will hear your confession. But remember, you will have to make it short and snappy.
HB:	(Departing perplexedly) Well, I'll be damned.[4]

MIRANDA v. ARIZONA

*T*HE OUTRAGEOUS SPOOF, "An Honest Confession May Be Good for the Soul, but not for the FBI," reflects the judicial backdrop of the Supreme Court's famous MIRANDA v. ARIZONA decision of 1966.[5] Ernesto Arturo Miranda had his first brush with the law when he stole a car at age fourteen. He was then in the eighth grade. He was placed on probation but was subsequently sent to the Fort Grant reformatory for three months. His mother had died when Ernesto was six years old, and his father, a painter, had remarried. "I never could get adjusted to her," Ernesto said of the stepmother who raised him. His father frequently beat him up when he got into trouble as an adolescent.

Ernesto never got beyond the first half of the ninth grade in school. Soon after release from Fort Grant, Ernesto at fifteen was sentenced to a year for attempted rape and assault. At age seventeen he was arrested in Los Angeles for being a Peeping

Tom and placed on probation. He was arrested twice more on suspicion of armed robbery.

Miranda then joined the U.S. Army. Things were no better there. He did time in the brig and was given an undesirable discharge fifteen months after enlisting for being a Peeping Tom. Within a half-year he was sentenced to a federal penitentiary for transporting a stolen car across state lines. When Ernesto was twenty-one he began living with a common-law wife seven years older than he, the mother of two school-age children from a previous marriage. By the time of his arrest the Mirandas were the parents of a ten-month-old daughter.

Ernesto Miranda was twenty-three and working as a truck driver when arrested at his home in Phoenix, Arizona, on March 13, 1963. Taken to the police station, he was picked from a four-man lineup and identified by an eighteen-year-old girl as the man who had kidnapped and raped her ten days before. Another woman also identified him as the man who had robbed her in November 1962.

Officers Carroll Cooley and Wilfred M. Young took Miranda to "Interrogation Room No. 2" for questioning about the offenses. Two hours later, at 1:30 P.M., they emerged with a written confession of guilt to the crimes in hand. The first paragraph of the signed document was a typed statement that the accused had made the confession voluntarily and of his own free will, "with no threats, coercion, or promises of immunity, and with full knowledge of my legal rights, understanding any statement I make may be used against me." The court record shows that the handwritten confession then continued as follows:

I, Ernest A. Miranda, am 23 years of age and have completed the 8th grade in school.

E.A.M. Seen a girl walking up street stopped a little ahead of her got out of car walked towards her grabbed her by the arm and

*asked her to get in the car. Got in car without force tied hands and
ankles. Drove away for a few miles. Stopped asked to take clothes
off. Did not, asked me to take her back home. I started to take
clothes off her without any force and with cooperation. Asked her
to lay down and she did could not get penis into vagina got about
½ (half) inch in. Told her to get clothes back on. Drove her home.
I couldn't say I was sorry for what I had done. But asked her to
say a prayer for me. E. A. M.*

*I have read and understand the foregoing statement and hereby
swear to its truthfulness.*[6]

The confession was signed by Miranda and witnessed by the
interrogating officers.

Miranda was given a jury trial. At it the officers testified he had
confessed to the crimes orally before signing the written confession. The officers admitted at the trial that Miranda was not
advised he had a right to have an attorney present during the
questioning. The written confession was entered into evidence
over the defense counsel's objection.

The jury found Miranda guilty of kidnapping and rape. In a
separate trial he also was convicted on the robbery charge. He
was sentenced to from twenty to thirty years' imprisonment on
each count, the sentences to run concurrently. He received a
sentence of from twenty to twenty-five years on the robbery conviction. The appeal to the Arizona Supreme Court was to no
avail; it held that Miranda's constitutional rights had not been
violated in obtaining the confession.

The Supreme Court Decision

Appeal to the U.S. Supreme Court on the kidnap-rape conviction resulted in reversal of the lower courts' decisions. Chief
Justice Earl Warren spoke for the Court's five-to-four majority.
He concluded that Miranda had not in any way been apprised
of his right to have a lawyer present during questioning and that

his right not to be compelled to incriminate himself was not otherwise sufficiently protected (Fifth Amendment). "Without these warnings," the Chief Justice said, Miranda's confession was illegal and inadmissible as evidence. What the Constitution requires is "knowing and intelligent waiver," if constitutional rights of an accused person are to be relinquished.

This was not the happy end of a sad and sordid story, however. Since Miranda also had been convicted on the robbery charge in a separate trial, and that decision had not been appealed, he was obliged to continue serving that twenty- to twenty-five-year sentence. In addition, the State of Arizona decided to press the kidnap-rape charges again, and this time—without using the confession—once more convicted Miranda and sent him to prison to serve the same sentence he had originally been given. He was ultimately stabbed to death during a brawl in a Phoenix barroom on January 31, 1976, at age thirty-four.

Implications of the *Miranda* Case

In the country at large, a great furor was aroused by the Court's decision in MIRANDA v. ARIZONA. The focus was on police brutality, station-house abuses, especially during police investigation prior to formal accusation. Every fan of "Adam-12" re-runs on television knows that "MIRANDA cards" were required to be printed up and promptly read to any person seriously suspected of a crime by police. As the Hillbilly-FBI skit showed, there was a strand of bitter, bemused reaction to MIRANDA: the hands of the police are tied; the crooks get all the breaks now; how can the police do their jobs of protecting society against criminals?

The elements of the MIRANDA "warnings" are simply those employed by the FBI for years prior to 1966. As Chief Justice Warren phrased the matter, the FBI advises "any suspect or arrested person, at the outset of an interview, that he is not required to make a statement, that any statement may be used against him in court, that the individual may obtain the services of an attorney of his own choice, and, more recently, that he has a right to free counsel if he is unable to pay. . . ." Chief Justice Warren also spoke to a point raised by the hillbilly skit, the status of freely given confessions:

> In dealing with statements obtained through interrogation, we do not purport to find all confessions inadmissible. Confessions remain a proper element in law enforcement. Any statement given freely and voluntarily without any compelling influences is, of course, admissible. . . . There is no requirement that police stop a person who enters a police station and states that he wishes to confess to a crime. . . . Volunteered statements of any kind are not barred by the Fifth Amendment and their admissibility is not affected by our holding today.

The sentiment of most law enforcement officers seems heavily against the restrictions placed on them by the Court in interrogating suspects. In a recent study,[7] 58 percent perceived Miranda negatively and 94 percent perceived recent Court decisions negatively. However, the Supreme Court in 1976 reaffirmed the MIRANDA principles in a case appealed from Ohio. The Court spoke of the MIRANDA rule as a "prophylactic means of safeguarding Fifth Amendment rights." It "requires that a person taken into custody be advised immediately that he has the right to remain silent, that anything he says may be used against him and that he has a right to retained or appointed counsel before submitting to interrogation." [8] A 1975 decision also included the dictum that even a wholly voluntary confession cannot be admitted into evidence over a defendant's objection if officers during subsequent interrogation have violated the specified procedures required by MIRANDA, as just summarized.[9]

How do you deal with the criminal element of society? Fairly. That is a theme from the Magna Carta onward, as seen in the quotation at the beginning of this chapter. But how "fairly" is defined has varied greatly over the centuries. Punishments are to be proportioned to offenses; judgments are to be rendered by fellow citizens of the neighborhood in which the offenses occur and penalties similarly imposed. Proceedings must be according to established laws, justice be swift and sure. At the time of the famous poet Samuel Taylor Coleridge, some feared English justice had "gone soft," provoking Coleridge to ridicule Edmund Burke's presentation of the fundamental law because it seemed too solicitous of the rights of thieves and robbers.

The tendency toward assuring impartial justice has taken startling turns in recent years, as the colloquy between the Hillbilly and the FBI suggests. Some say we are coddling offenders, that we need to untie the hands of law enforcement officers, strengthen law and order in the country. The major concern of American support of law and order was pungently expressed by the celebrated humorist Josh Billings: a good portion of our happiness does depend on security in our possessions and persons. We need to be able to walk down the sidewalk without being mugged and to park our cars without their being stolen or the tires slashed. A balance must be struck between society's claim to security and the suspected, accused, or convicted individual's claim to fair treatment and impartial justice. From the fifteenth century onward, Anglo-American jurisprudence has never lost sight of Sir John Fortescue's principle: "... one would much rather that twenty guilty persons should escape the punishment of death, than that one innocent person should be condemned, and suffer capitally." [10]

In the opening pages of this chapter I have reviewed the leading case in the field of criminal procedure (*Miranda* v. *Arizona*, decided in 1966). We shall now trace the general scope of individual rights as they apply today to a person who allegedly runs afoul of the law. The thrust of the account will be to display the specific constitutional protections triggered at each phase of the criminal justice process in a sequential, step-by-step fashion from initial investigation of a crime by the police to the suspect's final conviction or acquittal. The account is, of course, a generalized one. Exceptions are to be found in different state and local jurisdictions. It obviously lies beyond the scope of this kind of book to attempt to take these variations fully into account. For details in your jurisdiction, and for expert advice, consult an attorney!

Scope of American Criminal Rights

The whole criminal justice spectrum is well illustrated in Figure 4–1, including dimensions of the subject not immediately related to individual rights. The rights that are most "basic" are the ones you need when you are in trouble, or at least it seems that way to most people. A highly technical, complex, and extremely important body of basic rights, accordingly, protects each person in this country from arbitrary and abusive treatment by law enforcement officers and by the courts when accusations have been made. These rights take effect on the sidewalks and in the streets. That, surely, makes them basic in one important sense of the word. They regulate relations with the one kind of government official everyone has at least some contact with, law enforcement officials.

Americans are uniquely immune from that ubiquitous phenomenon of police states of every variety: the knock on the door in the middle of the night by faceless officials in state employ who spirit people away to unknown destinations for unknowable periods of time and unspeakable torments. This truly marvelous circumstance, this precious living heritage of personal protections—some of them many years in the making, as the excerpts from the Magna Carta quoted as a headnote to this chapter suggest—is not merely a matter of course. To the contrary. It is a distinctive feature of American justice, even by comparison with the justice systems of other free nations. Some of the specific protections, as the *Miranda* decision suggests, are of recent vintage. Selective incorporation of the specific protections of the Bill of Rights scarcely began before 1925. Since then virtually all provisions have been made applicable to the states. This complex

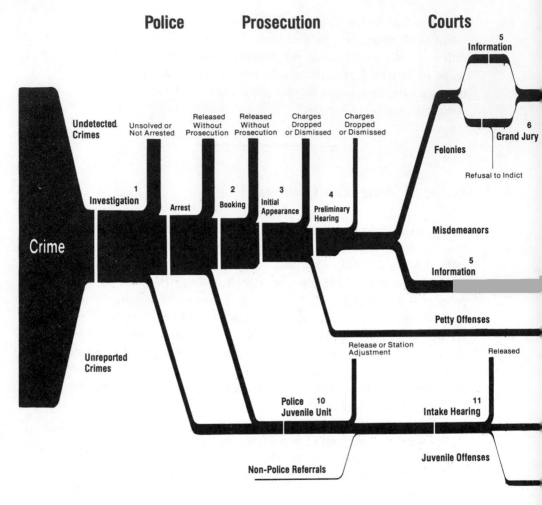

Police **Prosecution** **Courts**

Crime

Undetected Crimes

Unsolved or Not Arrested

Released Without Prosecution

Released Without Prosecution

Charges Dropped or Dismissed

Charges Dropped or Dismissed

1 Investigation

Arrest

2 Booking

3 Initial Appearance

4 Preliminary Hearing

5 Information

6 Grand Jury

Refusal to Indict

Felonies

Misdemeanors

5 Information

Petty Offenses

Unreported Crimes

Release or Station Adjustment

Released

Police Juvenile Unit 10

Intake Hearing 11

Non-Police Referrals

Juvenile Offenses

1 May continue until trial.

2 Administrative record of arrest. First step at which temporary release on bail may be available.

3 Before magistrate, commissioner, or justice of peace. Formal notice of charge, advice of rights. Bail set. Summary trials for petty offenses usually conducted here without further processing.

4 Preliminary testing of evidence against defendant. Charge may be reduced. No separate preliminary hearing for misdemeanors in some systems.

5 Charge filed by prosecutor on basis of information submitted by police or citizens. Alternative to grand jury indictment; often used in felonies, almost always in misdemeanors.

6 Reviews whether Government evidence sufficient to justify trial. Some States have no grand jury system; others seldom use it.

Figure 4–1   A general view of the Criminal Justice System. This chart seeks to present a simple yet comprehensive view of the movement of cases through the criminal justice system. Procedures in individual jurisdictions may vary from the pattern shown here. The differing weights of line indicate the relative volumes of cases disposed of at various points in the system, but this is only suggestive since no nationwide data of this sort exists.

Source: The President's Commission on Law Enforcement and Administration of Justice: The Challenge of Crime in a Free Society 7–12 (1967).

Corrections

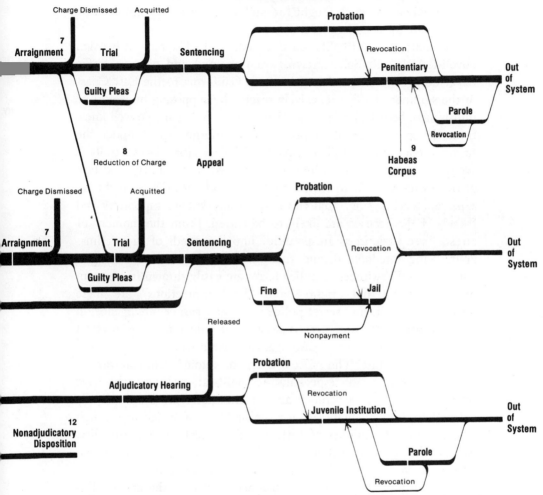

7 Appearance for plea; defendant elects trial by judge or jury (if available); counsel for indigent usually appointed here in felonies. Often not at all in other cases.

8 Charge may be reduced at any time prior to trial in return for plea of guilty or for other reasons.

9 Challenge on constitutional grounds to legality of detention. May be sought at any point in process.

10 Police often hold informal hearings, dismiss or adjust many cases without further processing.

11 Probation officer decides desirability of further court action.

12 Welfare agency, social services, counseling, medical care, etc., for cases where adjudicatory handling not needed.

process has taken place within a tradition where the liberties of free men have been coveted, fought for, and, in various ways, enforced by government for a millennium or more.

The contrast with totalitarian systems is stark. The famous Russian novelist Aleksandr Solzhenitsyn, when stopped and given a traffic ticket during a cross-country drive from California to the East Coast in the summer of 1976, reflexively reacted by supposing he would be imprisoned. Soviet justice works that way—as Solzhenitsyn well knew from eleven years spent in prison and a lifetime spent under the terror of constant surveillance. Arrested Soviet citizens—especially if accused of a "political" crime—are presumed to be guilty. The task of the Soviet police is to elicit a confession to be read in court during a perfunctory "public" trial from which any known supporters and friends of the accused are likely to be barred. From the moment of arrest, three basic ideas are pounded into the minds of the victims: guilt, being foredoomed, and the justness of the accusations. The "on" and "off" switches of police terror are easily thrown in a system where constitutional "rights" and "legal protections" are mere formalities. Public and secret police constantly garner intelligence on the citizenry from an enormous network of paid informers (*seksots*) as future "evidence" for a case against anyone who becomes inconvenient to the state. The process is one of studied dehumanization. The convicts, and most especially the "political" prisoners who have supposedly committed crimes against the state, are systematically reduced to "human material" for the building of socialism through highly refined techniques of torture and eradication of personality. America has no political prisoners. The very category is unknown here, whatever the radical left may assert to the contrary.

The reality of the Soviet system remains even in the era of "Detente" and the enlightened despotism of Leonid Brezhnev and his associates who direct the Communist Party of the Soviet Union (CPSU) in 1977. The Soviet prototype has been widely adopted by other communist countries of Europe and Asia. Thus, when the former dean of the law faculty of Catholic University Aurore in Shanghai, China, Father André Bonnichon, was arrested by the police of the People's Republic of China, the judge clarified his situation this way: "If you have been arrested, it is not without reason, for the government acts always in the right.... It is, therefore, certain that you are guilty." "Justice" at the hands of one country—when compared with that of some others on a global scale—can sometimes be merely a synonym for atrocity.[11]

The American devotion to preserving the rights of individuals is so utterly at odds with the system I have just been discussing that America is sometimes thought to have swung to the other extreme of anarchy. This was the point ridiculed by the great poet Samuel Taylor Coleridge in the barb directed at Edmund Burke. Even Supreme Court justices have had similar thoughts and expressed comparable misgivings. An instance is the concluding sentence of Justice Robert H. Jackson's powerful dissent in the *Terminiello* case (1949): "There is danger that, if the Court does not temper its doctrinaire logic with a little practical wisdom, it will convert the constitutional 'Bill of Rights' into a suicide pact." [12] Such has been the extraordinary degree of this nation's solicitude for the liberty of every person!

As crime rates soar (reported crimes up 150 percent between 1960 and 1975), the real dangers to the nation's safety seem to progress geometrically. It appears that we are increasingly driven toward the apparent dilemma of choosing between repression of the citizenry on the one hand and destruction by internal and external forces on the other. Either way we lose. Is the dilemma a real one? Is it avoidable? Is the cure for abuse of liberty yet greater protection of liberty, as Justice Louis D. Brandeis urged in his earlier manifesto defending free speech and assembly in 1927? "If there be time to expose through discussion the falsehood and fallacies, to avert the evil by the processes of education," Brandeis said, then "the remedy to be applied is more speech, not enforced silence. Only an emergency can justify repression." [13] The questions remain to be definitively answered.

The answers so far supplied by the Supreme Court in modern decisions harmonize with the Brandeis sentiment. Provisions of the Fourth, Fifth, Sixth, and Eighth amendments enumerate a series of rights to be observed in criminal procedures by the federal and state governments. These may be summarized, with certain exceptions to be discussed later, as follows:

Government is prohibited from: conducting unreasonable searches and seizures; putting persons in jeopardy twice for the same offense; compelling persons to testify against themselves; requiring excessive bail or exacting excessive fines; and imposing cruel and unusual punishments.

Government is required to: obtain warrants on the basis of sworn probable cause expressed in particular detail in order to conduct a search or an arrest; charge persons only on the basis of indictment by grand jury; try by a petit ("small" or petty) jury of the vicinity in which the alleged crime was committed; provide the accused with information about the nature and cause of the accusation; confront persons with their accusers; provide them with legal counsel, and with court processes to obtain witnesses on their behalf. Criminal proceedings are governed by the presumption that accused persons are innocent until proved guilty by the government, usually to the satisfaction of a unanimous petit jury, beyond a reasonable doubt. Convicted persons retain rights of appeal of convictions to higher courts, a process that permits the challenge of both matters of law and fact.

Specific Protections of the Judicial System

Habeas Corpus

The privilege of the *Writ of Habeas Corpus* is of prime importance in any discussion of civil rights. The Latin words literally mean "you should have the body"; they constitute the first phrase of a court order commanding that a person allegedly illegally detained be physically brought before a judge as a protection against wrongful imprisonment. *Habeas corpus* is available at *any* stage of the proceeding from arrest onward as a remedy for every unlawful detention or imprisonment. Chief Justice John Marshall defined the "writ of habeas corpus [as] a high prerogative writ ... the great object of which is the liberation of those who may be imprisoned without sufficient cause." [14] Called "The Great Writ," habeas corpus is sometimes regarded as *the* fundamental civil right, inasmuch as it is a summary procedure for compelling government agents having physical custody of prisoners to bring them before a judge and to show to the satisfaction of a court of law whether there is sufficient cause to hold them. It assures prisoners a hearing before a judge who will ascertain the facts and legality of the detention. Habeas corpus, then, stands for the fact that our governments cannot physically incarcerate someone arbitrarily.

Personal liberty of this basic kind is as old as our civilization itself, and for many centuries after the abolition of slavery in England it rested on no statute. It was the birthright of free men. Writs of habeas corpus occurred as early as the thirteenth century, however, and the relationship of the idea to the language of the Magna Carta is apparent even from the small excerpts given in the headnotes to this chapter. The idea of habeas corpus became formalized in writing in Britain's Petition of Right of 1628 after members of Parliament had been detained by order of King Charles I. It was written into a statute for the first time in the Habeas Corpus Act of 1679 during the reign of Charles II. The statute gave no new rights but merely provided a means of enforcing ones long held by English free men. We have seen that the writ was formally incorporated into United States law by inclusion as a provision in the Constitution (ART. I, SEC. 9, CL. 2), a provision cited by Chief Justice Marshall in the 1830 decision quoted above.[15]

Because of habeas corpus no person who has been arrested can be put in jail and held except for legally justifiable reasons. It should be stressed that, until very recently, whenever a prisoner in a state's custody raised a claim under federal law or the Constitution (before trial, after sentencing, or during parole and probation), a federal court could *always* be appealed to for federal habeas corpus relief.[16] This broad relief was initiated because of the carelessness of state and local courts in protecting the liberties of persons arrested and convicted within their jurisdictions. The need for ready access to federal courts for relief accelerated in the 1950s, along with the civil rights revolution. Because of the broad sweep of availability and the great increase of litigation that accompanied both desegregation and selective incorporation of the Bill of Rights, the number of habeas corpus petitions to federal courts increased steeply: from an average of 451 in the 1940s to 12,000 in 1969.

So burdensome, in fact, did this procedure become, that, when weighed against the benefits to justice derived from it, access to federal habeas corpus was restricted by the Court in 1976. In cases begun by convicted murderers serving time in California and in Nebraska, the Supreme Court decided this: (1) where a state had provided for full and fair litigation during trial and appeal of conviction of rights claimed under the Fourth Amendment's prohibition against the use of evidence gathered otherwise than through reasonable search and seizure procedures, then (2) a state prisoner could *not* be granted habeas corpus relief by a federal court review of his conviction by alleging that evidence used to convict him had been obtained by unconstitutional search and seizure. In thereby ruling, the Court spoke of "substantial societal costs" attending such reviews. And it did not fail to charge the states with this reminder: "State courts, like federal courts, have constitutional obligation to safeguard liberties and to uphold federal law." [17]

Individual rights in the area of criminal procedure rest on two main points: (1) the bias of the law to see to it that innocent persons are not convicted, even if this means allowing some guilty persons to go free; (2) the great emphasis placed on preserving the rights of the arrested and accused.

The Burden of Proof

The first main thrust of the law is supported especially by the requirement, mentioned above, that guilt be proved *beyond a reasonable doubt*. How is this accomplished? It must be done on the basis of a prosecutor's presentation of corroborated testimony showing, in the first place, that some offense actually was committed. Until this is shown, confessions generally are not admissible as evidence that the person charged committed the crime. The burden of proving guilt beyond reasonable doubt, then, extends to every element of the crime charged. What is proof beyond a *reasonable* doubt? It does *not* mean beyond every possible or imaginable doubt. Rather, the test requires jurors to arrive at the conviction based on a comparison and consideration of all the evidence, of the truth of the charge *to a moral certainty*. The process of deliberation and decision occurs during the course of a preliminary hearing (or examination) and, then, a trial; both must be conducted in public and in a fair and impartial atmosphere. During both preliminary hearing and trial the accused must be confronted by the accusers to cross-examine them with the assistance of competent legal counsel.

Protecting the Accused

The *second* main thrust, to assure by all reasonable means that the rights of the accused are nowhere violated, has elaborate protections. They include most prominently: (1) the rights of protection of privacy and from unreasonable searches and seizures by police looking for evidence; (2) the right to the services of a qualified lawyer at every "critical stage" in the process of criminal prosecution, from the time of custodial interrogation onward; and (3) the right to prompt arraignment and, in most cases, to release on bail.

Illegal Search and Seizure. The Fourth Amendment prohibition against unreasonable searches and seizures has been implemented by the *exclusionary rule,* a judicially-created remedy that draws strength from the Fifth Amendment's prohibition against compelling self-incrimination. The exclusionary rule requires both state and federal courts to exclude from consideration in a trial all evidence unreasonably obtained. And what is "unreasonable"? In general, it is all evidence not obtained on the basis of a warrant lawfully authorizing searches and seizures or by other valid means.

Mapp v. Ohio. This standard was first fully imposed on state officers and trials in the decision of *Mapp* v. *Ohio* (1961)[18] in which the Court also first directly spoke of "the right of privacy." It there overturned an Ohio conviction of the appellant, Ms. Mapp, for having in her possession contrary to state law "certain lewd and lascivious books, pictures, and photographs." The Ohio Supreme Court had sustained the conviction, even while acknowledging that it was "based primarily upon the introduction in evidence" of the lewd books, pictures, and photographs seized by unlawful search of the defendant's home.

What really happened? In brief, seven Cleveland policemen had staked out Dolly Mapp's residence for some hours because they supposed a suspect in a bombing incident might be hiding there. They tried to kick in the door and did break the glass in it to admit themselves through the back of the house. Ms. Mapp had refused them entry without a search warrant, on her attorney's advice gained by telephone. Some scuffling occurred. Ms. Mapp was handcuffed while the police forcibly took her into her bedroom and later upstairs in the course of a thorough search of the house and its basement, its closets, cabinets, dresser drawers, trunks, and elsewhere. "The obscene materials for possession of which she was ultimately convicted were discovered in the course of that widespread search."

Ohio argued that, even if the search had been illegal, this did not constitutionally prevent the state from using the evidence thereby gained at trial to secure a valid conviction. The Supreme Court rejected both parts of this argument. It held "that all evidence obtained by searches and seizures in violation of the Constitution is . . . inadmissible in a State court." It said that "evidence secured by official lawlessness in flagrant abuse of" the basic "right of privacy" secured by the Fourth Amendment could not be the basis of a constitutional conviction for a state crime any more than it could be for a federal crime. By this means the "exclusionary rule" became enforceable on the states.

This rule broadly serves to invalidate evidence gained by coercive means against the accused person (from beating to stomach-pumping) and by illegal wiretaps. It also extends inadmissibility to "fruits" of illegal searches including any objects, testimony, or information thereby discovered or obtained.

Today a number of qualifications attach to the application of the exclusionary rule. One limitation is that, although such tainted evidence is precluded from a trial, it can be used as the basis of questioning before a grand jury investigating a possible crime. Witnesses and defendants cannot refuse to answer grand jury questions, *unless* their answers would be self-incriminating.[19] The major exception to the requirement of a search warrant is that a lawfully arrested person ("arrest" is defined as "taken into physical custody") may be completely searched, along with the immediate environment ("areas within the immediate control or reach" of the arrested person). Discovery under this circumstance can provide admissible evidence of criminal activity. But such searches and discoveries *must* be incidental to a lawful arrest for probable cause: a mere traffic citation (not involving the taking of the person into custody) generally does not authorize police to conduct a search (beyond a "pat down") of the person or his automobile.[20]

United States v. *Janis.* A further and potentially far-reaching limitation on the applicability of the exclusionary rule was effected by the Court in 1976 in the case of *United States* v. *Janis*.[21] Police in Los Angeles, on the basis of a search warrant that was later found to be defective, discovered bookmaking and other gambling equipment in the apartments of Janis and his associate. They confiscated it, together with $4940 in wagering receipts in cash, and arrested both men. One of the police officers telephoned an agent of the Internal Revenue Service about the find of cash, and together they ultimately calculated that Janis had a wagering tax liability of $89,026 which had accrued during the seventy-seven days of surveillance leading up to the police raid. The IRS assessed Janis for this amount and, in partial satisfaction of it, levied upon the $4940 seized in the raid. Because the state warrant was defective, that case was dropped and everything but the $4940 was returned to Janis. Janis then sued the IRS for refund and to quash the assessment.

The District Court concluded that Janis was entitled to a refund, because the assessment "was based in substantial part, if not completely, on illegally procured evidence, in violation of [Janis's] Fourth Amendment rights"; the Circuit Court of Appeals affirmed. The Supreme Court posed the question this way: "Is evidence seized by a State criminal law enforcement officer in good faith, but nonetheless unconstitutionally, inadmissible in a civil proceeding by or against the United States?" Justice Blackmun, speaking for the Court, said it was not inadmissible. The exclusionary rule should not be so extended as to forbid the use, in the IRS's *civil* proceeding, of evidence seized by state law enforcement officers, even though the evidence had been illegally seized. The Court held that *not* personal constitutional rights of aggrieved parties *but* the intention to "deter future unlawful police conduct" was the basic justification for the exclusionary rule's existence. It was, in any event, merely a "judicially created" device.

Whether the exclusionary rule serves its prime purpose of deterring unlawful police conduct is still uncertain. But the present extent of the rule suffices, the Court argued. It need not be further expanded by now applying it to *civil* proceedings of the kind before the Court. However, the rule continues in force in both state and federal criminal trials to exclude evidence illegally seized by police. It is the distinction between civil and criminal trials that governs admissibility. The so-called "silver platter" doctrine, operative from 1928 to 1960, was not reintroduced completely. In this doctrine, evidence of a federal crime obtained illegally by state officers was admissible in federal prosecutions, provided there was no connivance with federal officers in obtaining it.

What further limitations on the exclusionary rule are contained in the *Janis* case is impossible to say. But it is evident that the present Court views with misgivings the procedural "punishment" (as Justice Blackmun called it) that the rule imposes on all law enforcement officers going about the difficult business of combatting organized crime, particularly of the Cosa Nostra-Mafia variety. *Janis* may be a straw in the wind.

Interrogation. Under procedures now required, especially because of the *Miranda* decision of 1966,[22] arrested persons must be warned that: (1) they have a right to remain silent when arrested; (2) if they volunteer any information it can be used against them in evidence; and (3) they have the right to the presence of an attorney during (custodial) interrogation, one of their choice or one appointed by the court if they are indigent. Defendants may waive these rights, if they can intelligently do so. If at any stage, however, they indicate a desire for a lawyer, there can be no questioning until one is retained or appointed. These *Miranda* guidelines are based on the Fifth Amendment's prohibition against compelling self-incrimination, and *not* on the Sixth Amendment's guaranty of legal counsel. Evidence obtained otherwise than under these restrictions is regarded as inherently coerced and falls before the exclusionary rule; it is thus not admissible in a trial.

Arraignment. Arresting officers are required to bring suspects before the court promptly, so that they may be advised of their rights by a member of the judiciary and be formally charged with (or accused of) a crime. This two-fold process is called "arraignment." Just how this occurs varies with circumstances. A suspect can arrive at a court for arraignment or formal accusation of a crime by at least four different routes: (1) directly after arrest for a misdemeanor (relatively minor offense) or felony (serious offense) observed by the arresting officer, when a "complaint" is filed with the magistrate (justice of the peace, municipal court judge) or the judge of a superior court; (2) in the wake of an arrest authorized by a court-issued arrest warrant based on a complaint showing probable cause that the suspect committed a crime; (3) subsequent to an arrest on the basis of a warrant authorized by a "presentment" or an "indictment" by a grand jury setting forth the probable cause of guilt for a crime and containing the accusation; (4) subsequent to an arrest on the basis of a warrant issued because of an "information" presented to a judge by the prosecuting attorney's office. (Arraignment after grand jury action and by information from the district attorney's office will be discussed shortly.)

In any event, arraignment must be speedy and always promptly follow the police's physically taking custody of a person by arrest (within six hours of arrest). Arraignment is done in open court within the jurisdiction where the alleged offense occurred.

Complaint. The formal charge is called a "complaint." A complaint may have been filed prior to the arrest as the basis of a warrant to arrest, but if not it must be filed at the time of the first appearance in court of the arrested person. A complaint is an affidavit (or sworn written statement) by a police officer setting forth: (1) the nature of the offense committed, and (2) summarizing evidence supporting the charge that the suspect probably ("probable cause") did the unlawful things described. The test or standard of "probable cause" is required by the Fourth Amendment; it means that the arresting officer as a "man of reasonable caution" has grounds at the time to believe that the arrested person committed (or was committing) the crime he is suspected of. Hearsay information can be the basis of the arrest and complaint, if it is corroborated by other facts known to the police.[23]

With the complaint filed, the judge immediately informs the arrested person of the charge. The person must be physically present in the court, as a rule. The judge outlines the person's constitutional rights, including the right to legal counsel. If the charge is a misdemeanor, the person is arraigned then and there and required to plead guilty or not guilty to the charge. But if the charge is a felony the person usually is ordered held for a more elaborate "preliminary examination" in court to determine if the charges are justified; hence, actual arraignment is delayed.

Bail is then set for misdemeanor offenses, but in serious felony cases (such as murder) it will not be set until after arraignment.

"Excessive bail" may not be required, although the Eighth Amendment is not yet incorporated by the Fourteenth Amendment in this respect. Release by posting bail is based on several considerations: the principle of presumed innocence until proved guilty; the need of the accused to prepare a defense against the charges made; the need to pursue one's livelihood without suffering economic hardship and without being imprisoned for an offense that one may not have committed. From the state's side, the amount of the bail is determined by the gravity of the offense and must be high enough to assure appearance in court to face the charges rather than forfeit through flight.

Under terms of the federal Speedy Trial Act of 1974, the goal is to

How to end his act
Source: © 1977 Don Hesse, St. Louis Globe Democrat.
Dist. by L. A. Times Syndicate.

bring all criminal cases in the country to trial within one hundred days of the suspect's arrest or within sixty days after arraignment.

If the arrested person has been indicted by a grand jury "preliminary examination" is not used. It is used in complaint- and information-based proceedings to determine whether there is, in fact, sufficient evidence to support probable cause. Uses of the preliminary examination (or hearing) vary. In federal cases it is used only to set bail. In some states, such as New York, it is used to decide whether to refer the case to a grand jury for investigation. In other states, such as California, it is the prelude to actual arraignment of the suspect or to dismissal of the charges.

But whatever its function, preliminary examination is conducted as an adversary proceeding between accuser and accused. The prosecution presents evidence and witnesses sufficient to show that the crime committed (if any) had probably been committed by the suspect. The defense need call no witnesses and may use the preliminary examination to gain some idea (for "discovery," in lawyer's parlance) of the "theory" of the prosecutor's case and to cross-examine accusers and witnesses. A transcript of the hearing may or may not be required, depending on the particular jurisdiction. But, the transcript may be used later in the actual trial.

When arraignment takes place, at least one day's delay in answering the accusation is given the suspect before being required to plead guilty or not guilty. If not guilty is the plea, then the suspect may be asked whether a jury trial is desired, and bail is set if this was not previously done. Some offenses of exceptional gravity (capital offenses for which the death penalty is optional) may not be bailable. If the suspect pleads guilty, the time is set for sentencing by the court.

Indictment and Presentment. At the heart of the American system of criminal justice lie two ancient institutions, the grand jury and the petit jury, through which a citizen's peers decide whether to formally accuse the citizen of a crime and whether to convict or acquit.

The grand jury consists of at least twelve and no more than twenty-three members from the county (or "vicinage") where the offense was committed. At least twelve of them must vote to indict the person or else the charge is dismissed. The prosecutor begins the proceeding by submitting a "Bill of Indictment" to the grand jury, spelling out in writing the accusation against the suspect and presenting the evidence supporting the charge in *secret* session. The person suspected has neither the right to be present to give evidence nor the right to legal counsel, *but* may decline to answer incriminating questions (Fifth Amendment).[24] If the grand jurors believe the evidence offered (unless explained and contradicted) would suffice for a conviction of the crime charged, then it votes a "true bill of indictment" against the person. The formal accusation then is filed with the court having jurisdiction. Otherwise, no accusation results.

The "presentment" of a grand jury is to the same effect as an indictment, the distinction being that the jury may itself (generally only on rare occasions), on its own motion, take notice of illegal acts it believes to have been committed and formally accuse without the district attorney's submitting the matters for consideration.

Information. When the grand jury is not used, formal accusation may be by "information": today the bulk of criminal procedures in the states is handled this way. This bypassing of the grand jury is possible because the clause of the Fifth Amendment requiring "presentment or indictment of a Grand Jury" has *not* been incorporated by the Fourteenth Amendment as a "fundamental right" applicable in state prosecutions.[25] An information is a formal written accusation of a crime by a prosecuting attorney; it is filed in court in the name of the state, usually only after probable cause has been ascertained by a judge through a preliminary hearing and jailing of the suspect has occurred.

In summary, then, by whatever route taken—policeman's complaint, presentment or indictment by a grand jury, or prosecutor's information—arraignment and, therewith, formal accusation of a crime is reached and the accused is required to enter a plea. The next step is the trial.

Confessions and Plea-bargaining. But before taking that step an important point must be made: most criminal cases never come to trial. In fact, in some jurisdictions up to 90 percent of the cases—according to the 1967 *Report* of the President's Commission on Law Enforcement and Administration of Criminal Justice—are disposed of in one way or another without trial during the various earlier stages of the administrative process. Just as a policeman has considerable discretion in deciding whom to arrest, so do prosecutors have wide discretion in deciding whom to prosecute.

Miranda and related decisions have not changed this basic fact: the vast majority of criminal cases that are cleared from the books result from guilty pleas. Often this involves "plea bargaining" in which a guilty plea by the suspected or accused person is exchanged for a lesser charge and penalty. The question of the meaning of "equal justice under the law" is posed by this frequent practice of prosecutors: the poor and the ignorant, who typically do not understand their rights or the laws, seldom come out as well in this (or any other) aspect of the administration of justice as do the wealthy *or* the operatives of big-time organized crime. The latter have the legal, financial, and political means to insulate themselves—whether through intelligence or influence—from the full force of the criminal laws.

Yes, we must reluctantly admit that there is inequity in the system, some of it arising from corruption. Despite heroic efforts by some to find remedies for defects apparent to everyone, this remains not the best of possible worlds, merely the only one we have.

Petit Jury

But now to resume our account. The trial jury is the *petit jury*. The purpose of the grand jury is to accuse, that of the trial jury to convict or acquit. Both are rooted in the principle basic to all free government, the principle of *consent*: accusation, conviction, and acquittal all depend upon the consent of the citizens in the neighborhood or county (vicinage, venue, judicial district) in which the alleged events occurred. The questions to be decided by the juries are: (1) did a crime occur? (2) did the accused person do it? The standards of proof already have been mentioned: *probable cause* is the standard to be met by the grand jury, proof *beyond reasonable doubt* by the petit jury.

The petit jury has been relied on in criminal trials steadily since the seventeenth century. But its origins are much older. In the long history since the first clear emergence of both juries in the thirteenth

"My client doesn't wish his trial to be televised,
your honor. . . . He plans to make a movie of it
himself."
GRIN AND BEAR IT by Litchty and Wagner. ©
Field Enterprises, Inc., 1977. Courtesy of Field Newspaper Syndicate.

century (with beginnings reaching back at least to the Frankish Empire of the ninth century), *unanimous verdicts* have been characteristic of the decisions of both kinds of jury. Acceptance of the principle of majority rule as a means of expressing consent has eroded this
somewhat today: not only will a vote of twelve members of a grand
jury composed of as many as twenty-three persons suffice to indict,
but a unanimous verdict is not always necessary from the smaller
petit jury. The reliance on the jury system in America as a central
institution of government is eloquently suggested by two facts. The
only legislation to survive the first five years of the Plymouth Colony
(1620) is a single regulation providing "that all criminal facts, and
also all manner of trespasses and debts between man and man, shall
be tried by the verdict of twelve honest men, to be impanelled by

authority in form of a jury, upon their oath." Second, there is the testimony that the inadequacy of the guaranty of trial by jury in the Constitution (ART. III, SEC. 2, CL. 3) was nearly fatal to its ratification in 1787; the issue "was pressed with an urgency and zeal ... well-nigh preventing [the Constitution's] ratification" by opponents.[26]

All the protections of the accused in criminal cases enumerated in the Sixth Amendment, including the "right to a speedy and public trial, by an impartial jury of the State and district wherein the crime shall have been committed," now are incorporated by the Fourteenth Amendment and apply to the states.[27] Although the number of jurors required in federal cases, as we noticed somewhat earlier, is the traditional twelve, this is not constitutionally required and a state jury of a lesser number (six) has been upheld. Again, a unanimous verdict is required in federal cases, but a nine-to-three verdict as "a substantial majority" has been upheld in a state case.

The petit jury is a body of (usually) twelve persons impanelled and chosen from the "vicinage" (surrounding district) who are sworn to try the facts of a case on the basis of the evidence placed before them by the prosecution and defense. The jury is conceived of as impartial and neutral, representing neither the state nor the accused. To secure this neutrality, challenges to eliminate prospective jurors are allowed in the impanelling process; these challenges may either be for cause or peremptory without cause. The jury makes the final decision with respect to the facts, and that decision must be a free one, uncoerced by interference from the judge or other outside influences. Although the judge has the duty to instruct the jury as to the law that is applicable to the case, and what facts constitute the crime charged, he or she is not entitled to express opinion on the adequacy of the evidence presented to convict the defendant or to reject a jury's verdict of acquittal (not guilty).

How far is the jury's judgment of the law (as distinguished from judgment of the facts) valid? The verdict of "not guilty" by a jury cannot be set aside by a judge—no matter how erroneous the judge thinks it is—or even by another court. Since a jury deliberates in secret and gives no reasons for its verdict, an acquittal usually is final, and necessarily embraces matters of both fact and law. The judge can, however, set aside a verdict of "guilty" and grant a new trial by finding the verdict to be contrary to law and unwarranted. Such a retrial does not involve double jeopardy, since it is an act of mercy by the court in the face of conviction by a jury.

Double Jeopardy. The key to understanding double jeopardy is that it relates to *offenses* and not *acts*. It means you may not be put in jeopardy (danger or hazard of legal punishment) a second time for the same offense. Thus, to retry on the basis of a jury's acquittal would violate the prohibition against double jeopardy of the Fifth Amendment, now incorporated into the Fourteenth Amendment and binding on the states.[28] But it should be noted that, even if a person is acquitted under a state proceeding by a jury, he still can be tried for a crime in a *federal* court, *if* the alleged act also constitutes an *offense* under federal law. The theory here is that two distinct crimes can be committed in a single act, one state and the other federal. A defendant can be acquitted of the one and convicted of the other, or be convicted and punished for both. Such dual state and federal convictions do not violate the protection against double jeopardy. However, some states (California) have abandoned this rule and recognize the defense of jeopardy whenever there has been a prior conviction or acquittal in another court of law for the same act. Also, it should be noted that conviction or acquittal in a municipal court (for example) bars the *state* from prosecution of the same offense because cities (and counties) are political subdivisions of the state.

Right to Counsel. The right to legal counsel assured by the Sixth Amendment applies from the time a person is *formally charged* with commission of a crime. This guaranty holds whether the person can afford to pay for a lawyer or not; and the court is obliged to appoint and pay a competent criminal lawyer if the defendant cannot.[29] This protection complements the requirements of *Miranda* (based on the Fifth Amendment privilege against self-incrimination) that legal counsel must be provided at all "critical stages" of the proceedings—even before formal accusation is made, beginning with "custodial interrogation," as noted earlier.[30]

Ex Post Facto Laws. The Constitution (ART. I, SEC. 9) limits prosecution of crimes by prohibiting punishment of an act that was not an offense when it was committed. Thus, a statute is invalid as an *ex post facto* law if it provides punishment for something that was not illegal when it was done, *or* if it increases the punishment beyond that authorized when a crime was committed.

Cruel and Unusual Punishment. Although not clearly defined by the Court, the prohibition of cruel and unusual punishments in the Eighth Amendment has been incorporated by the due process clause of the Fourteenth and applies to the states. Punishment violates this provision if it is either excessive or fails to fit the crime. Thus, fifteen years at hard labor in irons was excessive punishment for the crime of falsifying public records; and imprisonment of a person because he was a drug addict was not fit punishment, since it was like punishing someone for being sick. Other examples of cruel and unusual punishments prohibited are burning at the stake, use of rack and thumbscrews, crucifixion, and breaking on the wheel.[31] Other examples of "cruel and unusual punishment" in more recent cases are discussed below in connection with the death penalty.

The Death Penalty. Before 1972, death by hanging, firing squad, lethal gas, or electrocution was not considered cruel or unusual punishment. But eleven states banned the death penalty by statute, and no one in the country was executed between 1968 and 1976. Is the death penalty considered "cruel and unusual punishment" today? In 1972 the Court, despite the fact that nine opinions were written by the justices, seemed to say as much in the decision rendered in *Furman* v. *Georgia*.

Furman v. *Georgia.* In a concurring opinion in *Furman* v. *Georgia*,[32] Justice Brennan said this:

> From the beginning of our Nation, the punishment of death has stirred acute public controversy.... The country has debated whether a society for which the dignity of the individual is the supreme value can, without a fundamental inconsistency, follow the practice of deliberately putting some of its members to death. In the United States, as in other nations of the western world, "the struggle about this punishment has been one between ancient and

deeply rooted beliefs in retribution, atonement or vengeance on the one hand, and, on the other, beliefs in the personal value and dignity of the common man that were born of the democratic movement of the eighteenth century. . . ." It is this essentially moral conflict that forms the backdrop for the past changes in and present operation of our system of imposing death as a punishment for crime.

Justice Brennan approvingly cited the words of a lower court judge:

> "For myself, I do not hesitate to assert the proposition that the only way the law has progressed from the days of the rack, the screw and the wheel is the development of moral concepts, or, as stated by the Supreme Court . . . the application of 'evolving standards of decency' . . ." [33]

But there was little consensus among Brennan and his colleagues, and the five-to-four decision was marked by five separate opinions written by the majority justices.

In 1976 the Court's answer was *clearly* that the imposition of the death penalty is *not per se* "cruel and unusual punishment." For, in that year, the Court (by seven-to-two majorities) upheld the death penalty as applied in Georgia, Florida, and Texas—while at the same time it rejected death penalty statutes in North Carolina and Louisiana. In the former cases, the statutes were found constitutional by an essentially due process analysis that they so channeled the exercise of jury discretion as to carefully fit the penalty to the crime. The statutes of North Carolina and Louisiana, on the other hand, provided for *mandatory* capital punishment for first-degree murder convictions. That approach was unacceptable to the Court because it deprived the juries of the opportunity to weigh mitigating factors and secure, thereby, a proper "fit" of the penalties by allowing a less drastic punishment to be considered where warranted. The touchstone, then, seemed to be the requirement of mechanisms for careful and precise consideration of discretionary action in the sentencing phase of the trial. Such features were thought lacking in the North Carolina and Louisiana laws.

Gregg v. *Georgia.* All of the opinions mentioned that the "Eighth Amendment must draw its meaning from the evolving standards of decency which mark the progress of a maturing society," to quote Justice Stewart's formulation from the plurality opinion in the Georgia case, *Gregg* v. *Georgia*.[34] This was an echo of *Furman*. Dissenting Justice Brennan responded, saying that Justice Stewart's opinion for the Court held that " 'evolving standards of decency' require focus not on the essence of the death penalty itself but primarily upon the procedures employed by the State to single out persons to suffer the penalty of death. . . . [But] I read 'evolving standards of decency' as requiring focus upon the essence of the death penalty itself. . . ."

Some of the key points of the decision in *Gregg* v. *Georgia* should be noted. Troy Gregg was convicted by a jury of robbing and murdering two men outside of Atlanta who had picked him up in Florida while he was hitchhiking north. He was subsequently arrested in North Carolina. A search turned up the .25-caliber pistol later shown to have been the murder weapon. After receiving the *Miranda* warnings, and signing a written waiver of his rights, Gregg signed a statement admitting the shooting and robbing of the two victims. His first three shots (he said) dropped the men, who fell near a ditch; he then fired another shot into the head of each. He robbed them and drove away in their automobile.

After the jury found Gregg guilty, the judge instructed them as to the penalty they could recommend: *either* death *or* life in prison. He told them they could consider mitigating circumstances. They could *only* impose death if they first found beyond a reasonable doubt that: (1) murder was committed during the commission of other capital felonies (*viz.*, armed robbery); (2) the accused committed the murder so as to obtain the victims' automobile and money; *or* "(3) the murder was 'outrageously and wantonly vile, horrible and inhuman' in that it 'involved the depravity of the mind of the defendant.' " The jury found that the first and second of these *aggravating circumstances* were present, and they returned a sentence of death. The Georgia Supreme Court automatically reviewed the case, and affirmed the conviction and sentence.

The U.S. Supreme Court affirmed the judgment on appeal. It held that the punishment of death for the crime of murder does not always violate the Eighth and Fourteenth Amendments. The Court further said that the Eighth Amendment has been interpreted in a flexible manner so as to be in accord with the evolving standards of decency. The amendment "forbids the use of punishment that is 'excessive' either because it involves the unnecessary and wanton infliction of pain or because it is grossly disproportionate to the severity of the crime." The Court pointed to the fact that the framers of the Constitution accepted capital punishment, and that for nearly two centuries the Court had recognized that the death penalty for murder is "not invalid *per se*." The Court further noted that legislative determination has great weight, and cited the facts that, in the four-year interim since the *Furman* decision, Congress and thirty-five states had enacted new statutes providing for the death penalty.

The Court went on to conclude that *Furman's* objections to letting juries impose the death penalty, found as fatal defects in the earlier Georgia law, had been overcome in the new statute. The statute had been carefully drafted to include two processes: (1) the finding of guilt and (2) sentencing. It supplied standards to guide the sentencing phase. The Georgia State Supreme Court automatically thereafter reviewed each death sentence and compared it with precedent to "ensure that the sentence of death in a particular case is not disproportionate." Under these circumstances, then, the Court upheld the statute as constitutional and the sentence as justifiable.

In human terms, what did the Court's 1976 decision mean? It meant that 147 people then under sentence to die in Georgia, Texas, and Florida were likely to be executed. It paved the way for executions of another 100 to 140 persons in other states with statutes comparable to those approved by the Court. But it revoked the death sentences of 300 persons in some twenty states with statutes analogous to those struck down in North Carolina and Louisiana.

Status of the Death Penalty Today. Today our reluctance to use the death sentence contrasts with attitudes of earlier years. For example, British settlers in early Virginia had demanded death for such offenses as stealing grapes, trading with the Indians, or killing farm and household animals without permission. In the 1650s, colonists who cursed their parents or denied the true God could be executed. Even in Pennsylvania and West Jersey, where Quaker influence was strongest, death was imposed for treason and wilful murder during colonial times. In 1837 Maine was the first state to declare a moratorium on capital punishment; capital offenders were there sentenced to one year in solitary confinement and executed only on direct order of the governor. Electrocution as the means of execution was first adopted by New York (in 1890), and this triggered a wave of reform that led Congress in 1897 to reduce the number of federal capital crimes.

By 1917, twelve states had banned capital punishment and another six had passed such a prohibition through one house of their legislature. World War I reversed the trend, due to rising hatred of foreigners, fear of radicals, and reaction to a rising crime wave. The high year for executions was 1935 with 199 deaths; 1950 showed a drop to eighty-two, 1955 to seventy-six. After the National Association for the Advancement of Colored People (NAACP), through its Legal and Educational Fund, in appeal cases began defending blacks convicted of rape, murder, and other capital offenses in Southern courts, the statistics dropped markedly. In 1965 there were seven executions, in 1966 two, and in 1967 one. Ten years elapsed before another execution occurred in the United States, in 1977.[35]

The 1976 decisions cleared the way for execution by Utah of Gary Mark Gilmore on January 17, 1977, by firing squad for the brutal murder of a young motel manager six months earlier. A Harris poll released a week before Gilmore's execution showed that 71 percent of the American people believed capital punishment should be reinstituted, the ten-year moratorium ended, and that Gilmore should die for his crime.[36]

Conclusions

In conclusion, three principles underlie the process of criminal justice: (1) any person brought before the bar of justice in this country for a crime is entitled to be fairly treated at every step of the way, and this includes an impartial, neutral, and legally sound trial by jury; (2) any conviction of a defendant must be *solely* on the basis of legally obtained evidence properly admitted for the jury's consideration in a court of law; (3) any punishment meted out after conviction must "fit the crime." Any abuse by law enforcement officers or prosecutors, or serious errors by the presiding judge, or intrusion of prejudicial events such as a threatening mob or press notoriety, can serve to deprive the accused of the constitutionally protected rights enjoyed by all citizens. This is cause for a new trial. From the meticulous care with which criminal procedure must be approached, one might say that justice moves on "leaden feet" through its maze of intricacies, contrived over the centuries to assure (within the limits of all due care) that only the guilty are punished.

Summary

In this chapter we have sketched the rights assured persons who are accused of committing a crime. The process of criminal justice has been traced from its beginning in an investigation, through the search for evidence, interrogation, the filing of a complaint, and arraignment. The operation of the grand jury, the work of the prosecutor, the procedures of the petit jury, and the importance of confessions and plea bargaining all have been examined. The basis of the rights to a lawyer's assistance during the preliminary and trial phases of the process has been shown, and the protections against double jeopardy and cruel and unusual punishments explained. We have concluded by exploring the debate surrounding the death penalty and by showing the steps that led up to the first state-ordered execution in the country in a decade in 1977.

We turn now to consider the topic of race relations and the civil rights revolution that has occurred since 1954. Of particular concern will be the application today of the Equal Protection of the Laws Clause of the Fourteenth Amendment.

REVIEW QUESTIONS

1. Why is the decision in *Miranda* v. *Arizona* significant?

2. Does the Hillbilly-FBI skit accurately reflect problems facing the

law enforcement agencies today? When is a voluntary confession to a crime admissible as evidence?

3. What is *habeas corpus?* Why is it sometimes regarded as "the" fundamental civil right? How did the Court change habeas corpus jurisdiction?

4. What did the Fourth Amendment mean to Dolly Mapp?

5. What is the "exclusionary rule"? How does it affect procedures in criminal trials? What is the impact of the *Janis* decision?

6. Trace the essential steps of the criminal process from investigation to conviction or acquittal of a suspect. Explain the meaning of each key term in the process.

7. What are the roles of the grand jury and the petit jury? Must the states use grand jury indictment to charge a person with a crime? Must the petit jury be composed of twelve members in state procedures? Must their verdicts be unanimous?

8. Do most criminal suspects who are arrested come to trial? Why or why not?

9. Explain the meaning of "double jeopardy." What amendment protects against it?

10. Why is the "right to counsel" important? What is its scope? What basic rights is it designed to help protect? Is the right to counsel guarantied by the Fifth Amendment? Sixth? Both? Explain.

11. How has the prohibition against "cruel and unusual punishments" of the Eighth Amendment been defined by the Supreme Court?

12. Under what circumstances may the death penalty be constitutionally applied? Discuss *Gregg* v. *Georgia.* Do you agree or disagree with Justice Brennan's objections to Justice Stewart's logic?

13. At what points do you think protection of rights during criminal procedures ought to be modified? How and why?

14. Is American justice "too soft" on the criminal element? Why or why not? In your opinion what can be done to reduce crime in the country?

15. What distinctions can you draw between the Soviet and American attitudes toward a person arrested by the police?

16. Why was Justice Jackson concerned that the Bill of Rights might become a suicide pact? Were his fears justifiable?

17. How and why have American attitudes toward the death penalty changed since the early colonists settled in Jamestown and Plymouth?

CHAPTER FIVE

The Civil Rights Revolution: A New Birth of Freedom?

We hold these truths to be self-evident, that
all men are created equal, that they are endowed
by their Creator with certain unalienable
Rights, that among these are Life, Liberty and
the pursuit of Happiness.[1]

DECLARATION OF INDEPENDENCE (1776)

It is rather for us to be here dedicated to the
great task remaining before us . . . that this
nation, under God, shall have a new birth of
freedom; and that government of the people, by
the people, for the people, shall not perish from
the earth.[2]

ABRAHAM LINCOLN (1863)

. . . if the policy of the government, upon vital
questions, affecting the whole people, is to be
irrevocably fixed by decisions of the Supreme
Court, . . . the people will have ceased, to be their
own rulers, having, to that extent, practically
resigned their government, into the hands of that
eminent tribunal.[3]

ABRAHAM LINCOLN (1861)

BROWN v. BOARD OF EDUCATION

*T*HE CASES CAME FROM Kansas and Delaware, from South Carolina and Virginia. One came from the District of Columbia itself. There were five of them in all, brought to the Court on the same day by black elementary and high school children from Topeka, Kansas; rural Clarendon County, South Carolina; Prince Edward County, Virginia; industrial New Castle County, Delaware; and the District of Columbia. The suits were much the same, but BROWN v. BOARD OF EDUCATION (Topeka, Kansas) has become the most famous, and the one we shall discuss here.

The "pied piper" who led them all into the highest Court was himself black, a determined, impressive attorney in his midforties named Thurgood Marshall. The children's complaints seemed simple enough. They were black students and had been denied permission to set foot in the white schools of their communities, counties, and states. The children came before the Court for the first time. Thurgood Marshall had been there before. This son of a Pullman car steward, great grandson of a slave, and native Marylander, would eventually bring thirty-two cases before the United States Supreme Court, and win twenty-nine of them.

Tension ran high when the arguments first were heard on the case the country soon would identify as BROWN v. BOARD OF EDUCATION.[4] It was December 9, 1952. Chief Justice Fred M. Vinson presided. The distinguished lawyer, John W. Davis, then nearly 80, led the opposing cluster of attorneys. It was Davis who earlier that year had won the famous steel mills seizure case, against President Harry S Truman's assertion of Executive powers to take over the steel mills under the emergency conditions of the Korean Conflict.[5] The Court had responded at Davis's behest that neither statute nor constitutional provision authorized the President to legislate. Hence, Truman's seizure order was unconstitutional.

The confrontation between Marshall and Davis would be another battle of giants. Some 300 people, mostly blacks, packed the Chamber to witness it. Another 400 stood in long lines reaching through the marble corridor, far down white granite steps that lay before the towering bronze doors of the Supreme Court building.

The South was defiant in anticipation of a further desegregation ruling. Marshall had been there before on that issue, too. As principal lawyer of the NAACP Legal and Educational Fund since 1939 he had argued—and won—cases before this same Court which had cut down white primary elections, segregated seating on interstate buses, court-enforced covenants to maintain all-white neighborhoods, and the exclusion of blacks from the University of Texas Law School. A revival of the "American Confederate Army" was threatened by the Grand Dragon of the Ku Klux Klan if segregated schools fell. Georgia had enacted a statute to withhold public funds from any desegregated school district. South Carolina's Governor James F. Byrnes, himself a former associate justice of the U.S. Supreme Court, had led the fight to so amend the state constitution as to dissolve the public school system itself.

Background of the Brown Case

The decision in the case was far from a foregone conclusion, however. Case law generally supported Davis rather than Marshall. The Supreme Court had endorsed the doctrine of "separate but equal" in an 1896 case, after it first appeared in an 1849 Massachusetts school case.[6] It was sociology and the testimony of social scientists that Marshall would have to rely on most heavily. But he also had in his favor a string of recent decisions by the Court that threw grave doubts on the whole "separate but equal" doctrine. And some said that, best of all, justice was on his side. The show between the two great lawyers, Davis much senior to Marshall, was as good as everyone had anticipated. Davis claimed to have spent seventy-five hours preparing the case. He had the law in the palm of his hand, and he was a fine speaker. His task that day was to argue South Carolina's case.

Davis cited a "vast body" of legislation, judicial rulings, and learned argument that had supported segregation for ninety years. Segregation quite obviously had grown up after ratification of the Fourteenth Amendment and so could hardly be prohibited by it. He derided Marshall's over-reliance on the expert testimony of social scientists, recalling a line he had come across that characterized their findings as "fragmentary expertise based on an unexamined presupposition." He pointed to the reliance in educational matters placed on local government, the authorities closest to the people most concerned about the education of children. He urged the Court to preserve reliance on these local determinations, and also to preserve the wisdom of its own decisions of ninety years.

Marshall, on the other hand, bolstered the authority of the expert testimony. The best scientific thinking showed that segregated schools were in essence both inferior and degrading to black children. Segregated schools are no more justifiable than segregated buses, and the Court had already condemned those. He pointed to the developing body of law propounded by the Court itself to the effect that purely racial distinctions are "odious and invidious." Various justices questioned him sharply. Marshall always came back to his central point: state-imposed segregation is the principle that must go; it is this above everything that affects so adversely individual children, placing them beyond the pale of respectability. Just how the principle would be established through the schools' redistricting was a matter for legislatures to work out—once the Court had laid down the right principle.

After all arguments had been completed on all the cases, Davis felt he had won—unless the Court decided to remake the law! History and precedent were firmly on his side. The reporter for TIME magazine thought otherwise, for he pointed to Marshall's unique advantage: it was the law he had made yesterday that was controlling precedent today! By the following May, 1953, the Court had leaned in the direction of Marshall. But there were nagging doubts. So re-argument was demanded on a series of further questions that had arisen out of the justices' conferences on the case. The re-argument would occur in December, requiring both sides to spend another half year researching arguments, examining the legislative history of the Fourteenth Amendment and of the Civil Rights acts of 1866 and 1877.

On December 7, 1953, the scene of a year before was reenacted. But a judge in the case was changed. Chief Justice Vinson had died suddenly in September, and President Eisenhower had filled the vacancy through nomination of Governor Earl Warren of California. Before he had become governor, Warren had been attorney general of California, a successful and relentless prosecutor, but a man of profound compassion. Court convened at noon and the routine business of the day was transacted for sixty-five minutes. Then the five segregation cases were called up.

The second and decisive round of this battle of giants raged for five hours spread over three days of argument. Davis was disgusted to find Assistant U.S. Attorney General J. Lee Rankin taking the NAACP side and going almost to the length they did to distort the historical and judicial facts. The legislative history of both the Fourteenth Amendment and the Civil Rights acts, Rankin asserted, shows nothing to contradict the belief that Congress then intended to end all racial discrimination. How, then, had Congress indulged in the creation of segregated schools in Washington, D.C., in 1871, snapped Justice Frankfurter. Rankin could not explain it, but he stood his ground even if not very persuasively.

Marshall's presentation was powerful. Asked whether the Supreme Court was within its powers to outlaw segregated schools, Marshall responded with a "flat" yes. In fact, the Fourteenth Amendment imposes it as a duty of the Court, he argued. The South's segregation laws were in the same category as the "Black Codes" that sprang up following the Civil War and against which the Civil Rights acts originally were directed: those same federal statutes justify the Court's action to outlaw segregation as it exists under modern state authority. Was the Court to give force to the legislative will of Virginia and South Carolina or the authority of the Constitution?

Davis's argument ridiculed the historical constructions of Rankin and Marshall. He gave his own version, heavily relying on the discredited account of the old historian, Claude Bowers. He argued with good evidence that the Fourteenth Amendment could not be shown to prohibit segregation. He pointed to the Court's own decisions, and argued that if it adhered to these and followed stare decisis then it could not decide for the plaintiffs. He himself finally stooped to sociology, and argued that the doctrine of "reasonable classification" was sufficient to sustain segregation even if precedent were not relied on. He believed desegregation would be a disaster for all, black and white alike, and adduced evidence to show the historical and geographical depth of concurrence with that judgment. Such a view, he said, was not racism. He allowed that to include something in the Fourteenth Amendment which was not already there would be to amend the Amendment—a power not vested even in the Supreme Court. Davis spoke long and eloquently, and was only interrupted once by the Court during his entire presentation. But, then, it was listening to the lawyer who had appeared more frequently before it than had any other man in modern history: this was his 140th time to have his day in Court. It was to be his last.

To the distinguished legal scholar, Alexander Bickel, what came through most powerfully from Davis's argument that day in 1953 as he sat in the Chamber was the sense of the "pervasive" and "solidly founded" existing social order of the country, and the staggering difficulties to be "encountered in uprooting it."

The Supreme Court Decision

It was the Court's decision that the existing order must be uprooted. Remarkably, when the decision came at last on May 17, 1954, the Chief Justice spoke for a unanimous Court. His opinion was short and unadorned. "Today," Chief Justice Warren said, "education is perhaps the most important function of state and local governments." The clock cannot be turned back to 1868 when the Fourteenth Amendment was adopted nor to 1896 when the "separate but equal" doctrine was propounded by the Court. No child can be expected to succeed in life "if he is denied the opportunity of education. Such an opportunity . . . is a right which must be made available to all on equal terms."

The question was this: Does segregation in public schools on the basis of race alone, even in the presence of equal physical school facilities, deprive "the children of the minority group of equal educational opportunities"? The Chief Justice answered:

We believe that it does.... To separate them from others of similar age and qualifications solely because of their race generates a feeling of inferiority as to their status in the community that may affect their hearts and minds in a way unlikely ever to be undone.... We conclude that in the field of public education the doctrine of "separate but equal" has no place. Separate educational facilities are inherently unequal. Therefore, we hold that the plaintiffs and others similarly situated ... are, by reason of the segregation complained of, deprived of the equal protection of the laws guaranteed by the Fourteenth Amendment.

The conflicting 1896 precedent basic to the "separate but equal" position, was partially overruled (PLESSY v. FERGUSON). And, as we saw much earlier, the District of Columbia case was resolved to the same effect as the state cases, despite the slight inconvenience of having to rely on the due process clause of the Fifth Amendment. But for the Court's purposes, that due process clause was taken to be equivalent in meaning to the equal protection clause of the Fourteenth Amendment. How would desegregation be implemented? That complex question required further study, the Chief Justice said. Arguments would be heard later for the purpose of formulating decrees to give effect to the ruling announced in BROWN I.[7]

Implications of the Brown I and II Cases

This decision (together with its sequel, BROWN II, when implementation decrees were issued) marks an epoch in American social and legal history. It is without any doubt the most towering Supreme Court decision of the century, if the measure is social impact. BROWN I rejected the argument basic to PLESSY that it was within the police power of the states to segregate the black and white races in the interest of minimizing the likelihood of racial friction and violence. It found "that in the field of education the doctrine of 'separate but equal' has no place. Separate educational facilities are inherently unequal." Brown I thereby became the revolutionary matrix of all subsequent efforts to eliminate segregation "root and branch" from public education—and, indeed, from every other aspect of American life. This has proved to be a tall order!

As to the players in this historic drama, John W. Davis fell ill and was unable to further represent South Carolina. The oral arguments concerning implementation were held in April 1955. By then Davis was dead, some say killed by the Brown I decision. The final decrees were issued a bare six weeks later, almost one year to the day after Brown I was decided. Davis had thought it a bad decision, simply "unworthy" of the Supreme Court.

Marshall continued to fight and to succeed in the tumultuous years that were the aftermath of Brown, participating in many of the cases that I shall mention in the balance of this chapter. On June 13, 1967, President Lyndon B. Johnson nominated this Pullman steward's son to a vacancy on the bench he had so frequently pled before. Thurgood Marshall thereby became, after Senate confirmation, Associate Justice Marshall, the first black to sit on the Supreme Court.

———————

To fit the self-evident truths of the Declaration of Independence to American law and political and social life was the great task of both President Abraham Lincoln and Supreme Court Chief Justice Earl Warren. The sticking point was the race problem. Slaves were not men but things under the law when the Declaration and Constitution were drafted. As property rather than people, the Supreme Court had held in the *Dred Scott* [8] case of 1857 that Congress could not prohibit their being taken by their masters into the unorganized territories comprising the Louisiana Purchase (north of latitude thirty-six degrees thirty minutes), an area supposedly immunized against slavery by the Missouri Compromise of 1820. This was because Congress could not, Chief Justice Roger B. Taney said for the Court, constitutionally deprive persons of their private property. Hence, the Missouri Compromise was void. It was this decision, with the awful consequences leading to the Civil War, that Lincoln had in view in his remarks about the Supreme Court in the "First Inaugural Address," quoted at the beginning of this chapter. In the abstract, his observations lie close to those of Jefferson, quoted as a headnote in chapter 1.

Chattel slavery ended with the Emancipation Proclamation of January 1, 1863, as sustained by the surrender of the Confederacy to the Union by General Robert E. Lee at Appomattox court house on April 9, 1865. The Civil War did not so much reverse *Dred Scott* as circumvent it. The adoption of the "Civil War Amendments"— Thirteen, Fourteen, and Fifteen—to the Constitution supplied the constitutional gap basic to *Dred Scott* and basic to translating black slaves into black citizens. The irony is that it has been the Court of the post-World War II era that has led the way in achieving the promise of Lincoln's proclamation of a "new birth of freedom." For by applying, and broadening the meaning of, the Equal Protection of the Laws Clause of the Fourteenth Amendment, the nine-member Court—disparaged by Jefferson as "the despotism of an oligarchy," by Lincoln as potential usurpers to whom the people may have "resigned their government"—has created the civil rights revolution to be sketched in this chapter.

We have begun by reviewing the most famous of all modern Supreme Court decisions, *Brown v. Board of Education* (1954). We shall now trace some of the major ramifications of *Brown* and related decisions, showing how equal protection has been applied to give effect to the revolutionary decision. We will briefly consider civil rights legislation, and then voting rights, before investigating the emergent field of restrictions placed on private actions (as opposed to state actions) that result in illegal discrimination. We conclude with an overview of the characteristics of the present Court and of its renewed interest in the question of "intent" in discrimination controversies.

Desegregation of Education

Since 1927 when Justice Oliver Wendell Holmes disdainfully referred to the equal protection of the laws clause of the Fourteenth Amendment as "the usual last resort in constitutional arguments," that provision has grown to cardinal importance as a basis of civil rights in America. Today, it vies with the due process clause as the most frequently invoked constitutional provision in cases brought before federal courts. It also is the basis of extensive legislation enacted by the Congress immediately after the Civil War and, after a long interlude, after World War II. The target of most of this litigation and legislation has been *state* action. But a more recent development is to attack *private* action that has deprived citizens of rights. Much of this judicial and congressional activity has been directed toward ending racial discrimination, most especially toward securing the full rights of citizenship for the black American.

From the outset, American race relations has been a battlefield of legal—sometimes of physical—strife and contention. How to cope with the presence of the Negro in America has steadily proved to be *the* single most intractable domestic problem faced by the United States throughout its entire history. Our Civil War was fought over the issue. The very phrase, "civil rights," attaches preeminently to the race problems of minority groups, particularly to those of the black race which composes more than 10 percent of our citizenry. This is true even though solid progress has been made in race relations. Let us not blink the fact: racism is a distasteful and sordid fact of American life.

In the wake of the Civil War, the so-called "Civil War Amendments" were ratified (the Thirteenth, Fourteenth, and Fifteenth Amendments; see Appendix B). All three aimed at ending racial discrimination in all its aspects. Shortly after ratification, the Court acknowledged this by saying there is "one pervading purpose" of the three amendments: "we mean the freedom of the slave race, the security and firm establishment of that freedom, and the protection of the newly-made freeman and citizen from the oppressions of those who had formerly exercised dominion over him." [9] That the struggle continues to be reported in daily newspapers from Boston,

Detroit, Louisville, and Dallas tells us the arena of bitterest confrontation since 1954 has been education.

The *Brown* decision was not the beginning of the attack on segregated educational institutions. That began in the late 1930s, but it was not until the mid-1950s that full-scale "war" was declared. In summary, what happened? To begin with, the legal effect of *Brown I* [10] was this. It became the law of the land that the dual system of public education separating the races into different schools, even if the instruction and facilities were equally good, violated the Constitution's equal protection clause. As was seen, the Court corrected a "half-century of error" by partially overruling *Plessy* v. *Ferguson* and the "separate but equal" doctrine it had announced.

Admission of black pupils to school on a nondiscriminatory basis "with all deliberate speed" became the focal point of efforts from 1955 onward when the implementation decree was given in *Brown II*.[11] Numerous suits followed in a sustained attack conducted through every judicial and political means available under the law. They sought to break down the century-old pattern of racially segregated schools in the South on the rock-bottom premise that state-imposed "segregation by race in public schools denies equal protection of the laws." Primary reliance was on federal district courts to see that good faith implementation of the constitutional principles was pursued by local school authorities. Dual school systems must go.

But deliberate resistance of every form was encountered. A civilization was being uprooted through the judicial power of the United States, and, as the Court at length admitted, "Nothing in our national experience prior to 1955 prepared anyone for dealing with changes and adjustments of the magnitude and complexity encountered since then." How were these efforts carried forward?

"Freedom of choice" programs were acceptable to the Court only on condition that they "work" to end the dual school system. The shift from prohibiting discrimination to positively requiring integration of schools was expressed by 1968.[12] Positive integration meant a "unitary" system of faculty, staff, and services, composed in such a way that it was impossible to identify the *system* as either black or white. The Court wanted results. It said in the important *Swann* case, discussed below, that to be able to identify a school system (if not individual schools within the system) as either black or white constitutes a *"prima facie* case of violation of substantive constitutional rights under the Equal Protection Clause."

Swann v. Charlotte-Mecklenburg

The Court perceived the situation in *Swann* v. *Charlotte-Mecklenburg Board of Education* [13] as precisely the kind of undesirable situation as that of the *Brown* case decided seventeen years before. Charlotte, North Carolina, had for several years been under a court-approved desegregation plan; 30 percent of the total student population was black. But by 1969, only half of the black pupils were in formerly all-white schools, and the other half were still in virtually all-black schools. The federal district court ordered a more effective plan to be devised. It subsequently rejected several proposals submitted by the school board, and finally hired a consultant to draw up a plan, which it approved and ordered implemented. This mandated plan included busing suburban white pupils to inner city black schools and inner city black students to suburban white schools, to achieve better racial balance. The United States Court of Appeals for the Fourth Circuit set aside the busing feature devised by the district court's consultant. The case then came on appeal to the Supreme Court in 1971.

The question in 1971 was the same as in 1954: How to achieve what *Brown I* said must be done? The *Swann* decision spelled out for the first time since 1954 four guidelines that were to be used by school districts to establish unitary systems: (1) Mathematically calculated quotas might be prescribed by district courts. (2) One-race schools might be allowed within a system—but only if the fact of their existence could withstand close scrutiny proving they were not products of state-enforced segregation, the burden of proof lying on school authorities. (3) The techniques of gerrymandering (drawing district lines as to get the proper racial mix) and of pairing or grouping schools for student assignment purposes to achieve satisfactory balances were approved. (4) Busing was endorsed as a suitable tool to achieve balance, so long as it did not (a) carry risk to the health of the children involved, or (b) seriously impinge on the education process. "The objective is to dismantle the dual school system," the Court said bluntly.

Legally enforced (or *de jure*) school segregation in the South—not *de facto* segregation elsewhere—was the exclusive target of the Court's efforts for twenty years. In the wake of *Swann*, busing became a burning emotional issue reflected in political campaigns, including the presidential campaign of 1972 and reverberating ever since. Anti-busing legislation and constitutional amendments were introduced and passed by Congress with Administration support. National support for the counterattack on busing increased as Court decisions in 1973 and later pointed up the belatedly noticed fact that segregated school systems are found outside the South.

Keyes v. School District No. 1

An important case was brought before the Court in 1973, *Keyes v. School District No. 1, Denver,*[14] which paved the way for court-ordered integration in the North. Justice Powell, in a separate opinion, partly concurring and partly dissenting, cited data from a 1971 HEW study showing that segregation was more prevalent in the North and West than in the South itself. In the South 43.9 percent of the Negro pupils attended white-majority schools, while in the North and West only 27.8 percent attended such schools. Moreover, 57 percent of all "Negro pupils in the North and West attend schools with over 80 percent minority population as opposed to 32.2 percent who do so in the South."

Justice Brennan, speaking for the Court, defined *de jure* segregation as "a current condition of segregation resulting from intentional state action." The critical question, the Court said, was whether the high percentage of minority students in certain schools in Denver was due to a "racially neutral 'neighborhood school policy'" or "segregative intent" on the part of the school board. In the central passage of the opinion, the Court said this:

> ... we hold that a finding of intentionally segregative school board actions in a meaningful portion of a school system ... creates a presumption that other segregated schooling within the system is not adventitious. It establishes [as it does in Denver], in other words, a *prima facie* case of unlawful segregative design on the part of school authorities, and shifts to those authorities the burden of proving that other segregated schools within the system are not

also the result of intentionally segregative actions. . . . We emphasize that the differentiating factor between *de jure* segregation and so-called *de facto* segregation to which we referred in *Swann* . . . is *purpose* or *intent* to segregate.

The *Keyes* decision opened the way for court-ordered integration not only in Denver—in the first case of its kind outside of the South—but also in other cities in northern and border states.

Detroit, Boston, and Louisville Desegregation Cases

A new storm of public protest ensued. Mothers marched and prayed in the streets of South Boston, which by 1976 was nearly in a state of siege. The issue there, as in *Swann*, was busing to achieve racial balance.

In the Detroit desegregation decision, however, the Court spoke in lofty language of preserving "local autonomy" in school matters and declined to extend its ruling to integrate the suburban systems of the metropolitan area (despite the bitter dissent of Justice Thurgood Marshall, who thought the Court had chickened out). The Court majority distinguished *inter*district from *intra*district patterns of segregation. In so doing it held it merely to be the "constitutional right of the Negro respondents residing in Detroit . . . to attend a unitary school system in that district"—not an integrated one! Thus, for the first time since the 1930s, the Court in a signed opinion rejected the NAACP's position on race and the schools.[15] (For further related discussion of the school cases, see the concluding sections of this chapter, pp. 213–228.) Let us now review two decisions rendered in 1976 by the Court which are of particular interest.

Runyon v. McCrary

Michael McCrary and Colin Gonzales, two black children, filed through their parents a class action suit against Russell and Katheryne Runyon, proprietors of Bobbe's Private School in Arlington, Virginia.[16] They claimed they had been prevented from enrolling in that school because they were black. The defendants were joined by the Southern Independent School Association, a nonprofit organization whose membership extends to 395 private schools in six states. The creation of private all-white schools has been widespread as a means of avoiding integrated public schools throughout much of the South. The suit sought relief under the Civil Rights Act of 1866 (42 U.S.C. SEC. 1981), which prohibits racial discrimination in the making and enforcement of private contracts. The Court ruled that this statute "*does* reach private acts of racial discrimination." (We will discuss the Civil Rights Act in greater detail later in this chapter.)

The statute's constitutionality, as applied to this case, was challenged as an abridgment of the protected rights of free *association*, of *privacy*, and of a *parent's right* to direct the education of his children. The Court brushed aside these challenges by acknowledging the existence of the rights but curtly denying that they collided with the challenged statute. In considering the right of association, Justice Stewart spoke for the Court: "... it does not follow that the *practice* of excluding racial minorities from such institutions [as these] is ... protected...." Justice Stewart cited precedent to show that: "the Constitution . . . places no value on discrimination." And he cited the court of appeals' opinion that "there is no showing that discontinuance of [the] discriminatory admission practices would inhibit in any way the teaching in these schools of any ideas or dogma."

Arguments from asserted parental rights and the right of privacy were similarly disposed of. Simply because these rights are protected does not mean that they cannot be reasonably restricted and regulated in their exercise by government. Section 1981 of the Civil Rights Act, Justice Stewart declared, was such a reasonable exercise of the federal government's legislative power. The children were ordered admitted to the private schools.

Pasadena City Board of Education v. Spangler

A different and rare result was reached in a Pasadena, California, case [17] in which the school board challenged the federal district court judge's integration decree. The Supreme Court concurred with the challenge and restricted the scope of the district court's order. It found that the lower court in the person of Judge Manuel L. Real of the U.S. District Court for the Central District of California had abused judicial discretion by requiring an annual reassignment of pupils to maintain racial balance and by insisting "that at least during my lifetime there [will] be no majority of any minority in any school in Pasadena."

This decree had been issued by the district court judge in the course of carrying out the original desegregation order, which had identified *de jure* segregation in the Pasadena school system. Two things had already occurred: (1) the Pasadena school board had satisfactorily complied with the original order by 1970, but (2) by the next year population moves were such that the system no longer complied with the judge's mandate that there be no schools in the district with a majority of minority students. These population changes, the Court noted, apparently were random and not caused by the desegregation order. The Court concluded that Pasadena had done all it need do under the *Swann* guidelines, once it had achieved a racially neutral attendance pattern, as it had done by 1970.

Civil Rights Legislation

In the Reconstruction Era immediately following the Civil War, a number of statutes were enacted pursuant to the "enforcement" clauses of the Thirteenth, Fourteenth, and Fifteenth Amendments. These statutes were designed to help assure the civil rights of the former slave population in the southern states. Some of the provisions of these acts, as was just noticed in the *Runyon* case, still remain in force today. They have been augmented by a considerable amount of national legislation enacted much more recently, specifically since 1957 and the Court-inspired civil rights revolution.

Early Legislation

The Civil Rights Act of 1866. The Civil Rights Act was aimed at the "Black Codes" enacted but never actually put into effect by several southern states. It was designed to implement the Thirteenth Amendment, which gave constitutional support to Lincoln's Emancipation Proclamation (1863). It provided that all persons born within the United States are "citizens of the United States" who possess certain rights regardless of "race and color . . . [or] previous condition of slavery," including "the same right [to] make and enforce contracts, to sue, be parties, and give evidence, to inherit, purchase, lease, sell, hold, and convey real and personal property, and to full and equal benefit of all laws [for] the security of persons and property, as is enjoyed by white citizens, and shall be subject to like punishment, [and] to none other, any law, statute, ordinance, regulation or custom, to the contrary notwithstanding." [18]

The criminal enforcement provisions of this Act have been retained in modern law and, as amended, state the following:

> *Deprivation of rights under color of law.* Whoever, under color of any law, statute, ordinance, regulation, or custom, willfully subjects any inhabitant of any State, Territory, or District to the deprivation of any rights, privileges, or immunities secured or protected by the Constitution or laws of the United States, or to different punishments, pains, or penalties, on account of such inhabitant being an alien, or by reason of his color, or race, than are prescribed for the punishment of citizens, shall be fined not more than $1,000 or imprisoned not more than one year, or both; and if death results shall be subject to imprisonment for any term of years or for life.[19]

The Enforcement Act of 1870. The Enforcement Act was enacted in 1870 to implement the provision of the Fifteenth Amendment that the vote was not to be denied to any citizen "on account of race, color, or previous condition of servitude" and to supply remedies against any such denials. But it also made it a felony for two or more persons to enter into a conspiracy, "or go in disguise upon the public highway, or upon the premises of another, with intent to violate any provision of this act, or to injure, oppress, threaten or intimidate any citizen with intent to prevent or hinder his free exercise and enjoyment of any right or privilege granted or secured to him by the Constitution or laws of the United States, or because of his having exercised the same." [20]

The Civil Rights Act of 1871. Known as the Ku Klux Klan Act, this 1871 Act established both civil and criminal liabilities for denial of rights. It also included a conspiracy provision that applied to private action, an increasingly important theme in recent rights litigation.

As preserved in modern law, the provisions of these various statutes have been the bases of several important decisions.[21]

This procession of legislation is, of course, a clue to understanding the trying social and political conditions that characterized life in the post-Civil War South. It was a vanquished and occupied territory. A great percentage of its population had, just yesterday, been chattel property without rights or a formal place as human beings in the political and legal order. The problems were enormous; abuses and suffering marked the era. One authority characterized the plight of the blacks in 1865 this way:

> At the end of the Civil War, Negroes were perhaps as near to minimal survival in the psychological sense, as human beings, as they had been since their initial transportation from Africa. They had lost the security of provision for food, clothing, shelter, and physical safety that had been fairly well assured them as long as they docilely accepted their position as slaves. They could no longer be sure that the master would provide for them. They had, often, to forage for themselves, like war refugees everywhere when crops have been destroyed and normal patterns of collaboration in productive work have been shattered. Overjoyed at their emancipation, they could use their freedom no more effectively than could concentration camp inmates in Germany when the doors at last swung open in early 1945. They could concern themselves really with only the satisfaction of their physical needs, which freedom is not and equality and dignity are not.[22]

In addition to the normal vicissitudes, there burst upon the scene the Ku Klux Klan. Its activities, especially in 1868 and 1870, were a source of anguish, disruption, and, to some, hope. Their initial justification was vigilante justice in a society that believed in white supremacy, even if it could no longer practice slavery. Their own institutions had collapsed or been taken over by carpetbaggers, scalawags, and their compliant black friends. The mission of the Klan was to protect old white interests and to preserve order on the old pattern. And it was against those efforts that the Act of 1871, and its curious provisions, as well as other measures were directed.

To begin with, Klansmen posted warnings and frightened the newly freed Negroes into submission. But when these methods grew ineffective—especially after the impressionable and superstitious blacks found that a rifle ball would kill Klansmen who were, then, after all, not superhuman spirits—then the atrocities began. The Klan hanged, burned, shot, and drowned Negroes, scalawags, and carpet-baggers. They drove them out of the country. The sorry state of affairs bordered on anarchy and mob rule. As one authority tells it, on one occasion the Klan "came to the rescue of a Mississippi court by executing three Negroes who had burned Meridian and who had then killed the judge who was trying them. Seven hundred Klansmen in black robes and masks stormed the Greenville, South Carolina, jail, loosed two of their comrades, and hanged six of their enemies. Less violent, but equally effective, was the work of the Klan in subduing the spirits of violent troublemakers, inducing Negroes to abide by their contracts to work, and scaring them away from elections."

The respectable elements of society who once had widely joined the Klan ultimately withdrew, leaving it "in the hands of cutthroats and riffraff, for private gain and vengeance. . . . It left a heritage which was to bedevil and disgrace the South thereafter, as mobs took the law into their own hands and engaged in barbarous lynchings—unjustified under any code of civilized rule." [23]

The Civil Rights Act of 1875.   The second civil rights act provided, among other things, "that all persons within the jurisdiction of the United States shall be entitled to the full and equal enjoyment of the accommodations, advantages, facilities, and privileges of inns, public conveyances on land or water, theaters, and other places of public amusement; subject only to the conditions and limitations established by law, and applicable alike to citizens of every race and color, regardless of any previous condition of servitude."

Civil Rights Cases of 1883.   In the landmark *Civil Rights Cases* of 1883, involving the states of Kansas, California, Missouri, New York, and Tennessee, the Supreme Court declared the Act of 1875 unconstitutional.[24] These cases are important today for they put "private action" into perspective. So-called "radical reconstruction" had by this time ended through the political compromise that in 1877 had seen the final withdrawal of occupying federal troops from the southern states. Thereby ended a turbulent decade during which the Radical wing of the Republican party had wrested control of reconstruction of the defeated South away from President Lincoln and President Andrew Johnson to place Congress directly in charge of policy. The result, especially during the period from 1868 to 1874, was a punitive, often corrupt rule of the southern states by Radical state governments dependent on federal bayonets and composed of northern carpetbaggers, southern scalawags, and the newly enfranchised freedmen. President Rutherford B. Hayes finally withdrew the last of the federal troops from Columbia, South Carolina, and New Orleans, Louisiana, in April 1877, shortly after he took office and ended an era.

The Court voided the Civil Rights Act of 1875 because it "pro-

"You can't have a balanced Court if they all believe in Civil Rights."
Source: from Herblock's State of the Union (Simon & Schuster, 1972).

ceeds *ex directo* to declare that certain acts committed by individuals shall be deemed offenses"; and on that basis, "the law in question cannot be sustained by any grant of legislative power made to Congress by the Fourteenth Amendment. . . . This is not corrective legislation; it is primary and direct; it takes immediate and absolute possession of the subject of the right to admission to inns, public conveyances, and places of amusement."

The appeal to the Thirteenth Amendment was not valid, in the Court's eyes, since that amendment only abolished slavery and had nothing to say regarding private refusal of public accommodations, conveyances, or admission to places of amusement, even if such acts might be the "badges of servitude." "It would be running the slavery argument into the ground to make it apply to every act of discrimination. . . ." Redress against any such discrimination must be sought from state laws.

That is where the matters stood, in the hands of the states, for a long time. For this decision had the far-reaching effect of dampening further legislative activity and discouraging it along three lines: (1) the Fourteenth Amendment itself did not reach private acts of discrimination, only state action. (2) The Thirteenth Amendment (SEC. 2) did not allow general enforcement of the law against acts of racial discrimination, the mere "badges of servitude," but more narrowly, only against slavery itself. (3) The congressional enforcement of the Fourteenth Amendment (under SEC. 5) could not go beyond limiting state action (under SEC. 1) to reach purely private actions.

Modern Civil Rights Legislation

It was not, then, until over eighty years later that national civil rights legislation was again successful. Then a surge of congressional activity began. The complex developments of this long stretch of time cannot be satisfactorily traced in a paragraph here. To summarize, after 1877 and the final withdrawal of occupying federal troops from the South, state and local governments fully reverted to white supremacy. The nation's concern for the well-being of the black population was swallowed up by the onrush of the industrial revolution that belatedly came to America. The sharecropping system in southern agriculture emerged as a fixture lasting down to World War II. The Supreme Court's rejection of the Civil Rights Act of 1875 as well as of other key policies of Reconstruction opened the way for white terrorism. A deteriorating Ku Klux Klan (in the final two decades of the nineteenth century) enlisted the criminal elements of the white population to harass the black population. Negro voters were systematically intimidated and disfranchised. During the 1890s the "Jim Crow" system of segregation was thoroughly established by custom and statute as the formal substitute for the old form of slavery.

The "new" Ku Klux Klan was organized in Atlanta, Georgia, in 1915, and spread its hatred and burnt its fiery crosses not only in the South but far away, in such unlikely places as the Middle West, Pennsylvania, and eastern Massachusetts. It had nothing in common with the old Klan that arose to help salvage some basic order after the Civil War, except its name, costume, and purpose to keep the Negro down. For good measure, it added to its most hated list Catholics, Jews, and foreigners. It was a part of the general upsurge of nativism that characterized this period in our history. For a decade or more it spewed the vilest hate imaginable into American life.

Lynchings—killing by mob rather than by legally authorized force—were almost commonplace. From 1882 when records first began to be kept till 1941, lynchings averaged seventy-eight per year. The figure does not include many isolated instances that went unreported. In the three decades after 1888 and down to World War I, lynch mobs claimed at least 3225 victims—78.2 percent of them blacks, including 50 women, 88 percent of them occurring in the southern and border states. This approach to execution was not necessarily overly fussy about humane treatment and often was accompanied by torture and mayhem. For instance, the November 20, 1922, New York *Times* carried a full-page advertisement bought by the NAACP captioned "The Shame of America." It asked: "Do you know that the United States is the Only Land on Earth where human beings are BURNED AT THE STAKE?" It went on to report that twenty-eight persons had been so killed in the four-year period from 1918 through 1921. While the Congress wrangled fruitlessly for two years (1921–1922) trying to enact the Dyer anti-lynching bill, 121 more people were lynched. In short, the blacks—especially but not exclusively—of the South lived in constant fear of being killed, castrated, or otherwise maimed or injured, particularly before the early 1920s. By 1940, the yearly average was five lynchings, and by 1948 it had dropped to three.

A number of factors accounted for this drop and for a revitalized concern to "do better" by the black American. One of those was the rise of a kind of neo-Abolition movement aimed at crushing segregation and minimizing abuses and crimes. The starting point of this effort was the formation of the Niagara Movement in 1905, led by W. E. B. Du Bois and other militant black intellectuals. The National Association for the Advancement of Colored People (NAACP) was founded in Lincoln's hometown of Springfield, Illinois, in 1909—a direct aftermath of the Springfield race riots of the previous year. The National Urban League appeared in 1910, and Marcus Garvey's short-lived Universal Negro Improvement Association began implanting the notion "Black is Beautiful."

No doubt the turning point, however, was the rise of the New Deal of Franklin D. Roosevelt after 1932. The lock on the Negro long held by the Republican Party—the party of Lincoln, after all—finally was broken. Blacks increasingly found place in public life and began their long agonizing ascent to admitted respectability reflected in the breakthrough of the *Brown* decision in 1954.[25]

The Civil Rights Act of 1957 and the Act of 1960 were primarily aimed at securing voting rights. They attempted to provide remedies against racial discrimination in that field. These protections were substantially expanded in the Voting Rights Act of 1965 as renewed and expanded in 1970 and in 1975. The Civil Rights Commission was established by the 1957 act and made important contributions to subsequent legislation through studies and recommendations.

Civil Rights Act of 1964. Based partly on Article I powers of Congress and partly on Civil War amendments, the first comprehensive civil rights legislation in modern times—the first to go beyond voting rights—was the Civil Rights Act of 1964. It dealt with public accommodations, additional voting rights, equal employment, and desegregation of schools and other public facilities. It established a Community Relations Service and authorized federal intervention in suits where denial of equal protection is claimed.

These congressional enactments were prompted by numerous factors, not least of all by the steady crescendo of civil rights agitation

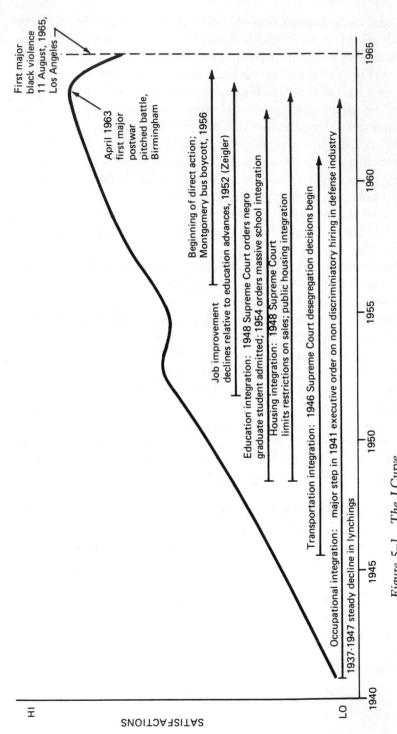

Figure 5-1   The J-Curve
Source: Hugh Davis Graham and Ted Robert Gurr, Violence in America, Staff Report
to the National Commission on the Causes and Prevention of Violence (Washington,
D.C.: U.S. Government Printing Office, 1969), p. 253.

which followed the 1954 and 1955 *Brown I* and *Brown II* Court decisions. Litigation to secure rights swelled to enormous proportions. The embattled white populations of the southern states fought to obstruct these efforts. Northern college students engaged in "freedom rides" into the South to bolster the effort toward black equality. Sit-ins, marches, street demonstrations, and rallies became a way of life. New or reinvigorated older militant organizations such as the Congress of Racial Equality (CORE), the Southern Christian Leadership Conference (SCLC) and the Student Nonviolent Coordinating Committee (SNCC) mobilized national sentiment and resources to help eliminate segregation "root and branch."

Federal troops were called into Little Rock, Arkansas, by President Eisenhower to enforce school desegregation in 1957. President Kennedy dispatched a federal force of 30,000 troops to Oxford, Mississippi, to see that James Meredith got admitted to the University of Mississippi in 1962. On and on it went, the irresistible force colliding with the proverbial immovable object of southern massive resistance. In the end, one by one, the barriers—legal and *de facto*—fell. Nothing about the process was either easy or simple, however. Riots in the summer of 1964 in New York City's Harlem district and in Rochester, New York, were followed in 1965 by a massive riot in the Watts district of Los Angeles. These are but three out of an estimated 329 important riots in 257 cities during 1964–1968. Property destruction was widespread in all of them. These rebellions brought out into the open that poverty, deprivation, and racial discrimination were national problems. Some people asserted, as did black power activist H. Rap Brown, that violence was as American as cherry pie.

The desegregation and student "New Left" movements partly converged, then, as the battleground shifted to the colleges and university campuses in the mid-1960s. That phase abated in 1970 with the Kent State University incident, but only after destruction on many campuses by demonstrating students. At Kent State, National Guard troops called in by Ohio's governor to quell the disturbance, fired into the demonstrators, killing four students. The nation reacted with shock at the incident. Solid progress, the ending of the Vietnam War, and perhaps plain old fatigue have contributed to making the 1970s a quieter time than the 1960s, at least so far as large public demonstrations go. Meanwhile, much of the country sat hypnotized and aghast at the horrors of the Watergate scandal, climaxed by President Richard M. Nixon's resignation from office on August 9, 1974.[26]

In the wake of the assassination of Dr. Martin Luther King, further elaborate legislation was enacted in 1968, which strengthened the laws against violence when related to civil rights violations, created a comprehensive fair housing law, dealt extensively with Indian rights, contained a Civil Obedience Act of 1968 (Title X), and included provisions on rioting.

Affirmative Action in Employment. A sizable field of rights is emerging from a combination of congressional legislation, Court decisions, and presidential executive orders, which converge in the policy called "affirmative action" in employment practices. Affirmative action is based on provisions of the Civil Rights Act of 1964, Title VII, as amended, making it unfair in employment practices to discriminate against, or segregate, anyone on the basis of race, color, religion, sex, national origin, or age between the years of forty and sixty-five. It applies to all employers affecting interstate commerce and having fifteen employees or more, including all businesses, trade unions, state and local governmental agencies, and universities.

Title VII has been amended and strengthened by various other acts, including the Equal Pay Act of 1963, the Equal Employment Opportunities Act of 1972, and by the addition of Title IX (prohibiting sex discrimination) to the Higher Education Act of 1965. The enforcement power of the administering agency, Equal Employment Opportunity Commission (EEOC), was augmented in 1972. The cumulative effect of affirmative action programs is to prevent and correct employment practices that discriminate against any of the listed minority groups or women by imposing requirements that are not job-related. It applies to all aspects of employment: hiring, promotion, firing, wages, testing, training, and apprenticeship.

A presidential executive order, which applies affirmative action to all federal contractors and subcontractors and requires them to establish and maintain a racially and sexually balanced labor force (quota hiring and promotions), was sustained by the Court in cases decided in 1971 and 1973. EEOC seeks to put voluntary affirmative action programs into effect through conciliation of grievance complaints as filed through regional offices and litigation centers. The upshot is to make Title VII and Title IX proceedings, through the administrative attention of the EEOC and the power of the United States Attorney General and the federal courts, a formidable fact of life in the employment field in this country today. Affirmative action has become a byword.[27] (See the related discussion in the concluding sections of this chapter, pp. 218–228.)

Voting Rights Legislation

Expansion of suffrage (the right to vote in elections) has been a basic trend in American politics from the time of the adoption of the Twelfth Amendment in 1804, which modified the presidential electoral system. This trend is part of the general tendency toward more and more democracy in American government. While not arising entirely from race-related matters, the bulk of the government's activity has been directed toward a host of legal obstacles that hinder the voting rights of minority groups among the citizenry.

Present Court Standards

It will be useful to focus our discussion on key formulations of the "right to vote" as defined in recent Court decisions and by noting the analytical approach now employed by the Court in voting rights cases.

"Undoubtedly," the Court said in *Reynolds* v. *Sims*,[28] a case in which malapportionment of the Alabama legislature was challenged in 1964, "the right of suffrage is a fundamental matter in a free and democratic society. Especially since the right to exercise the franchise in a free and unimpaired manner is preservative of other basic civil and political rights, any alleged infringement of the rights of citizens to vote must be carefully and meticulously scrutinized."

In 1969, in *Kramer* v. *Union Free School District*,[29] the Court went further. It stated that any unjustified restriction of participation in political affairs or the selection of public officials "undermines the legitimacy of representative government. . . ." If a challenged state law gives the right to vote to some residents but not others, then the Court will decide "whether the exclusions are necessary to promote a compelling state interest."

State legislators, therefore, do not have the power to decide which resident citizens may participate in the election of legislators and other public officials. On the contrary, the general presumption that state statutes are constitutional does not hold ". . . the traditional approval given state classifications if the Court can conceive of a 'rational basis' for the distinctions made is not applicable" when restriction of voting rights is attempted by any state.

By starting from the premises just outlined, the Court in recent years has struck down as unconstitutional a wide variety of state laws restricting eligibility to vote and ability of candidates to be placed on the ballot. It has also forced the redrawing of the lines of voting districts throughout the country to achieve better voting representation. Let us review the sequence of events.

Removing Obstacles to Voting

The initial attack on voting rights discrimination arose on the basis of the Fifteenth Amendment's provision against denial or abridgment of the right to vote by "any State on account of race, color, or previous condition of servitude." The focus of the attack was elimination of a series of ingenious devices restricting voting by Negroes from the end of the Civil War onward.

Grandfather Clauses. The first of the devices to fall was the so-called "Grandfather Clauses" enacted by a number of states whereby proof of literacy need not be given if a person were a descendant of an ancestor who had been a voter on January 1, 1867. In a 1915 Oklahoma case, a unanimous Court held this device to be unconstitutional because it perpetuated those very conditions the Fifteenth Amendment was meant to destroy.[30]

Oklahoma immediately enacted another law, this one providing that, unless a resident citizen had voted in 1914, he must register to do so between April 30 and May 11, 1916, or be perpetually disfranchised. It was twenty-five years before the Court found this statute unconstitutional and declared that the Fifteenth Amendment "nullified sophisticated as well as simple-minded modes of discrimination. It hits onerous procedural requirements which effectively handicap exercise of the franchise by the colored race although the abstract right to vote may remain unrestricted as to race." [31]

White Primary. Next device to fall was the "White Primary." In many southern states the Democratic Primary was (and often still is) the only significant election, because the Democratic Party dominates the politics of the region. In 1927, the Court applied the equal protection clause of the Fourteenth Amendment to strike down a Texas statute requiring a white primary election. But the political parties themselves then assumed the enforcement of the "whites only" restriction, even after the statute had been voided. The question of state action *versus* private action re-emerged. The political parties were private associations, and their rules and regulations were also construed to be private and not public in nature. Hence, they were not subject to federal constitutional guaranties.

This position, that political parties are private and not subject to federal action, was enshrined in the old *Civil Rights Cases* of 1883. It was only abandoned in 1944 when the Court at last declared it null and void, in *Smith* v. *Allwright*.[32] It ruled that, wherever state laws entrust the selection of candidates to political parties, the party thereby becomes a state agency when conducting elections for the purpose. By this rationale, political parties are subject to the Fifteenth Amendment's requirement not to exclude Negroes from voting in their primary elections.

Literacy Tests. Passing a "literacy test" as a qualification for voting first fell (after a long period of Court support) in 1949. The Court decided in *Davis* v. *Schnell* (1949)[33] that the intent of a challenged Alabama statute as actually administered was to disfranchise black voters. This was so because the test required the citizen to "understand and explain" part of the U.S. Constitution to the satisfaction of the Voter Registrar. The discretion given to that official was found to be unconstitutionally broad—in view, especially, of the fact that blacks tended to fail the test. The Alabama literacy test was merely a device to make racial discrimination easy and to appear legitimate.

From Court Proscription to Statutory Prescription. Discriminatory "tests and devices" came more broadly under the scrutiny of Congress when it enacted the remedial legislation outlined earlier. The relevant provisions of these statutes have been upheld against state attack by the Court in a series of sweepingly supportive decisions. By a 1957 act, the Attorney General of the United States may seek injunctive relief from a federal court to prevent interference with citizens' voting rights. A 1960 act then expanded this to permit the Attorney General to seek a court determination of a "pattern of practice" of discrimination in a locality. In the wake of any such finding, court-appointed voter referees could register to vote any citizen being discriminated against by local authorities. Still further provisions were added to the law in 1964.

The Voting Rights Act of 1965 finally barred the use of *any* "test or device" to restrict voting in districts where less than 50 percent of the voting age population either (1) was unregistered to vote, or (2) had failed to vote in the 1964 presidential election. A 1970 act "went the whole distance," as a justice remarked, and outlawed literacy tests nationwide for five years for use in any election, state or national.

By these acts of Congress, the tedious case-by-case *proscription* of unconstitutional hindrances to voting by blacks and other minority groups gave way to affirmative congressional *prescription* of voting rights. In the approving words of Justice Stewart, "Congress may paint with a much broader brush than may this Court, which must confine itself to the judicial function of deciding individual cases and controversies upon individual records." [34]

Important Court decisions upheld the most controversial parts of recent legislation. The Voting Rights Act of 1965 was sustained in the following year, when the prohibition against using any "test or device" to decide voter eligibility was broadly defined. Outlawed are *any* devices that are used to prove: (1) the ability to read, write, understand, or interpret any matter; (2) educational attainment; (3) good moral character; or (4) qualification by being vouched for by a registered voter. [35]

The Court also expanded the meaning of the Enforcement Clause of the Fifteenth Amendment. Now, federal law requires *prior* approval by the U.S. Attorney General (or by a three-judge federal district court in the District of Columbia) before a state can put into effect any new voting standard, practice, or procedure. In addition, the law requires the same procedure if a state makes: changes in apportionment or districting; changes from district to at-large voting; changes in candidate qualifications; and changes in the administrative handling of illiterate voters. Chief Justice Warren identified "one fundamental principle" underlying Court decisions and congressional enactments alike, namely: "As against the reserved powers of the States, Congress may use any rational means to effectuate the constitutional prohibition of racial discrimination in voting."

The Court justified Congress's activity in this sphere as anchored in the Necessary and Proper Clause of Article One no less than in the Fourteenth and Fifteenth Amendments of the Constitution, in voiding New York's and Oregon's requirement that voters pass a reading test. In the New York case, the Court held the pertinent provision of the 1965 act to be "a proper exercise of the powers granted to Congress by Section 5 of the Fourteenth Amendment and that by force of the Supremacy Clause, Article IV, the New York English literacy requirement cannot be enforced...." [36]

In the Oregon case, the Court unanimously upheld the literacy test proscription included in the 1970 act. Justice Black explained that the power of the states to set the "qualifications of voters in congressional elections was made subject to the power of Congress to make or alter such regulations if it deemed it advisable to do so.... In short, the Constitution allotted to the states the power to make laws regarding national elections, but provided that if Congress became dissatisfied with state laws, Congress could alter them." [37]

The tendency of the Court has been to endorse a wide exercise of congressional discretion in enforcing provisions of the Fourteenth and Fifteenth Amendments and also to extend the *principle of deference* to congressional judgment. In other words, the Court has been willing to defer to Congress's judgment in two respects. First, it has deferred to congressional judgment of the unconstitutionality of certain kinds of actions *not* previously declared to be in violation of the Constitution by any court. Second, it has deferred to the substantive expansion of civil rights by Congress beyond those either explicitly contained in the Constitution itself or previously found by the Court to be implied there.

A number of other restrictions on voting rights have been struck down by Court decisions. These include the *poll tax* and the requirements of *owning property* or of *having children in school* in order to qualify to vote in revenue bond or school board elections.[38]

Legislative Apportionment and Redistricting

Tammany Hall political boss George Washington Plunkitt of New York City in 1905 was prophetic when he railed against the upstate rural Republicans who dominated the state's legislature. He called them "hayseeds" who "think we are like the Indians to the National Government—that is, sort of wards of the state, who don't know how to look after ourselves and have to be taken care of by the Republicans of St. Lawrence, Ontario, and other backwoods counties. . . ." He was unwittingly forecasting the bankruptcy of the "Big Apple," as New York is sometimes affectionately called, during the regime of another Democratic statesman, Mayor Abraham Beame, in the mid-1970s; and he was intimating the rebellion of the big cities and heavily populated suburbs against conniving state legislatures that refused to adjust representation to fit population distribution.[39]

The pattern was a national one by the mid-1950s, with many cities and suburbs heavily Democratic and vastly underrepresented in legislatures controlled by rural constituencies, frequently Republican ones. The reason was that often the states' constitutions laid the burden of reapportionment on the legislative bodies themselves. The legislatures were reluctant to act, since incumbents would risk putting themselves out of office. The results were sometimes grotesque. In California, for instance, Los Angeles County contained 38 percent of the population of the state in 1960 but elected only one of the state's forty senators. Miami's Dade County in Florida contained about 20 percent of the state's population and elected but three of the ninety-five members of the legislature's lower house and only one of the thirty-eight senators. Comparable disparities could be observed in congressional districting throughout the country. A paralysis induced by foot-dragging had set in over the decades. The courts refused to intervene because deciding questions of representation, apportionment, setting district boundaries, and tampering with elections was long regarded as taboo. These were "political questions" to be dealt with by the "political" branches of government (legislatures and governors).

Baker v. Carr. The situation finally came to a head in Tennessee. There, the constitution directed the legislature to reallocate every ten years the available seats in both houses to districts "according to the number of qualified voters in each." Nothing of the kind had been done in sixty years, with the result that by 1960, when Memphis voters (in Shelby County) cast their ballots for state representatives, they counted only about one-twentieth as much as did votes in some rural counties of the state. Some 37 percent of the qualified voters there controlled twenty of the thirty-three members of the Tennessee Senate, and 40 percent of the voters elected sixty-three of the ninety-nine members of the House.

To seek remedy for this inequity, certain citizens as a last resort brought suit against state election officials in 1959 in federal district court. Under terms of the Civil Rights Act of 1871, they claimed that they had been deprived of federal constitutional rights. The district court judges rejected their suit, citing a similar Illinois case decided by the Supreme Court in 1946, *Colegrove v. Green*. In *Colgrove*, Justice Frankfurter had spoken for a Court divided four to three in ruling against the Illinois voters, on the ground that to do otherwise would impermissibly plunge the judiciary into the political thicket. The matter was political and must be resolved politically.[40]

On appeal to the Supreme Court, the Tennessee suit was supported by the United States Justice Department, and the ruling in *Baker v. Carr* (1962)—although cautious in language—precipitated a revolution.[41] In it the Court significantly narrowed the political question doctrine and plunged headlong into the political thicket by ruling in favor of the Tennessee voters. What did the Court decide in *Baker*? Merely this: it agreed to rule on complaints about legislative apportionment and districting. Both had heretofore been regarded as matters for resolution by the "political" branches of government and, hence, "nonjusticiable" (not a proper matter for Court determination). In *Baker*, the principle was first laid down that the equal protection of the laws clause extends to redistricting and to the reapportionment of legislative bodies. The specific holding in *Baker* was, however, only a preliminary one. It decided only three things: (1)

that the federal district court possessed *jurisdiction* to order reapportionment; (2) that (contrary to the decision in the *Colgrove* case of 1946), a *justiciable grievance* was at issue for which the appellants were entitled to relief; and (3) that the appellants had *standing* to challenge Tennessee's apportionment statutes.

The Supreme Court added this statement: "We have no cause . . . to doubt the District Court will be able to fashion relief if violations of constitutional rights are found. . . ." These words do not sound terribly exciting—much less revolutionary. Yet they triggered a social and political revolution. Within one year of the *Baker* decision, suits challenging apportionment were filed in over thirty states. Within two years, suits were in progress in forty-one states. In 1964, the Court read into Article One, Section Two, of the Constitution the requirement that Georgia's congressional districts be composed of substantially equal populations.[42] And later that same term, on June 15, 1964, the Court so ruled in six reapportionment cases that (in effect) changes were mandatory in election districts for virtually every legislative body in the United States. The principle of "one man, one vote" was judicially anointed.

Reynolds v. Sims.   As the Court then put it in the Alabama case of *Reynolds* v. *Sims:*

> We hold that, as a basic constitutional standard, the Equal Protection Clause requires that the seats in both houses of a bicameral state legislature must be apportioned on a population basis. Simply stated, an individual's right to vote for state legislators is unconstitutionally impaired when its weight is in a substantial fashion diluted when compared with the votes of citizens living in other parts of the State.

This meant that each state must redraw the boundaries of election districts of both legislative houses so that each state representative and senator represented as nearly the same number of people "as is practicable." Whatever "practicable" meant, the Court explained only that an "identical number of residents, or citizens, or voters" was not mandatory, since "[m]athematical exactness or precision is hardly a workable constitutional requirement." [43]

Quite apart from the obviously sweeping nature of these requirements, some not-so-obvious questions remained unanswered: (1) What units of government were affected by this ruling? (2) How exactly must population among districts be equivalent? (3) What other aspects of apportionment and districting were affected?

The Court settled the first question with an unambiguous answer: *any* elective body exercising "governmental functions" must be composed of representatives from equally populous districts.[44]

But the second question (how equal must they be?) proved more troublesome and involved the courts in numerous slide-rule exercises. The decisions distinguish *legislative* apportionment (for seats in a state legislature) from *congressional* districting (for seats in the U.S. House of Representatives). They are more tolerant of mathematical inconsistencies in legislative than congressional districting. Thus, the traditional standard of "rationality," rather than the stricter test of "compelling necessity," was applied in deciding reapportionment of a state legislature when the Court upheld a 16.4 percent maximum deviation. It found this variance from absolute equality justified by the state's policy of maintaining the integrity of boundary lines among its political subdivisions.[45] But it rejected Missouri's congressional redistricting plan because deviations from absolute population equality varied from 2.8 percent below to 3.1 percent above. The Court turned a deaf ear to urgent arguments to preserve traditional political subdivisions and to deter political gerrymandering, a posture it maintained in a similar decision in 1973. It directed the state to "make a good-faith effort to achieve precise mathematical equality."[46]

As to the further, third, question of other implications of *Baker* and *Reynolds*, the problems of gerrymandering and multimember districts are illustrative. Since 1960, gerrymandering to *foster* racial discrimination through the manipulation of district lines has been unconstitutional under the Fifteenth Amendment.[47] But here *intent* appears to have been the controlling consideration. For the Court has upheld a purposely gerrymandered apportionment plan from Connecticut. It accepted a plan which was contrived so as to balance the partisan political strengths of the Republicans and Democrats, excusing its evident inconsistency by saying: "we have not ventured far or attempted the impossible task of extirpating politics from what are the essentially political processes of the sovereign States."

At the same time the Court warned, however, against the widespread state and local use of multimember electoral districts when they serve to fence out racial or political groups from the political process and invidiously minimize their voting strength.[48] For example, this can occur when substantially large populations of minority group citizens, but under a majority of the population of an entire election district, are grouped with a white majority. By this device it becomes virtually impossible for (say) a black or a Chicano to be elected. The warning was given teeth in a 1973 decision declaring multimember districts unconstitutional for the first time. The Court then sustained the challenge of a Texas redistricting plan which included two multi-member districts, saying that the proposed arrangement tended "to cancel out or minimize the voting strength of racial groups." [49]

Other Race-Related Rights

The race-related rights so far inventoried do not, by far, exhaust the subject. Systematic exclusion of a minority or racial group from a *grand jury* that indicts a member of that group, or from a *petit jury* that tries him, constitutes a denial of equal protection and may require dismissal of the indictment or reversal of the conviction.[50] Racially restrictive *housing* ordinances, and restrictive private covenants when judicially enforced, violate equal protection.[51] The passage by referendum of a constitutional amendment repealing "fair housing" legislation and prohibiting further local and state fair housing action was declared unconstitutional.[52]

In the field of *transportation,* the "separate but equal" doctrine, which began there, did not long survive its repudiation in the field of education. In 1956, the Court declared unconstitutional a state statute requiring segregated seating on buses, and fully overruled the famous *Plessy* v. *Ferguson* case of 1896, the bone of contention in *Brown I.* In 1962 the Court wrote this epitaph: "We have settled beyond question that no State may require racial segregation of inter-state transportation facilities. . . . The question is no longer open; it is foreclosed as a litigable issue." [53] Similar fates awaited segregated *public facilities* and segregated activities when held in publicly supported parks and other places. It was decided, however, that a trust might revert if integration were prohibited by its terms and that public swimming pools might be closed instead of integrated, if operation ceased entirely.[54]

Laws against *miscegenation,* whether through marriage or cohabitation, are unconstitutional.[55] The practice of discrimination in *public accommodations* by retail merchants selling goods and services was made illegal by the Civil Rights Act of 1964, after a long period of Court vacillation over the issues involved.[56]

Discriminatory Private Actions

You will remember that a major emphasis of the decision in the *Civil Rights Cases* (1883) was this: "It is State action of a particular character that is prohibited. Individual invasion of individual rights is not the subject matter of the [Fourteenth] amendment." [57] Its

"*Thanks for coming in. It's such a relief to be able to deny someone a loan when there's no possibility of being charged with sex, race, age, or ethnic bias.*"
Source: Drawing by Ed Gisberg. © 1976 The New Yorker Magazine, Inc.

scope is to nullify all *state* legislation (or any other state action) that invades the privileges and immunities of our citizens, or "injures them in life, liberty, or property without due process of law, or denies to any of them the equal protection of the laws." The nub of the matter, then, was this: neither the Congress nor the courts should invoke the constitutional guaranties of the Fourteenth and Fifteenth Amendments directly to curb private actions.

Moreover, the *Civil Rights Cases*'s interpretation of the *Thirteenth* Amendment also narrowly confined any attack on private acts of discrimination. That amendment omits the words contained in the other two amendments—the words basic to the *state action* doctrine: "No State . . ." *and* "nor shall any State . . ." engage in the prohibited conduct. It was narrowly construed by the Court to prohibit only the actual enslavement of others by private action, in the strict meaning of the words. As Justice Felix Frankfurter said in defining state action much later, "The vital requirement is State responsibility [for violations of rights protected under the Fourteenth and Fifteenth Amendments], that somewhere, somehow, to some extent, there be an infusion of conduct of officials, panoplied with State power, into any scheme" against whose effects federal court succor is sought, if relief is to be granted.[58]

The range of state action admittedly is great, however. As the Court said on another occasion, the prohibitions of the Fourteenth and Fifteenth Amendments

> have reference to actions of the political body denominated by a State, by whatever instruments or in whatever modes that action may be taken. A State acts by its legislative, its executive, or its judicial authorities. It can act in no other way. The constitutional provisions, therefore, must mean that no agent of the State, or of the officers or agents by whom its powers were exerted, shall deny to any person within its jurisdiction the equal protection of the laws. Whoever, by virtue of public position under a State government, deprives another of property, life, or liberty, without due process of law, or denies or takes away the equal protection of the laws, violates the constitutional inhibition; and as he acts in the name of and for the State, and is clothed with the State's power, his act is that of the State.[59]

Recent congressional legislation and Court decisions have not essentially altered the traditional understanding of state action. But they have modified greatly the degree to which direct federal remedies are available against discriminatory *private actions*, heretofore beyond the reach of both federal legislation and judicial decree. This is yet another major rights development, one whose effects are only just beginning to be seen.

Modern national civil rights legislation applies directly to private action. For instance, voter intimidation as defined in the 1965 Voting Rights Act is prohibited, and carries the penalties attached to any such intimidation. Can this expansion to include private action be reconciled with the Court's settled views on the scope of the amendments under discussion as spelled out in earlier decisions? Apparently so. But no full answer to this complex question can yet be given. The drift of things to come can be illustrated from litigation arising from Congress's efforts to prevent private conspiracies, and other private actions, whose intent and result is to deprive citizens of their rights.

United States v. Guest

The majority of the Court showed considerable caution at first, as seen in *United States v. Guest*.[60] This case, appealed from Georgia in 1966, involved the indictment of five persons for conspiracy to shoot, beat, hinder in interstate travel, and otherwise infringe on the rights of Negro citizens. The federal district court dismissed the indictment because it did not charge any offense under U.S. law. These were private actions, not public ones by state authority, the district court noted.

The U.S. Supreme Court, however, sustained this indictment of private persons for criminal conspiracy. It gingerly skirted the private action question and found traces of state involvement. In so doing, the Court departed from its reliance on the Fourteenth Amendment's equal protection clause and leaned heavily on the "federal right of interstate travel," whose primary source they found in the Commerce Clause (ART. I, SEC. 8, CL. 3). The Court explained itself this way: "Although there have been recurring differences in emphasis within the Court as to the source of the constitutional right of interstate travel, ... [a]ll have agreed that the right exists. . . . We reaffirm it now."

Three justices (Justice Tom Clark, joined by Justices Hugo Black and Abe Fortas), were irked by the majority's avoidance of the private action issue. They bluntly stated in a brief concurring opinion:

> Although the Court specifically rejects any such connotation, it is, I believe, both appropriate and necessary under the circumstances here to say that there now can be no doubt that the specific language of Section 5 empowers the Congress to enact laws punishing all conspiracies—with and without state action—that interfere with Fourteenth Amendment rights.

Three other justices (Justice William J. Brennan, joined by Chief Justice Warren, and Justice Douglas) emphatically found that Section 5

> empowers Congress to enact laws punishing all conspiracies to interfere with the exercise of Fourteenth Amendment rights, whether or not state officers or others acting under the color of state law are implicated in the conspiracy.

Griffin v. Breckenridge

By 1971 the Court was able to rule unanimously that a federal statute punishing civil conspiracy to deprive persons of rights was valid and applicable to private action. The case of *Griffin* v. *Breckenridge* [61] was similar in ways to the Georgia case. A group of white men had conspired to detain, beat, and harass several Mississippi blacks who were traveling in a car, operated by a Tennessean, in Mississippi near the Alabama state line! The lower court had dismissed the complaint. The Court here found that the *sources* of Congress's power to enact such a statute are at least twofold: (1) the right of interstate travel, and (2) Section 2 of the Thirteenth Amendment. The Court said:

> Congress was wholly within its powers under Section 2 of the Thirteenth Amendment in creating a statutory cause of action for Negro citizens who have been the victims of conspiratorial, racially discriminatory private action aimed at depriving them of

the basic rights that the law secures to all free men. . . . In identifying these two constitutional sources of congressional power, we do not imply the absence of any other . . . the allegations of the complaint in this case have not required consideration of the scope of the power of Congress under Section 5 of the Fourteenth Amendment.

Jones v. Mayer

Another dimension of the attack on private discrimination came to view in *Jones* v. *Mayer* (1968),[62] a case involving private refusal to sell a house to the Negro plaintiff in a predominantly white community on the outskirts of St. Louis, Missouri. The Supreme Court reversed dismissals of the suit by the lower courts (because no state action was involved) and ruled in favor of the plaintiff on the basis of the Thirteenth Amendment. The Court held, despite vehement dissent from two justices, that federal law "bars *all* racial discrimination, private as well as public, in the sale or rental of property, and that the statute thus construed, is a valid exercise of the power of Congress to enforce the Thirteenth Amendment."

What of the power of Congress so to legislate? The majority swept all objections aside in a ringing opinion written by Justice Potter Stewart:

> Does the authority of Congress to enforce the Thirteenth Amendment "by appropriate legislation" include the power to eliminate all racial barriers to the acquisition of real and personal property? We think the answer to that question is plainly yes. Surely Congress has the power . . . rationally to determine what are the badges and incidents of slavery, and the authority to translate that determination into effective legislation. . . . At the very least, the freedom that Congress is empowered to secure . . . includes the freedom to buy whatever a white man can buy, the right to live wherever a white man can live.

We have seen the application of this doctrine to the Virginia private school desegregation case of *Runyon* v. *McCrary* (1976) discussed previously (see pp. 184–85). But the Court also applied the doctrine to the potentially enormous field of "reverse discrimination."

McDonald v. Santa Fe Transportation Co.

In the *McDonald* case decided in 1976, the Court stoutly affirmed that the Constitution "affords protection from racial discrimination in private employment to white persons as well as non-whites." [63] The case involved a complaint from two white employees who brought suit against a transportation company and their teamster union local. They had been disciplined by the union and fired by the company for allegedly stealing cargo. But a black employee who had also been charged with the same offense was neither disciplined nor fired. The whites, L. N. McDonald and Raymond L. Laird, brought suit under terms of the Civil Rights Act of 1870 (SEC. 1981) and the Civil Rights Act of 1964 (Title VII), which prohibit racial discrimination in private employment. A federal district court in Texas dismissed the suit, contending that these provisions were inapplicable to whites. The U.S. Supreme Court reversed that finding and remanded the case for further hearings by the district court. It held that both the company and the union are liable under Title VII and that "all persons"—white and black—are protected against discriminatory practices by Section 1981.

These two 1976 cases, considered against the backdrop of the other decisions reviewed here, signal the likelihood of major new developments. They clear the way for application of civil rights statutes both to private actions and to the reverse discrimination claims of white employees across the entire spectrum of American industry and institutions that engage in hiring and firing, from steel mills to day care centers.

Bakke v. Regents of the University of California

How the Court will deal with the explosive issues of reverse discrimination, and the attendant issues of reparations and of compensatory justice for blacks, other minorities, and women who have long been discriminated against, is today anybody's guess. For although the questions have been raised in a variety of statutory contexts, the Court has yet to deal squarely with the very troublesome constitutional issues. This it may do in a California case that has excited much public comment, *Bakke* v. *Regents of the University of California,* which it heard argument on during the 1977–1978 term. This case involves a challenge by Allan Bakke, a white applicant, of the admissions policy of the University of California medical school, which excluded him while at the same time admitting on a quota basis sixteen minority candidates, all of whom scored lower on the scale of admissions criteria than did he. Does such preferential treatment on the basis of a racial classification violate the principle of equality under the Constitution? The constitutional dilemma was well-stated by Alexander Bickel in his last book, *The Morality of Consent:* "Those for whom racial equality was demanded are to be more equal than others. Having found support in the Constitution for equality, they now claim support for inequality under the same Constitution." [64]

Present Character of the Court: A Focus on Intent

A changing emphasis can be observed in the Court's handling of some recent discrimination cases. It focuses on *intent* to discriminate in determining the nature of challenged official action and statutes. The cases have arisen in a variety of contexts, cutting across a wide range of discriminatory practices. The recent tendency of the Court is to take a harder look at the motivation, intention, and purpose that may, or may not, underlie allegedly discriminatory practices. This approach constitutes a shift in perspective that could have substantial impact on future civil rights litigation.

If discrimination is plain on the face of a statute, then the only question is whether it is in a form prohibited by some provision of the Constitution. Thus, as early as 1880, the Court decided that a black who had been convicted of murder by a jury from which all blacks were excluded (by virtue of a West Virginia law that made only white male citizens who were twenty-one years old eligible to serve on state juries) was thereby within his rights to demand removal of his trial to a federal court. The black had been denied the equal protection of the laws guaranteed by the Fourteenth Amendment whose "aim was against discrimination because of race or color." [65]

Since then, the law has so far changed as to shift from a focus on equal protection to a focus on the substantive right to a jury trial before a petit jury selected from a "representative cross section of the community [as] an essential component of the Sixth Amendment right to a jury trial," as Justice White said for the Court in 1975. Thus, a white defendant has successfully challenged a conviction because blacks were systematically excluded from the jury, and a male defendant because women were excluded.[66]

But what if discrimination is not evident on the face of a statute? That issue, too, faced the Court long ago when in 1886 it dealt with the conviction of a Chinese alien who had violated a San Francisco city ordinance that forbade operating a laundry in a wooden structure without a permit. The Court reversed the conviction on the basis of the equal protection clause. It determined that, while all but one non-Chinese applicant for a permit to operate a laundry in a wooden structure had been approved by the city's Board of Supervisors, Yick Wo and some 200 other Chinese had not. Justice Matthews in speaking for the Court found discrimination in the administration of a law that was neutral on its face, and he said:

> Though the law itself be fair on its face and impartial in appearance, if it is applied and administered by public authority with an evil eye and unequal hand, so as practically to make unjust and illegal discriminations between persons in similar circumstances, material to their rights, the denial of equal justice is still within the prohibition of the Constitution.[67]

In the years since 1954 when *Brown I* was decided, many more subtle forms of apparently neutral discriminatory statutes and administrative actions have appeared than faced the Court when Yick Wo stood before it. In most cases the Court has not explored intentions; rather, it has looked to practical effects, impact, or results of policies and decisions. The rules applied by the Courts in attempting to break down unconstitutional discriminatory practices have been sketched in the foregoing sections of this chapter.

In the area of school litigation—the matrix of all other civil rights adjudication—a turning point was reached in the Denver case (*Keyes*) decided in 1973. For in the Detroit case (*Milliken I*, decided the following year) the Court was seen to backpedal by holding that the constitutional requirement is not school racial mixing for its own sake but only the desegregation of school systems segregated *"de jure"* by official or state action. This decision, as we saw, provided that the fifty-three metropolitan (suburban) school systems of Detroit did not constitutionally have to be joined through a common desegregation plan with the central city of Detroit so as to achieve racial balance. The decision, then, found *de jure* segregation within Detroit and ordered that remedied, but it left intact the city's system with its 70 percent black and 30 percent white enrollment. By so ruling the Court effectively narrowed the "remedy" prescribed by *Brown II* and gave it this pointed statement: "... the remedy is necessarily designed, as all remedies are, to restore the victims of discriminatory conduct to the position they would have occupied in the absence of such conduct." [68]

Milliken I clung to (but did nothing to develop) the *de facto/de jure* distinction which in *Keyes* the Court had for the first time stressed. The two types of segregation were distinguishable by *"purpose* or *intent"* to segregate on the part of the state or its agents. How is such purposeful or intentional, hence *de jure*, segregation to be proved? As I have suggested, in all of the desegregation cases up to *Keyes* in 1973, the answer was simple enough. Intention did not significantly enter the question of determining *de jure* segregation, because from *Brown I* (1954) onward *all* of the cases arose in the South where *de jure* segregation of schools in 1954 was a matter of public record. This was the case no less than it was in the 1880 West Virginia jury case with which this discussion began.

A "prior history of segregation" automatically meant the segregation was state-compelled or *de jure*. Intentions need not be inquired into. Through a sort of Grandfather Clause assumption by the Court, ironically, if there existed state-imposed segregation in a school district at the time of *Brown I*, then (as the Court re-emphasized in *Keyes*) "the State automatically assumes an affirmative duty ... to eliminate ... 'all vestiges of State-imposed segregation.' " [69]

In tracing the matter backward through major decisions, it can be seen that this, too, was the situation in the landmark *Swann* decision in 1971, where the *de jure/de facto* categories were developed. Since North Carolina education was officially segregated in 1954, the Charlotte-Mecklenburg school system obviously had a "history of segregation." Under that decisive circumstance, the Court then said (and repeated in *Keyes*): "Where it is possible to identify a 'white school' or a 'Negro school' simply by reference to the racial composition of teachers and staff, the quality of school buildings and equipment, or the organization of sports activities, a *prima facie* case of violation of substantive constitutional rights under the Equal Protection Clause is shown." [70]

Similarly, the 1968 Virginia case of *Green* v. *County School Board* began from the threshold premise of a prior history of state-compelled segregation and focused on *effects*—that is, the impact or results of policies—not on intentions or purposes. In *Green* the Court had stated that, as a matter of principle, "School boards . . . operating state-compelled dual systems [are] . . . clearly charged with the affirmative duty to convert to a unitary system in which racial discrimination would be eliminated root and branch." After quoting this passage in *Keyes*, the Court added: "*Green* remains the governing principle." [71]

The trouble with *Keyes* was that it was the first "Northern" desegregation case to be decided by the Court. Denver, Colorado, could scarcely be found to have had a prior history of *de jure* or legalized segregation such as had been found ready to hand in all of the Southern cases. Herein, then, lay the genesis of the touchstone *intention to segregate* as a test for establishing *de jure* school segregation. Why was development of the test so important? The answer is that it is only by showing official segregation that the "burden-shifting principle" used by the Court in desegregation cases is triggered. In other words, it is by showing as a threshold premise the actual presence of state-compelled segregation that a "*prima facie* case of violation of substantive constitutional rights under the Equal Protection Clause is shown," to again quote *Swann*. On that ground—and unless the school board can then rebut or prove to the contrary the presumption that it has fostered segregation as a matter of policy—the judiciary fashions the remedy to integrate and brings into play the full arsenal of weapons developed since 1954 to secure compliance with constitutional demands.

Justice Powell's powerful separate opinion in the *Keyes* case pointed to the anomalies and difficulties of this abrupt switch from an effects to an intent test by the Court. Two points from his argument should be noticed. First, he regarded the focus on intentions ("segregative intent") to be both unreliable as a guide and contrary to previous law on the subject. He said that the "results of litigation—often arrived at subjectively by a court endeavoring to ascertain the subjective intent of school authorities with respect to action taken or not taken over many years—will be fortuitous, unpredictable and even capricious." And he illustrated from the Denver case itself, stressing the unreliability of ruling on the basis of "an issue as slippery as 'intent' or 'purpose,' especially when related to hundreds of decisions made by school authorities under varying conditions over many years."

Moreover, he argued that the Court was flying in the face of its own most recent holdings. Thus, he cited a 1971 decision in which Justice Black spoke for the majority, saying: "This Court has recognized repeatedly that it is 'extremely difficult for a court to ascertain the motivation, or collection of different motivations, that lie behind a legislative enactment.'" [72] The second point to be noticed was Justice Powell's charge that the *Keyes* approach created a "dual standard" for deciding desegregation cases, one for use in the South and the other for use in the North. Not only did he speak disdainfully of the "murky, subjective judgments inherent in the Court's search for 'segregative intent'" in this connection, but he also pointed to the Court's holding just a year before in a school case, that intention is irrelevant:

> ... an inquiry into the "dominant" motivations of school authorities is as irrelevant as it is fruitless ... we have said that "[t]he measure of any desegregation plan is its effectiveness." ... Thus we have focused upon effect—not the purpose or motivation—of a school board's action ... the courts' holdings [have steadily] rested not on motivation or purpose but on the *effect* of the action upon the dismantling of the dual school systems involved.

Justice Powell then continued:

> I can discern no basis in law or logic for holding that the motivation of school board action is irrelevant in Virginia [the setting of the case just quoted] and controlling in Colorado. ... The net re-

sult of the Court's language, however, is the application of an *effect* test to the actions of southern school districts and an *intent* test to those in other sections, at least until initial *de jure* finding for those districts can be made.[73]

Justice Powell proposed that the *de jure/de facto* categories be abandoned together with the intent test. As an alternative the Court should then foster the affirmative duty to maintain integrated school systems by laying down this principle: "A *prima facie* case of constitutional violation exists when segregation is found to a substantial degree in the schools of a particular district." [74]

The Court has not so far followed Justice Powell's suggestion. Rather, it has shown a resolve to rely on the intent test and has expanded its application in important 1976 and 1977 decisions, which we will now consider.

Washington v. Davis

A 1976 employment discrimination case (styled *Washington v. Davis*) arose in the District of Columbia where two black applicants for jobs with the police force were rejected because of low scores on a standardized written test of verbal skill given all prospective federal employees. The applicants challenged the ruling in federal district court on the grounds that the employment procedures were racially discriminatory and violated the due process clause of the Fifth Amendment, federal statute, and provisions of the District of Columbia *Code*. They lost on both constitutional and statutory grounds in district court. The Court of Appeals reversed the decision and ruled in their favor, relying on the *Griggs* decision of 1971. *Griggs* held that Title VII of the Civil Rights Act of 1964, as amended, prohibits the use of tests that operate to exclude minority groups unless the employer demonstrates that the tests are directly related to job performance. Discriminatory intent was held to be irrelevant; decisive was that four times as many blacks as whites failed the test. This "disproportionate impact" was held to demonstrate a constitutional violation.

The Supreme Court reversed the Court of Appeals's decision and ruled in favor of the police department, on the grounds that Title VII legal standards had been erroneously applied to a Fifth Amendment due process case. The Court, however, went on to stress the Court of Appeals's error in supposing that Title VII claims "need not concern themselves with the employer's possibly discriminatory purpose but instead may focus solely on the racially differential impact of the challenged hiring or promotion practices. This is not the constitutional rule."

In a majority opinion written by Justice White, the Court reaffirmed (citing *Bolling* v. *Sharpe,* 1954) that the due process clause of the Fifth Amendment "contains an equal protection component prohibiting the United States from invidiously discriminating between individuals or groups...." The central purpose of the equal protection clause (Fourteenth Amendment) "is prevention of official conduct discriminating on the basis of race." Justice White then proceeded to cite a series of decisions and opinions stressing that a " 'purpose to discriminate must be present ...' " if actions are to be held violative of equal protection rights. While the Court conceded that "[t]here are some indications to the contrary in our cases," it nonetheless firmly held that a showing of intentional discrimination is essential if a *prima facie* case is to be "made out" and " 'the burden of proof' " shifted " 'to the State to rebut the presumption of unconstitutional action. . . .' "

Justice White continued: "Disproportionate impact is not irrelevant, but it is not the sole touchstone of an invidious racial discrimination forbidden by the Constitution. Standing alone, it does not trigger the rule." Later on, he said: "Negroes ... could no more successfully claim that the test denied them equal protection than could white applicants who also failed." [75] Precisely how this discussion relates to Title VII proceedings is unclear from the Court's opinion and appeared confusing to Justice Brennan (joined by Justice Marshall), who wrote a long dissenting opinion that treated the case in terms of Title VII standards.

Justice White in *Davis* stated that the "rule is the same in other contexts." His range of citations—to criminal cases where convictions were set aside because of exclusion of blacks from the grand jury, a reapportionment case, a school desegregation case, and a licensing case, among others—indicated wide applicability of the intent test in discrimination cases.

Village of Arlington Heights v.
Metropolitan Housing Development Corp.

Just how wide was further suggested in the *Arlington Heights* zoning case, decided in 1977.[76] The Village of Arlington Heights, a suburb of Chicago, had refused to rezone a particular district to permit construction of multifamily dwellings in a single-family district. A real estate developer had contracted to purchase a tract of land to construct low- and moderate-income dwellings for racially integrated occupancy. The developer, along with individual minority persons who wished to reside in such dwellings, brought suit, asking for injunctive relief. They claimed that denial of the rezoning request was racially discriminatory and violated the equal protection clause of the Fourteenth Amendment, as well as provisions of the Fair Housing Act of 1968. The District Court ruled for the Village, and the Court of Appeals reversed, finding that the "ultimate effect" of the denial was racially discriminatory and, therefore, violative of the equal protection clause. The Supreme Court, in turn, reversed the Court of Appeals and held for the Village.

Justice Powell (!) relied heavily on the *Davis* decision in speaking for the majority of six judges. That decision, he said, "made it clear that official action will not be held unconstitutional solely because it results in a racially disproportionate impact. . . . Proof of racially discriminatory intent or purpose is required to show a violation of the Equal Protection Clause." He acknowledged that the proof of "invidious discriminatory purpose" is difficult and demands a "sensitive inquiry." The matter of "impact" is only a "starting point" for such a proof, for unless there is a consistent pattern "as stark as that in . . . *Yick Wo*, impact alone is not determinative."

Justice Powell went on to suggest other kinds of evidence to be considered in proving discriminatory intent: historical background, the specific sequence of events leading up to a challenged decision, legislative or administrative history (including statements of the decision-makers), and direct testimony in a trial court were specified as useful. The list, he said, was not "exhaustive." In this case, Metropolitan Housing had "simply failed to carry [its] burden of proving that discriminatory purpose was a motivating factor in the Village's decision." And that, the Court emphasized, "ends the constitutional inquiry. The Court of Appeals' . . . finding that the Village's decision carried a discriminatory 'ultimate effect' is without independent constitutional significance."

General Electric v. Gilbert

A sex-discrimination case, *General Electric* v. *Gilbert* [77] (decided in 1976, six months after *Davis*) was decided on the basis that bordered on application of the intent test. Significantly, it was a suit brought under Title VII, Civil Rights Act of 1964, against an employer by female employees who asserted discrimination on the basis of sex because the company's insurance program denied benefits for disabilities arising from pregnancy. Both the district and circuit courts held for the employees, but the Supreme Court reversed their decisions. While twice being moved to observe that "it is true that only women can become pregnant," the Court through Justice Rehnquist nonetheless ruled that no sex discrimination was present in the company's decision to list pregnancy among other conditions excluded from coverage. Title VII and equal protection concepts of discrimination explicitly interpenetrated in this opinion, just as they had done in the Court's opinion in the *Davis* case—again to the confusion and, even, consternation of some of the justices. The Court denied that "every legislative classification concerning pregnancy is a sex-based classification." Unless it can be *shown* that "distinctions involving pregnancy are mere pretexts designed to effect an invidious discrimination against the members of one sex or the other, lawmakers are constitutionally free . . ." to include or exclude it from program benefits on any reasonable basis, just as they (or employers) might exclude any other physical condition.

Justice Rehnquist acknowledged with evident reluctance that, under Title VII, "a *prima facie* violation . . . can be established . . . upon proof that the *effect* of an otherwise facially neutral plan or classification is to discriminate against members of one class or another . . . even absent proof of intent. . . . Even assuming that in this case it is not necessary to prove intent to establish a *prima facie* violation . . . the respondents have not made the requisite showing of gender-based effect."

This grudging language, almost implying that intent might be demanded even in Title VII cases, provoked alarm among three of the judges, two of them dissenters. More to the point, however, is that the demand of proof that exclusion of pregnancy from the list of disabilities covered by the company's program is a pretext "designed to effect an invidious discrimination" against one sex seems to be virtually equivalent in fact to the intent test. It might as well be asked: "By excluding pregnancy from the list, did the company intend to discriminate against women?" As Justice Stevens remarked in concurring with the *Davis* decision, ". . . the line between discriminatory purpose and discriminatory impact is not nearly as bright, and perhaps not quite as critical, as the reader of the Court's opinion [in this case] might assume." [78]

Conclusions: Equal Protection and the Higher Law Tradition

From the sweep of decisions that we have inventoried in this chapter, it is evident that the higher law spirit in jurisprudence, which we found infusing substantive due process, also infuses substantive equal protection. Not only did the promise of the Declaration of Independence become constitutional law in 1868 through ratification of the Fourteenth Amendment's provision that states may not deprive persons of "life, liberty, or property, without due process of law," but that promise also was fulfilled by constitutionalizing equality. Thereafter, states were prohibited from denying "to any person within [their] jurisdiction the equal protection of the laws." *Brown I* and its progeny, when taken all together and viewed in retrospect, comprise a chorus of judicial voices singing the praises of justice in the mode of equality before the law. To be sure, the chorus has not always been music to the ears. But it is indubitable that litigation in the numerous cases decided under the equal protection clause, especially those with a bearing on racial discrimination, is unified by the higher law theme of mending the torn mantle of justice in America, especially for its black citizens.

One index of this unifying strand is the sense of righteous indignation with which many of the court decisions are filled. The opinion in

Brown I itself was not so much a specimen of admirable juristic craftsmanship—indeed, it was quite the opposite—as an appeal to the hearts and minds of the nation. The flavor has not since been lost in subsequent decisions, such as impatience of results reflected in Justice Brennan's opinion for the majority in the *Green* case in 1968 or the frustration reflected in Justice Marshall's dissent in *Milliken I* in 1974.[79] In *Green*, the remedy of "desegregation" almost became the right of black children to attend integrated schools, fourteen years after *Brown I*. But in *Milliken I* the administrative detail of school district boundary lines around the metropolitan center of Detroit became a pretext for denying meaningful racial balance—and therewith meaningful integration—of the fifty-four districts composing the metropolis.

Another index of the higher law dimension in substantive equal protection cases, related to the fervor for justice just noticed, is the Court's utilization of complex standards or tests of constitutionality that sweep all opposition before them. Down to the 1950s when the civil rights revolution began—with the Court leading the charge and with equal protection the battering ram—the court test usually relied upon was a mild one. As classically stated in 1911,[80] the traditional test was "minimum rationality."

Insofar as an essential aspect of legislation is classification as a prelude to regulation, the minimum rationality test only demanded that there be a rational connection between the legislative means (the classification) and the end in view (regulation, taxation, or discrimination, for example). So long as there was a general "fit" of means to end, the courts generally deferred to the legislatures' judgments. Classifications were voided only when "without any reasonable basis and therefore . . . purely arbitrary." Mathematical precision was not required. "When a classification in such a law is called in question, if any state of facts reasonably can be conceived that would sustain it, the existence of that state of facts at the time the law was enacted must be assumed." Challengers had to carry the burden of proving that state classifications were irrational and arbitrary.[81] As the test was stated in a 1920 case: "[T]he classification must be reasonable, not arbitrary, and must rest upon some ground of difference having a fair and substantial relation to the object of the legislation, so that all persons similarly circumstanced shall be treated alike." [82]

In the jargon of the lawyers, this is called the traditional or "first tier" equal protection test. It remains in use today in legislative areas peripheral to, or outside of, the super-charged arena of civil rights. But, "first tier" analysis was relied on in the most important equal protection decision of the early 1970s, *San Antonio Independent School District* v. *Rodriguez*,[83] when the Court upheld Texas's system of financing the public school system partly through local property taxes, against an attack that contended this system invidiously discriminated against the poor (and favored the wealthy districts) and, hence, poor persons who reside in such districts. The *Rodriguez* decision displayed the deference of traditional equal protection court review characteristic of the earlier period (from the 1870s until the 1950s) when discrimination was seldom at issue. During that time, one scholar has shown, only 14.2 percent of a large sample of cases decided under the equal protection clause dealt with discrimination. The greatest number of cases dealt with economic matters: 426 out of 554 cases studied or 76.9 percent of the total.[84]

In contrast with the minimum rationality, first tier judicial review when the Court takes a "tolerant quick peek" to see if equal protection has been violated, there is the "strict scrutiny," second tier test when challenged statutes are greeted with a "conclusive frown" of disapproval from the bench.[85] All of the race-related cases considered in the foregoing sections of this chapter were decided on the basis of some variety of "strict scrutiny." The test is triggered in one of two ways, either by a statute's relating to a "suspect classification" or its implicating "fundamental rights" or "interests." Under either of those circumstances, mere rationality in the ends-means relationship is not enough, as it is under first tier review. Reasonableness is intensified to become a "necessary means," not merely to a legitimate governmental goal, but to a "compelling state interest." In other words, to meet this rigorous test, the government must display a high degree of need to legislate or otherwise act as it has done, and it enjoys little (or no) presumption before the judiciary that its classification or invasion of fundamental rights is valid.

Only one case decided by the Supreme Court that involved a statute detrimental to an ethnic group has survived strict scrutiny, *Korematsu* v. *United States*, the World War II Japanese-American case that validated the federal government's forced evacuation of these people from the West Coast.[86] In fact, as late as 1972 Chief Justice Burger could say this: "To challenge [a statute] by the 'compelling state interest' standard is to condemn them all. So far as I am aware, no state law has ever satisfied this seemingly insurmountable standard, and I doubt that one ever will." [87]

Heading the list of triggering "suspect classifications," of course, is race. Another classification in statutes that automatically bring second tier review into play includes nationality or alienage. Sex discrimination and illegitimacy are borderline at present. The triggering "fundamental rights" were clarified by the Court in the *Rodriguez* decision of 1973 to include only those rights explicitly or implicitly protected by the Constitution. Thus the list includes all of the rights now nationalized, most aspects of voting and access to the ballot, and some aspects of access to the justice system—such as free trial transcripts and filing fees for indigents who are defendants in criminal cases. It does not, however, include education—as *Rodriguez* stressed.

The statistical record of cases decided by the Supreme Court under strict scrutiny shows nearly universal rejection of challenged measures. This apocalyptical approach to judicial review for twenty years (the mid-1950s to the mid-1970s) swept before it every challenged state action which was such as to trigger the strict scrutiny-compelling state interest analysis. That kind of review imposed on the state the nearly insurmountable problems of: overcoming the presumption of unconstitutionality in a statute through the burden-shifting principle applied; proving a classification to be vital; and showing that an interest was both utterly compelling and the means of attaining it unavoidably necessary. This slight overstatement of the rule, compared with Court phraseology, is justified by the record. As Professor Dixon put it: "Once a classification was found 'suspect' per se or to trench on a 'fundamental interest,' the state's burden to show a 'compelling interest' became so heavy that invalidation was almost automatic."

Moreover, the Court also fashioned another lethal test called "irrebuttable presumption" and by it, too, regularly invalidated "on nominally objective basis, those extremes in classification that offend[ed] the Court's sense of justice." [88] This doctrine was the test applied in striking down Connecticut's law pertaining to out-of-state tuition charges at state colleges because the law contained the "irrebuttable presumption" that a student's legal address outside the state when he applied for admission meant that he was a nonresident of Connecticut during his entire enrollment at a college there. Hence, such a student was precluded ever from qualifying as a *bona fide* resident for instate tuition rates. In *Vlandis* v. *Klein* (1973),[89] the Court voided that statute because it permitted no challenge of the initial determination. The irrebuttable (or conclusive) presumption doctrine has been applied to the Department of Agriculture's food stamp program and to a school board's mandatory (unpaid) maternity leave program for teachers, with fatal results for the regulations.[90]

Finally, it can be said that there are several signs of the wane of apocalyptical judicial review in equal protection cases. To begin with, the strict scrutiny test now has been met by at least three states in recent decisions by the Court. In 1974, election laws of California and Texas met the test of strict scrutiny, and in 1975 a divorce residency requirement of Iowa's passed muster as a compelling state interest.[91] In the California case, *Storer* v. *Brown*, the test met was characterized this way: "[T]he Court finds compelling the State's interests in preventing splintered parties and unrestricted factionalism and protecting the direct-primary system...." [92] Upholding the tradition of the mysterious science of the law, Justice White in speaking for the majority did not clearly explain the criteria used in arriving at the holding. Here is his statement:

> Decisions in this context, as in others is very much a "matter of degree" ..., very much a matter of "considering the facts and circumstances behind the law, the interests which the State claims to be protecting, and the interests of those who are disadvantaged by the classifications." ... What the result of this process will be in any specific case may be very difficult to predict with great assurance.[93]

At the same time, a "middle tier" test of means-ends relationships has clearly emerged in recent decisions after a long period of hedging and vacillation by the Court. Lying somewhere between mere rationality and rigorous strict scrutiny, the middle tier test may be called the "strong rational basis" or "substantial relationship" test. By it the Court greets challenged legislation with an "unfriendly quizzical look." [94] It was formulated this way in 1976: "[The state's enactment] must serve important governmental objectives and must be substantially related to achievement of those objectives." [95]

The Court applied the middle tier test to an Oklahoma statute and invalidated it as an invidious gender-based discrimination that allowed sale of 3.2 percent beer to women at age eighteen but to men only at age twenty-one. Remarking in response to Oklahoma's statistical arguments that "proving broad sociological propositions by statistics is a dubious business, and one that inevitably is in tension with the normative philosophy that underlies the Equal Protection Clause," the Court held that the "beer statute invidiously discriminates against males 18–20 years of age."

Another gender-based case was decided in 1977 utilizing the substantial relationship test. [96] In it a section of the Social Security Act was voided which authorized survivors' benefits to widows regardless of dependency, but to widowers only if the husband had been receiving at least half of his support from his wife prior to her death. The Court found this to be invidious discrimination against female wage earners because it afforded them less protection for their surviving spouses than that provided to male employees.

In addition, other signs of moderation and restraint by the Court can be seen. The irrebuttable presumption doctrine was sharply curbed in a 1975 case. [97] The Court there brought the traditional rationality test to bear—in an equal-protection-like consideration of a case containing due process challenges!—to a provision of the Social Security Act limiting survivors benefits to persons married at least nine months prior to the death of the insured decedent. The Court upheld the provision whose objective was to disqualify persons who married terminally ill spouses solely to become eligible for benefits. It declined to apply irrebuttable presumption doctrine to the issue saying that "extensions" of that doctrine to such entitlement classifications as this one would turn it "into a virtual engine of destruction for countless legislative judgments which have heretofore been thought wholly consistent with the Fifth and Fourteenth Amendments to the Constitution." Subsequent handling of the irrebuttable presumption doctrine, such as its pointed avoidance even when raised as an issue by the district court's decision in the Massachusetts mandatory police retirement-at-fifty case [98] (decided on the rationality basis), may signal its demise: "the irrebuttable presumption doctrine may be dead without a decent burial." [99]

The gist of the matter, then, is this. Higher-law-grounded judicial review is to be seen prominently displayed in the modern cases decided under the equal protection clause. The major evidence of this is to be seen in the wide range of issues handled under strict scrutiny since the 1950s, especially in the area of racial classifications and fundamental rights. But this kind of apocalyptic judicial review today seems to be waning. Strict scrutiny has been circumscribed as a test in the following ways. Triggering suspect classifications are not being expanded. The list of fundamental rights is now defined (through *Rodriguez*) to be limited to rights mentioned or implied by the Constitution, and thereby it, too, is not being expanded. The middle tier test of substantial relation has emerged, one which allows the Court more flexibility in reviewing challenges than does strict scrutiny. There is evident reluctance to apply irrebuttable presumption doctrine. There is new vitality in traditional due process analysis, utilizing rational relationship-legitimate purpose criteria, as in *Rodriguez* where strict scrutiny was rejected. And in the fertile field of racial discrimination, the more probing intent test (discussed in the previous section) has displaced the disproportionate impact test as a *prima facie* means of triggering reversal of the burden of proof doctrine and, with it, the presumed invalidity of challenged statutes.

Summary

In this chapter we have surveyed the vast and prominent field of civil rights litigation. Beginning with the famous *Brown* case, we have traced the emergence of a host of rights secured since 1954 on the basis of protections claimed against race discrimination. The principles developed during the nearly two decades in which the courts were preoccupied with eliminating segregation in the southern education system were seen applied to northern segregated schools in cases arising in Denver and Detroit in the 1970s. The new setting of antisegregation cases provoked the rise of a new emphasis by the Supreme Court on the state to show intentional action in achieving an unsegregated pattern of education. The Court showed a diminished reliance—if not an outright abandonment—on the effect or discriminatory impact test relied on in earlier decisions.

We have briefly reviewed the legislative and historical background of American racial matters and then examined the federal government's policy in the period of Reconstruction following the Civil War. We saw a renewed interest in racial matters by Congress in the period following enactment of the first rights statute since that time, the Civil Rights Act of 1964. The importance of voting rights in our democracy, and the significance of the conflict over the question of who should vote, required us to give detailed attention to this facet of civil rights by considering both legislative and court activity in the field. The related topic of legislative and congressional apportionment, then, we considered and analyzed the revolutionary implications of Supreme Court decisions mandating the "one man one vote" principle.

The recent interest of the Court in private action involving discrimination was stressed, and we considered the significance of the "intent" test for the Court and the nation as applied since 1976 to a wide spectrum of cases arising in virtually every corner of the discrimination field. In a concluding section we saw how the entire discussion related to the higher law theme and dealt in some detail with the array of tests and their rationales applied by the Court when state laws are challenged on equal protection grounds.

We next turn to draw this study of American individual rights to a close by briefly considering the relationship of citizenship to liberty and the performance and prospects of our legal and political order today.

REVIEW QUESTIONS

1. What were the issues in *Brown I?* Summarize the arguments of John W. Davis and Thurgood Marshall. How did the Court deal with *stare decisis* in this instance? What did it finally decide? Why was the decision of such great importance?

2. Illustrate the various ways in which the equal protection of the

laws clause of the Fourteenth Amendment has been applied in the civil rights field.

3. Do you think the country has been too reliant on the Supreme Court in the field of civil rights and race relations generally? Why or why not? What alternatives do you see?

4. What did *Brown II* do? Identify and explain the main aspects of school desegregation ordered by the courts.

5. What are the *Swann* guidelines? How have they been received? To what degree in the 1970s are segregated schools a national problem? Where? Why? How?

6. Does desegregation apply to private elementary and secondary schools? How? How do issues here relate to the rights of association, privacy, and to a parent's right to educate his children? Is the power to order desegregation unlimited? Illustrate your answers with examples from cases covered in this chapter.

7. What happened after the Civil War to foster civil rights? What happened to endanger them? What situations led to federal civil rights legislation in that period?

8. What was decided in the *Civil Rights Cases* of 1883? What are the contemporary implications of that decision?

9. Summarize the events between the end of Reconstruction in the South and enactment of the first modern civil rights law. When was that law adopted?

10. List the main objectives of modern civil rights legislation. How have the courts administered justice under these various laws? Illustrate your answer with examples of statutes and laws covered in this chapter.

11. What does "affirmative action" mean? How has it been applied? Do you think it is necessary? How is its application limited by recent decisions?

12. Why are voting rights especially important? How have black and other minority groups been deprived of their right to vote in the past? May literacy be demanded of a voter today? Why or why not?

13. What is meant by "court proscription" and "congressional prescription"? How has the "principle of deference" been applied in the voting rights field by the Supreme Court?

14. What was decided in the case of *Baker* v. *Carr*? Discuss the consequences of that case as shown in later decisions. What were the political consequences?

15. What is "legislative" as contrasted with "congressional" reapportionment? What standards apply in these areas? How precisely equal must populations be in election districts?

16. How have civil rights been implemented in the areas of grand jury and petit jury action, housing, transportation, public accommodations, and interracial marriage or cohabitation?

17. Are private acts of discrimination beyond the reach of the U.S. Constitution? Of federal legislation? Explain and illustrate.

18. What is meant by "state action" in contrast to "private action"? On the basis of what provisions of what amendments have these concepts been defined by the Court? Compare and contrast the viewpoints of the *Civil Rights Cases* (1883) and *Jones* v. *Mayer* (1968). Can the two views be reconciled? Why or why not? What are the implications?

19. What major new fields of civil rights litigation now seem to be about to open up? Is the Court going too far? Why or why not?

20. Is the Supreme Court a policy-making body? Does it legislate or merely adjudicate? Is there a difference? Where does the old democratic principle of "consent of the governed" stand these days?

21. What is meant by the "intent test"? In what kinds of cases—and

to what effect—has it been applied? What has been the reading of it by Justice Lewis F. Powell, Jr., in the *Keyes* and the *Village of Arlington Heights* cases?

22. How is equal protection related to the higher law theme in judicial review?

23. Distinguish among the first, second, and middle tier court tests applied under equal protection and give a case illustration of the application of each of them.

24. What is meant by "irrebuttable presumption"? Is it widely used today?

25. What are the signs that the Court may rely less on rigorous strict scrutiny in deciding equal protection challenges henceforth? Are there counter-signs?

Citizenship, Liberty, and the American Prospect

The nations of our day cannot prevent condi-tions of equality from spreading in their midst. But it depends upon themselves whether equality is to lead to servitude or freedom, knowledge or barbarism, prosperity or wretchedness.[1]

ALEXIS DE TOCQUEVILLE (1840)

We all declare for liberty; but in using the same word we do not mean the same thing. . . . The shepherd drives the wolf from the sheep's throat, for which the sheep thanks the shepherd as his liberator, while the wolf denounces him for the same act, as destroyer of liberty. . . . precisely the same difference prevails today among us, human creatures, even in the North, and all professing to love liberty.[2]

ABRAHAM LINCOLN (1864)

We have a government of limited power under the Constitution, and we have got to work out our problems on the basis of law. Now, if that is reactionary, then I am a reactionary.[3]

WILLIAM HOWARD TAFT (1909)

*M*UCH HAS BEEN SAID of rights in this volume. What of duty? What of future prospects? Many of the rights discussed, such as protection of due process and equal protection of the laws, extend to all persons in the United States including aliens. But their full enjoyment depends upon the holding of national citizenship. I shall conclude the discussion by summarizing the terms and meaning of American citizenship, by briefly exploring the subject of duty, and by considering the performance and promise of the American system.

Citizenship

How Citizenship Is Gained

National citizenship is conferred in three ways: by birth in the United States, by birth outside the United States to U.S. citizens, and by naturalization.

Birth in the United States. Most Americans have citizenship by virtue of their birth in the United States. This principle is called *jus soli*, or "right of the soil." Children born in this country are "natural born" citizens, whether their parents are citizens or not, unless their parents are foreign diplomats or other persons not "subject to the jurisdiction" of the United States (Fourteenth Amendment).

Birth to U.S. Citizens Abroad. By an act of Congress, citizenship is conferred to children born to U.S. citizens abroad, provided at least one of the parents is a citizen and has lived for a time in the United States prior to the birth of the child. This principle is called *jus sanguinis* or "right of blood relationship."

Naturalization. The extension of citizenship by the United States to aliens through the process of naturalization is a privilege to be given or withheld. The power is not restricted by any constitutional limitation (see ART. I, SEC. 8, CL. 4). Congress at first extended naturalization only to "free white persons" (1790), then expanded it to include those of "African nativity and . . . descent" (1870). Orientals were specifically excluded in 1882, although the children of resident aliens of Oriental or any other descent became citizens simply by being born here. Since 1952, restrictions on attaining citizenship through naturalization have been eliminated so far as conditions of sex, race, or marriage are concerned. Remaining restrictions, however, prohibit naturalization of persons who are members of the Communist Party or other totalitarian organizations, those who advocate or teach overthrow by force or violence of the government of the United States, and persons not of "good moral character," such as convicted felons.

Requirements for naturalization include these: residence for five years in the United States, possession of good moral character for all of that period, and the taking of an oath of allegiance. The oath includes these pledges: to support the Constitution of the United States; to renounce absolutely any allegiance to a foreign power; to defend the country against enemies by bearing arms (or to do equivalent noncombative service instead) whenever required by law to do so.

How Citizenship Is Lost

Only persons who have gained citizenship by birth *in* the United States are, of a certainty, "natural-born" citizens (ART. II, SEC. 1, CL. 5), since the citizenship of others rests upon acts of Congress. But the rights attached to citizenship (however attained) are supposed to be the same for all. Naturalization does not confer "a second-class citizenship" but "carries with it the privilege of full participation in the affairs of our society." [4] Nevertheless, some differences exist: only a "natural-born" citizen can be President of the United States, and the naturalized citizen stands in much greater jeopardy of loss of United States citizenship than do other citizens.

Under current law, ten ways are spelled out whereby a naturalized citizen may lose American citizenship.[5] Thus, a naturalized citizen's good faith in taking the oath of allegiance to the United States can be inquired into at any time, and citizenship be revoked if bad faith can be demonstrated. Moreover, if a naturalized citizen joins a questionable organization within five years—one devoted to the overthrow of the United States Government, for example—citizenship may be imperiled. Or if a naturalized citizen assumes residence in a foreign country within five years, a *prima facie* case of bad faith in taking the oath of allegiance may thereby be demonstrated.

Of course, any citizen may at any time *voluntarily* renounce citizenship, and hence expatriate himself. But whether deprivation of citizenship can be authorized as punishment by congressional act is, today, uncertain. This uncertainty extends even to punitive loss of citizenship by naturalized citizens, due to conflicting conclusions of recent Court decisions. In a 1967 decision, the Court held that the first sentence of the Fourteenth Amendment vested citizenship (born or naturalized) as an absolute right that Congress is powerless to take away. Thus, the voluntary renunciation of citizenship must apparently be explicit. For example, the fact of voting in the elections of another nation was not regarded as sufficient proof implying a voluntary renunciation. The Court denied that "Congress has the power to ... take ... away citizenship. ... [T]he Government is without power to rob a citizen of his citizenship." [6]

Rights of Citizens

The rights held by United States citizens include the privileges and immunities protected as fundamental to Americans, those that belong by right to the citizens of all free governments and are enjoyed by citizens of all the states. These privileges include the right to travel freely from state to state and move from place to place, the right to acquire and possess private property of all descriptions, to engage in lawful commerce, occupations, and professions, and the right to have access to the courts and to judicial remedies in protection of rights.

Duties of Citizens

The simplest and truest way of conceiving of the duties of Americans is through the common notion that every right implies a correlative duty. In an era when civil disobedience sometimes has taken on the luster of a divine calling, civil duty requires great emphasis.

Respect for Limits. What does the duty of an American citizen encompass? To begin with, a sense of limits—a respect for the rights of others. Your rights end where "the other fellow's nose begins," it is commonly said. Our government assures liberty under law. "Even liberty itself, the greatest of all rights, is not unrestricted license to act according to one's own will," the Court once said in making the fundamental point.[7] Limits must be observed because rights are never absolute—notwithstanding what Justice Douglas may have said to the contrary from time to time.

Obedience to the Law. A general duty is obedience to the law. Conversely, disobedience to its dictates is rightly punishable in varying degrees of severity by all governments. The duty to obey the law applies with exceptional force to citizens of a country whose laws rest squarely on the principle of consent: where an independent judiciary armed with the power of judicial review sedulously considers the constitutionality of provisions of the laws; where minority rights are energetically protected by the judiciary, administrative agencies, and political processes; where repeal of unfair and obnoxious laws is within relatively easy reach of citizens through their elected representatives; where constitutional amendment is a recourse; where the adaptation of the meaning and application of constitutional provision is a constant, never-ending process; and where general governmental policy at all levels is responsive to popular will. Consider the utter contrast of all this with the conditions that obtain in the apolitical regimes of the communist world, for example, where the government dictates law to the people, the Party to the government, and the controlling few to the Party *via* the Central Committee. To petition or dissent is to become an enemy of the people—and thereby to risk dire if not deadly consequences.

Duty of Opposition. The duty to obey the law does not impair the duty to oppose the government by legal and constitutional means whenever you think the government is wrong. Opposition and debate are the very stuff of politics itself. The principle of "loyal opposition" is a fundamental balance wheel in the operation of American no less than of British government. But, again, within limits. We are not entitled to break the law or to use violence against political opponents. The political opposition in this country emphatically, however, is not the public enemy. Political office holders, at times, may be. We have only to recall the Nixon Administration "horror" in which the FBI and other federal agencies were abused by the Chief Executive's demands that political opponents and critics be spied on and that a secret White House's "Enemies List" be maintained.

We are forever engaged in adversary activities as the very stuff of all our political processes: in courtroom trials, in partisan campaigns for elective office when it is Republican against Democrat, in seeking compromise of legislative and executive policy decisions, in seeking remedy for inequities through administrative processes of innumerable kinds, in the constant streams of news reporting and editorial comment in the press. But when verdicts are rendered and appeals exhausted, we are bound by the results of due process even if we lose. When the election is over, we are bound to accept the results of the ballot box even if "our" candidate is defeated. We are not entitled to assassinate public officials, candidates, or victors in elections for high office because we happen to oppose them. When Congress has voted and the President has signed, we are bound by the law and the demands it makes even if they are distasteful. When administrative remedies are exhausted, and judicial appeals have been made, we are bound to abide by the decision of the final arbiter, whether it be an administrative board or a court of law. At least for a time. For the processes of opposition, accommodation, and resolution compose a vital unending strand of American political existence itself.

Assertion of Rights. Some argue that it is a citizen's positive duty to assert the rights assured by the Constitution and, thereby, to realize and preserve them. It is evident that rights not asserted are lost, and this is technically the case in the strict atmosphere of many courtroom proceedings. But the rights assured by the Bill of Rights clearly are dead letters on the page unless they are constantly asserted by individual citizens and by associations of citizens. It was precisely this view that breathed life into the equal protection clause. Through tirelessly asserting rights believed to be protected by the

Constitution, Thurgood Marshall and the NAACP ultimately brought about the civil rights revolution. Their motivation for action was their conviction that the Constitution represents liberty and justice. And so it does, but not simply of itself without a steadfast insistence from individuals who care sufficiently to pursue liberty and justice against all adversity. Without that effort, the equal protection clause would probably be as dead today as it was in 1927 when Holmes disparaged it as the usual last resort of hopeless cases. Solely in this way do we preserve and vivify our living Constitution. Another term for this is "eternal vigilance."

Duty to Vote. Good citizenship includes the familiar duty to vote and to take part in politics. Free government cannot be sustained unless the people interest themselves in their political well-being and actively participate in the processes of self-government. It is evident that most nations of the world are not free and not concerned with fostering the liberty and soundness of the United States. Those are the special concerns of American citizens. There are no more than two dozen free democratic governments among the 150 nations in the world today.

Civic Duty and Public Order. The outer limits of rights and the province of duty overlap and merge at some points. All officials of both state and national governments formally take an oath tacitly taken by all citizens of the United States: they swear to "preserve, protect and defend the Constitution of the United States." [8] Like the coronation oaths of old, this oath binds together the national community. It obligates its citizens to exercise the rights and powers of government according to the restrictions imposed by the Constitution and the laws pursuant to it. A corollary is the duty of all government officials to maintain the liberty of the people.

No rights held by citizens, however, prevent the government from enacting laws (through the police power, for example) to foster the general welfare, the protection of the people, and the orderly conduct of government. Thus, government rightly demands certain residency and citizenship qualifications to vote and hold public office and to engage in certain professions, such as the practice of medicine or law. Liberties are not absolute, therefore. The fundamental "Privileges and Immunities of Citizens" secured by the Constitution (ART. IV, SEC. 2) are common to all the states under their various constitutions and laws, because Americans are citizens of their states as well as their nation. On the other hand, the privileges and immunities of American citizens (expressly protected by the Fourteenth Amendment) arise from the character of the national government as expressed by the Bill of Rights, the other provisions of the Constitution, and by laws and treaties made pursuant to them. In this volume we have been most concerned with the latter range of liberties: those that arise from the nature and essence of our republican form of government.

Modern philosophical writers may mumble incoherently when asked to speak about civic duty. But this was not always so. Socrates, in a powerful passage of the *Crito* over two millennia ago, wrote these remarkably relevant words:

> ... if you cannot persuade your country [to the contrary] you must do whatever it orders, and patiently submit to any punishment that it imposes, whether it be flogging or imprisonment. And if it leads you out to war, to be wounded and killed, you must comply, and it is right that you should do so. You must not give way or retreat or abandon your position. Both in war and in the law courts and everywhere else you must do whatever your city and your country command, or else persuade them in accordance with universal justice, but violence is a sin against your parents, and it is a far greater sin against your country.[9]

Performance and Prospects of American Liberty

In this as in so much else, it was James Madison who set forth the standard whereby to judge the performance and prospects of our constitutional regime as a structure of ordered liberty. In *The Federalist (No. 51)* he wrote: "Justice is the end of government. It is the end of civil society. It ever has been and ever will be pursued until it be obtained, or until liberty be lost in the pursuit."

The pursuit of justice in America's two centuries has been at one and the same time a pursuit of liberty. The considerable materials surveyed in the foregoing pages amply attest to that. In a thousand detailed ways the nation conceived in liberty has sought, continues to seek, to measure, and moderate the complex inner workings of its political, economic, and social structures by the standard of justice. The nation has insisted, as has no other people before, that the standard of justice be extended to the least among us. As we have seen, it has viewed justice as comprehending and embracing perfect liberty.

I know of no better way to measure American success or failure than by its achievement of justice and liberty for all. No doubt we fall well below the perfection envisaged as the ultimate goal by Madison. As Winston Churchill once remarked in the House of Commons, "No one pretends that Democracy is perfect or all-wise. Indeed, it has been said that Democracy is the worst form of government except all those other forms that have been tried from time to time." [10] Churchill's wisdom can be applied here. We can readily concede the truth of almost any criticism advanced against America's system of liberty and justice—and still rightly maintain that it is better than any of the alternatives that we might embrace. Ours is, in fact, one of the great achievements in the history of civilization.

Madison linked the pursuit of justice with the possible demise of liberty. What could he have meant? There seem to be three main, interrelated ways in which this could happen, and all three are threatened today: the way of *anarchy*, *zealotry*, and *lassitude*. All three are ancient enemies of ordered liberty, however they may be decked out in new twentieth-century costumes.

The demise of liberty through *anarchy* was warned against by Justice Jackson in the *Terminiello* dissent. Liberty can become such an absolute goal, as the alpha and omega of justice, that the fabric of free government no longer can tolerate the internal stresses, and is ripped to shreds. The tensions of the 1960s distinctly showed tendencies in this direction. When citizens conceive of liberty as a license to do "what you will, when you will, to whomever you will," they threaten the security and safety of persons and property. In such a contest, the latter will prevail—even if repression of a high order of brutality is entailed. Justice Jackson, in pondering what to do with the inciter of a riot, thought the Court ought to temper its doctrinaire logic with a little common sense. In principle, he was right.

Zealotry is a second possible way for the pursuit of justice to extinguish liberty. This can occur through the dogmatic imposition of standards of perfect justice upon society, thereby making it ever more perfectly free. The Supreme Court in the years since 1954 has not infrequently been accused of moving precisely in that direction. The tendency is also seen in the exorbitant administrative demands made by "Big Government" on institutions and the rank and file citizenry. Both the courts and the bureaucracy have come in for harsh criticism in this regard. Soon we will be so free through court decree and administrative edict, it sometimes seems, that we will have no choices of our own left to make. Consider, for example, the British scholar Maurice Cranston's remark in June, 1976:

> Even the most hardened *étatiste* in Europe today finds it hard to believe the extent to which the American Department of Health, Education and Welfare and the American courts dictate not only what shall not be done but what shall be done about abortion, the upbringing and schooling of children, the hiring of academic faculty, and dozens of other matters which are properly the concern of the family or of private institutions.[11]

Apprehension about this multifaceted dimension of pursuing justice is not new. Jefferson and Lincoln voiced similar fears, as can be seen in headnotes to the first and fifth chapters of this book. I have previously suggested that reliance on the Court to set major public policy clearly violates the principle of government by consent of the governed and is, in fact, an authoritarian derailment of our democratic system.

The matter is not always grim, however. Consider the plight of the Perry Local School District of Stark County, Ohio. In 1976 the school trustees were taken to task by Mr. Cranston's friends at HEW, it seems, for discriminating against the sexes, contrary to Title IX requirements. The HEW officials formally complained that the school board's dress code, which limited the length of male students' hair and forbade them to grow "facial hair," was discriminatory against men, since women were not so restricted. Whereupon the afflicted school board—who well understood the bureaucratic mentality—promptly adopted a new regulation prohibiting female students in their schools from growing beards and mustaches. The U.S. officials had taken the new regulation under advisement and were (at last report) studying it to determine whether Perry Local School District was now in full compliance.

This mode of extinguishing liberty in the pursuit of justice may be called damned foolishness by the great unwashed. And it is also the tell-tale mark of an ideological zealotry of venerable ancestry. Thus, Jean-Jacques Rousseau wrote this memorable line in 1762: "...it may be necessary to compel a man to be free...." [12] This is the root of the totalitarian mentality whose aspiration is to perfect justice and liberty, by formula. This used to be called tyranny—a familiar enemy of Madison and his friends. It has taken many forms and has always aroused fear, whether of a majority, or a chosen few who compose a revolutionary elite, or a despotical strong man. The spirit of the thing was captured by Lord Bryce, in his opening lines of the chapter on "Tyranny of the Majority," in *The American Commonwealth*: [13]

> O it is excellent
> To have a giant's strength, but it is tyrannous
> To use it like a giant.

Lassitude is a third mode of fulfilling Madison's prophecy. It arises out of the torpor of the people, their carelessness of things public, their preoccupation with private satisfactions to the exclusion of all else, their willingness to let the politicians run the country while "I do my thing." The vacuum to be filled in a free government when it is abandoned by the people is no more tolerable than the vacuum in physics—it will be filled, for "Nature abhors a vacuum," as Spinoza once said. And a vacuum in the public sphere is created when individuals turn away from public concerns and immerse their lives in purely private pursuits, whether they are "workaholics" or hedonists. The fitful pursuit of a life that meets the aspirations of atomized individuals who compose such a radically privatized society may be understood as "living well" in one established sense of the phrase. Lassitude is disastrous for free institutions. The man on horseback who despises his fellow men and lusts after power for its own sake is saddled and ready, waiting for his opportunity. Some say the Watergate affair may have been symptomatic of such a state of things in the country. Whether that is true or not, the familiar litany of the apathetic and disaffected need not be mumbled again here.

Everybody knows quite well that many Americans aren't just "sitting out" this (or that) election, but the whole political life of the nation. Among the traits to be traced in the late 1970s in America are the deadening of public spiritedness, patriotism, the decline of confidence in government, the recoil from disclosures of deep corruption in the political process, and the disintegration of the community itself into contending factions each seeking private gratification at public expense. These traits are inimical to the scheme of ordered liberty that is the heritage of the country. Add to them the debauchery of education, to the point that entering college students are hardly expected to read above the eighth-grade level, and the configuration of a substantial crisis takes shape.

My conclusion is, then, that internal factors make our prospects hazardous at best, and that James Madison's prescience was great. And this leaves out all of the dreadful things that external forces could also bring about, which need not be inventoried here. From the onset of the Cold War in 1947, if not before, it has been clear that the odds are against free government in the United States. The drift into an authoritarian regime from external pressures alone has seemed almost inevitable in a country whose foundations rest on maximizing individual liberties so as better to pursue happiness. Pursuit of survival contradicts this fundamental thrust of our institutions, and the strain on them shows everywhere.

Yet I would end on a brighter note. There was substance, I thought, to Patrick Henry's famous exclamation: "Give me liberty or give me death." This is not because it betrays a suicidal mentality. Rather, it is because Henry rightly saw that liberty is the root of humanity. The history of this country is a testament to that belief. And those who identify themselves with that tradition know that liberty is essential to existence. It is both a constant in history and a great dissolvent of despotic regimes past and present. Liberty is the fresh air of existence, as a Solzhenitsyn repeatedly reminds us. It is an intrinsic part of everyone's humanity, hence it is inextinguishable.

There is, indeed, more to existence than biological process, even if (as Georges Santayana once said) biologically we are all proletarians.

The sense of dignity and nobility that attaches to free people—and to all people in quest of liberty—places them in communion, not only with the framers and founders of America, but with the framers of the Magna Carta on the field at Runnymede eight centuries ago. They are members of a universal community reaching toward the dawn of civilization—back to distant philosophers and prophets who led their people out of bondage. They join the mythical figure of Homer's Achilles, who knew (once dear Patroclus had been slain wearing Achilles's armor) that friendship and faithfulness to one's true self are ultimately more important than even life itself.

It is from the deep sense of liberty rooted in everyone and in history itself that our enduring higher law stems, and our tradition of institutional concern for rightness. Sir Isaiah Berlin once remarked that the irresistible in human affairs usually is only that which is not resisted. That statement I take to be true. Historical inevitability or "determinism" is propaganda to be thrown aside. *Resist!* Despite all of the calculated odds against it, have no doubt at all that liberty will survive as long as men do. Nor doubt that, for all its shortcomings, the American institutionalization of liberty under law is the greatest monument to truth shaping the future of human beings today.

Notes and References

PREFACE

1. "First Charter of Virginia" (1606) quoted from Bernard Schwartz, ed., *The Bill of Rights: A Documentary History,* 2 vols. (New York: Chelsea House Pubs., McGraw Hill, 1971), 1:59–60.
2. President Jimmy Carter's "Inaugural Address" quoted from W. L. Miller, "The Yankee From Georgia," *New York Times Magazine* (July 3, 1977), 18.

INTRODUCTION

1. Aristotle, *Nicomachean Ethics,* bk. 1, ch 3, 1119b5–6; trans. M. Ostwald (Indianapolis, Ind.: Bobbs-Merrill Co., Library of Liberal Arts, 1962), 6.
2. Quotes from Ralph H. Gabriel, *Main Currents in American History* (New York: D. Appleton-Century Co., 1942), 32. For the quotations in context see Edmund Burke, *Speech on Conciliation with the Colonies,* ed. Jeffrey Hart (Chicago: Henry Regnery Co., Gateway Edition, 1964), 62, 137–38.
3. Charles C. Tansill, ed., *Documents Illustrative of the Formation of the Union of the American States* (Washington, D.C.: Government Printing Office, 1927), 952.
4. Quoted from Philip S. Foner, ed., *The Complete Writings of Thomas Paine,* 2 vols. (New York: Citadel Press, 1945), 1:50.
5. Bernard Schwartz, ed., *The Bill of Rights: A Documentary History,* 2 vols. (New York, Toronto, London, Sydney: Chelsea House, 1971), 1:256, 179–379 *passim.*
6. *Buckley* v. *Valeo,* 96 S. Ct. 612 (1976); *see* the discussion in *Muskrat* v. *U.S.,* 219 U.S. 346 (1911).
7. *The Federalist* is a collection of essays written by Alexander Hamilton, James Madison, and John Jay. It was first published in book form in May 1788, but most of its 85 "Papers" had been published earlier in New York newspapers. Its purpose was to defend the proposed new Constitution against its detractors and, thereby, persuade New Yorkers to ratify the Constitution. The three authors used a common pseudonym, "Publius," and thus some of the Papers are of disputed authorship. *The Federalist* is widely regarded as not only an authoritative commentary on the original meaning of our Constitution but "the most significant contribution Americans have made to political philosophy . . ." *See* Jacob

E. Cooke, ed., *The Federalist* (Middletown Ct.: Wesleyan University Press, 1961), ix.
8. Arguments of Hamilton, summarized from *The Federalist* No. 84.
9. Letter of Jefferson to Madison, December 20, 1787.
10. *Cf.* Edward S. Corwin, *The "Higher Law" Background of American Constitutional Law* (1928–29; reprint ed., Ithaca, N.Y.: Cornell University Press, 1955) *and* Thomas C. Grey, "Do We Have An Unwritten Constitution?," *Stanford Law Review*, 27 (1975):703–18.

CHAPTER ONE Liberty, Law, and Due Process

1. Jefferson to Rowan, Sept. 26, 1798, in Thomas Jefferson, *Works,* ed. Paul Leicester Ford, Federal Edition, 12 vols. (New York, 1904–05), 8:448.
2. *Marbury* v. *Madison,* 5 U.S. (1 Cranch) 137 at 176, 177.
3. Jefferson to Jarvis, Sept. 28, 1820, in *Works,* ed. Ford, 12:162.
4. Quoted from Albert J. Beveridge, *The Life of John Marshall,* 4 vols. (Boston and New York: Houghton Mifflin Co., 1916–19), 3:158.
5. *Marbury* v. *Madison,* 5 U.S. (1 Cr.) 137 (1803). *See* Beveridge, *The Life of John Marshall,* 3:52–222.
6. Aristotle, *Politics,* bk.3, ch.16, 1287a19–20, 27–32, trans. B. Jowett (New York: Modern Library, 1943), 162.
7. Cicero, *Pro A. Cluentio Oratio,* c. 53, sec. 146. Quoted from Edward S. Corwin, *The "Higher Law" Background of American Constitutional Law* (Ithaca, N.Y.: Cornell University Press, repr. ed., 1955), 11.
8. *Palko* v. *Connecticut,* 302 U.S. 319 (1937).
9. William Blackstone, *Commentaries on the Laws of England,* ed. William B. Hammond, 4 vols. (San Francisco: Bancroft-Whitney, 1890), 1:60.
10. *Barron* v. *Baltimore,* 32 U.S. (7 Pet.) 243 (1833).
11. *Connally* v. *General Construction Co.,* 269 U.S. 385 (1926). *Cf. Mathews* v. *Eldridge,* 96 S. Ct. 893 (1976).
12. *Grayned* v. *Rockford,* 408 U.S. 104 (1972); *Lanzetta* v. *New Jersey,* 306 U.S. 451 (1939).
13. Sir Henry Sumner Maine, *Dissertations on the Early Law and Custom* (London: John Murray, 1883), 389.

14: *Bolling* v. *Sharpe*, 347 U.S. 497 (1954).

15. *Bolling* v. *Sharpe*, 347 U.S. 497 (1954); *Hampton* v. *Mow Sun Wong*, 96 S. Ct. 1895 (1976). *See also* Justice Potter Stewart's concurring opinion in *Fronteiro* v. *Richardson*, 411 U.S. 667 (1973), and the Court's express statement in *Johnson* v. *Robison*, 415 U.S. 361 (1974), that anything invalid under the equal protection clause of the Fourteenth Amendment also is invalid under the due process clause of the Fifth Amendment. Robert J. Harris commented: "In all of constitutional history the reading of the equal protection clause of the Fourteenth Amendment into the due process clause of the Fifth was one of the more remarkable feats of judicial thaumaturgy, because it converted the due process clause of the Fifth into something substantially more than the same clause in the Fourteenth and thereby created the anomaly that the same thing is not really itself." Harris, "Judicial Review: Vagaries and Varieties," *Journal of Politics*, 38 (Aug., 1976), 193.

16. William Blackstone, *Commentaries on the Laws of England*, ed. William B. Hammond, 4 vols. (San Francisco: Bancroft-Whitney, 1890). The *Commentaries* first appeared in 1765, 1766, 1768, 1769. Hammond's edition collates all changes made by Blackstone through the first eight editions; the eighth edition (1778) was the last published during Blackstone's lifetime.

17. Edward Coke, *The Institutes of the Laws of England*, 4 parts (London, 1628–1644). *The Reports of Sir Edward Coke ... of Divers Resolutions and Judgements ... of Cases in Law.* (First published in entirety in London, 1658.) For further elaboration *see* A. E. Dick Howard, *The Road from Runnymede: Magna Carta and Constitutionalism in America* (Charlottesville, Va.: University Press of Virginia, 1968), chap. 6 and *passim*.

18. *See Adamson* v. *California*, 332 U.S. 46 (1947), the dissenting opinion of Justice Black in which Justice William O. Douglas joined; also, *FPC* v. *Natural Gas Pipeline Co.*, 315 U.S. 575, 600 note 4 (1942). For discussion, *see* Wallace Mendelson, "Mr. Justice Douglas and Government by the Judiciary," *Journal of Politics*, 38 (Nov., 1976), *esp.* 934–37.

19. *Calder* v. *Bull*, 3 U.S. (3 Dallas) 386 (1798). *See* p. 61, Ct. Judge Iredell's opinion in this case.

20. *Fletcher* v. *Peck*, 10 U.S. (6 Cr.) 87 (1810).

21. *Bank of Columbia* v. *Okley*, 17 U.S. (3 Wheat.) 235 (1819).

22. *Dred Scott* v. *Sandford,* 60 U.S. (19 How.) 393 (1857).
23. *Wynehamer* v. *New York,* 13 N.Y. 378 (1856).
24. *Butchers' Benevolent Association* v. *Crescent City Livestock Landing and Slaughterhouse Co.,* 83 U.S. (16 Wall.) 36, 21 L.Ed. 394 (1873).
25. *Munn* v. *Illinois,* 94 U.S. 113 (1877). The end of the doctrine of business "affected with a public interest" came in *Nebbia* v. *New York,* 291 U.S. 502 (1934). *Cf. Wolff Packing Co.* v. *Industrial Court,* 262 U.S. 522 (1923). For discussion, *see* Carl B. Swisher, *American Constitutional Development* (2nd ed.; Cambridge, Mass.: Houghton Mifflin Co., 1954), 397–406, 630–38, 815–20, 829–30, 924.
26. *Allgeyer* v. *Louisiana,* 165 U.S. 573 (1897).
27. *Lochner* v. *New York,* 198 U.S. 45 (1905).
28. *Budd* v. *New York,* 143 U.S. 517 (1892), Justice Brewer dissenting.
29. For details *see* Harold U. Faulkner, *American Economic History,* 8th ed. (New York: Harper and Row, 1960), 449–76.
30. *West Coast Hotel* v. *Parrish,* 300 U.S. 379 (1937).
31. The decision cited and quoted is that of Justice Washington in *Corfield* v. *Coryell,* 6 Fed. Cas. 546 (No. 3230) (C.C.E.D.Pa., 1823).
32. *Slaughter-House Cases,* 83 U.S. (16 Wall.) 36 (1873).
33. *Lynch* v. *Household Finance,* 405 U.S. 538 (1972).

CHAPTER TWO A Scheme of Ordered Liberty

1. *Calvin's Case,* Court of King's Bench, 4 Coke's Reports 1, 77 English Reports 377 (1609).
2. Learned Hand, *The Bill of Rights* (Cambridge, Mass.: Harvard University Press, 1958), 73.
3. Martin Luther King, Jr., "Letter from Birmingham Jail," in *Why We Can't Wait* (New York: Harper and Row, 1964), 82.
4. New York Penal Laws, Sects. 160, 161; Laws of 1909, chap. 88; Consol. Laws 1909, chap. 40. Originally enacted in 1902; Laws 1902, chap. 371.
5. *Gitlow* v. *New York,* 268 U.S. 652 (1925).
6. *Schenck* v. *United States,* 249 U.S. 47 (1919). *Cf. Debs* v. *United States,* 249 U.S. 211 (1919). *See also* Carl B. Swisher, *American*

Constitutional Development (Boston and New York: Houghton Mifflin Co., 1943), chap. 32.

7. *Brandenburg* v. *Ohio*, 395 U.S. 444 at 447, which overruled the *Whitney* case (ref. 8).
8. *Whitney* v. *California*, 274 U.S. 357 (1927).
9. Thomas C. Grey, "Do We Have an Unwritten Constitution?", *Stanford Law Review* 27 (1975):717.
10. *Griswold* v. *Connecticut*, 381 U.S. 479 (1965). The "right of privacy," it should be noted, was first called that in *Mapp* v. *Ohio*, 367 U.S. 643 (1961) where it was anchored to the Fourth Amendment.
11. *Skinner* v. *Oklahoma*, 316 U.S. 535 (1942).
12. *Lochner* v. *New York*, 198 U.S. 45 (1905).
13. *West Coast Hotel Co.* v. *Parrish*, 300 U.S. 379 (1937).
14. *Morey* v. *Doud*, 354 U.S. 457 (1957), overruled by *New Orleans* v. *Dukes*, 96 S. Ct. 2513 (1976) with the Court saying at 2518: "Morey was the only case in the last half century to invalidate a wholly economic regulation on equal protection grounds, and we are now satisfied that decision was erroneous." The present discussion of substantive due process is generally indebted to notes in Gerald Gunther, *Cases and Materials on Constitutional Law*, 9th ed. (Mineola, N.Y.: Foundation Press, Inc., 1975), chaps. 8–10.
15. *Meyer* v. *Nebraska*, 262 U.S. 390 (1923).
16. *Pierce* v. *Society of Sisters*, 268 U.S. 510 (1925).
17. *Whitney* v. *California*, 374 U.S. 355 (1927), concurring opinion of Justice Brandeis.
18. *Skinner* v. *Oklahoma*, 316 U.S. 535 (1942).
19. *Prince* v. *Massachusetts*, 321 U.S. 158 (1944).
20. *Buck* v. *Bell*, 274 U.S. 200 (1927).
21. *Aptheker* v. *Secretary of State*, 378 U.S. 500 (1964).
22. *Kent* v. *Dulles*, 357 U.S. 116 (1958); *Shapiro* v. *Thompson*, 349 U.S. 618 (1969).
23. *Poe* v. *Ullman*, 367 U.S. 397 (1961).
24. *Loving* v. *Virginia*, 388 U.S. 1 (1967).
25. *Roe* v. *Wade*, 410 U.S. 113 (1973); *see also* the companion case, *Doe* v. *Bolton*, 410 U.S. 179 (1973).
26. *Roe* v. *Wade*, 410 U.S. 113 (1973), dissenting opinion of Justice Rehnquist.
27. *Bolling* v. *Sharpe*, 347 U.S. 497 (1954). In 1976 the Court stated:

"The Fifth Amendment's due process clause encompasses equal protection principles." *Mathews* v. *de Castro*, 97 S. Ct. 431 (1976).

28. Louis Henkin, " 'Selective Incorporation' in the Fourteenth Amendment," *Yale Law Journal*, 73 (1963):78.
29. *Griswold* v. *Connecticut*, 381 U.S. 479 (1965).
30. *Roe* v. *Wade*, 410 U.S. 113 (1973), concurring opinion of Justice Douglas (emphasis as in the original).
31. Jefferson to Jarvis, September 28, 1820, cited in Albert J. Beveridge, *The Life of John Marshall*, 4 vols. (Boston and New York: Houghton Mifflin Co., 1916–19), 3:144.
32. *Calder* v. *Bull*, 3 U.S. (3 Dall.) 386 (1798). In 1977 Justice Powell, with three other justices concurring, said: "Appropriate limits on substantive due process come not from drawing arbitrary lines but from careful respect for the teaching of history and solid recognition of the basic values that underlie our society." *Moore* v. *City of East Cleveland, Ohio*, 97 S. Ct. 1932 (1977).
33. *Adamson* v. *California*, 332 U.S. 46 (1947) with a concluding quotation from *Federal Power Commission* v. *Natural Gas Pipeline Co.*, 315 U.S. 575 (1942).
34. *Griswold* v. *Connecticut*, 381 U.S. 479 (1965), Justice Black dissenting.
35. *Duncan* v. *Louisiana*, 391 U.S. 145 (1968).
36. *Calder* v. *Bull*, 3 U.S. (3 Dall.) 386 (1798); *Murdock* v. *Pennsylvania*, 319 U.S. 105 (1943); *Palko* v. *Connecticut*, 302 U.S. 319 (1937).
37. *Roe* v. *Wade*, 410 U.S. 113 (1973), concurring opinion of Justice William O. Douglas.
38. *Gitlow* v. *New York*, 268 U.S. 652 (1925); *Duncan* v. *Louisiana*, 391 U.S. 145 (1968).
39. *Chicago, B. & Q. Railroad* v. *City of Chicago*, 166 U.S. 226 (1897).
40. *Twining* v. *New Jersey*, 211 U.S. 78 (1908).
41. *Snyder* v. *Massachusetts*, 291 U.S. 97 (1934). *Palko* v. *Connecticut*, 302 U.S. 319 (1937).
42. *Palko* v. *Connecticut*, 302 U.S. 319 (1937); the internal quotation near the end is from *Hebert* v. *Louisiana*, 272 U.S. 312 (1926). Double jeopardy was incorporated into the Fourteenth Amendment by *Benton* v. *Maryland*, 395 U.S. 784 (1969) which partially overruled *Palko*.

43. NAACP v. *Alabama ex rel. Patterson,* 357 U.S. 449 (1958).
44. *Benton v. Maryland,* 395 U.S. 784 (1969).
45. *Williams v. Florida,* 399 U.S. 78 (1970) partly concurring and partly dissenting opinion of Justice Black, quoting from *Maloy v. Hogan,* 378 U.S. 1 (1964).
46. *Williams v. Florida,* 399 U.S. 78 (1970).
47. *Apodaca v. Oregon,* 406 U.S. 404 (1972); *Johnson v. Louisiana,* 406 U.S. 356 (1972).
48. *West Virginia State Board of Education v. Barnette,* 319 U.S. 624 (1943); *Thomas v. Collins,* 323 U.S. 516 (1945); *United States v. Carolene Products Co.,* 304 U.S. 144 (1938).
49. *License Cases,* 46 U.S. (5 How.) 504 (1847); Thomas M. Cooley, *A Treatise on the Constitutional Limitations* (1848; reprint of 1st ed., New York: Da Capo Press, 1972), 572; Christopher G. Tiedeman, *A Treatise of the Limitations of Police Power in the United States* (St. Louis: F. H. Thomas Law Book Co., 1886), 4–5; *cf. Gibbons v. Ogden,* 22 U.S. (19 Wheat.) 1 (1824); *Brown v. Maryland,* 25 U.S. (12 Wheat.) 419 (1827); *Atlantic Coast Line v. Goldsboro,* 232 U.S. 548 (1914).
50. *Young v. American Mini Theaters, Inc.,* 96 S. Ct. 2440 (1976).
51. *Schenck v. United States,* 249 U.S. 47 (1919).
52. *Palko v. Connecticut,* 302 U.S. 319 (1937).
53. *Terminiello v. Chicago,* 337 U.S. 1 (1949).
54. *Dennis v. United States,* 341 U.S. 494 (1951); the Court embraced Federal District Chief Judge Learned Hand's formula.
55. *American Communications Association v. Douds,* 339 U.S. 382 (1950); *see Young v. American Mini Theaters, Inc.,* 96 S. Ct. 2440 (1976).
56. *Chaplinsky v. New Hampshire,* 315 U.S. 568 (1942).
57. *Lanzetta v. New Jersey,* 306 U.S. 451 (1939).
58. *Gooding v. Wilson,* 405 U.S. 518 (1972).
59. *Shelton v. Tucker,* 364 U.S. 479 (1960).
60. In the "summary" I am indebted to Edward S. Corwin, *The Constitution and What It Means Today,* rev. by Harold W. Chase and Craig R. Ducat (13th ed.; Princeton, N.J.: Princeton University Press, 1974), 238–68.
61. *Village of Arlington Heights v. Metropolitan Housing Development Corp.,* 97 S. Ct. 555 (1977) at 561.
62. *Warth v. Seldin,* 422 U.S. 490 (1975) which has quoted from *Baker v. Carr,* 369 U.S. 186 (1962).

CHAPTER THREE A Preferred Position: First Amendment Liberties

1. Pericles's "Funeral Oration" (*Eulogium*) as given by Thucydides, *Peloponnesian War*, bk. 2, ch. 6, para. 44; trans. Rex Warner; reprinted in Charles M. Sherover, ed., *The Development of the Democratic Idea* (rev. ed.; New York: New American Library, Mentor Books, 1974), 16.
2. Representative James Madison of Virginia in a speech to the House of Representatives recommending the Bill of Rights, April 8, 1789, *Annals*, First Congress, First Session, p. 437; quoted from Charles S. Hyneman and George W. Carey, *A Second Federalist* (New York: Appleton-Century-Crofts, Meredith Pub. Co., 1967), 264.
3. Representative John Nicholas of Virginia in a speech to the House of Representatives opposing a bill to enact a sedition law, July 10, 1798, *Annals*, Fifth Congress, Second Session, p. 2144; quoted from Hyneman and Carey, *A Second Federalist*, 284.
4. *Near v. Minnesota ex rel. Olson*, 283 U.S. 697 (1931). Cf. *Nebraska Press Association v. Stuart*, 96 S. Ct. 2791 (1976). *See also* C. Herman Prichett, *The American Constitution* (New York: McGraw-Hill Book Co., 1959), chap. 23.
5. Cited by Chief Justice Hughes as "Report on the Virginia Resolutions," Madison's *Works*, 4:543; *Near v. Minnesota*, 283 U.S. 696 at 717–18.
6. *Palko v. Connecticut*, 302 U.S. 319 (1937); *Murdock v. Pennsylvania*, 319 U.S. 105 (1943).
7. *Gitlow v. New York*, 268 U.S. 652 (1925).
8. *Stromberg v. California*, 282 U.S. 359 (1931); *Near v. Minnesota, supra*.
9. William Blackstone, *Commentaries on the Laws of England*, 4:151–53.
10. Quoted from Thomas M. Cooley, *A Treatise on the Constitutional Limitations* (Boston: Little, Brown and Co., 1868), 431 n.
11. *Nebraska Press Association v. Stuart*, 96 S. Ct. 2791 (1976).
12. *New York Times v. Sullivan*, 376 U.S. 254 (1964).
13. *Brandenburg v. Ohio*, 393 U.S. 444 (1969).
14. Dallas *Times Herald*, Oct. 9, 1976 (Associated Press accounts).
15. Dallas *Times Herald*, Mar. 2, 1977, p. A-15 (Associated Press accounts). *Disorders and Terrorism: Report of the Task Force on Disorders and Terrorism*, ed. Joseph Foote, National Advisory

Committee on Criminal Justice Standards and Goals, U.S. Department of Justice (Washington, D.C.: Government Printing Office, 1977).

16. Dallas *Times Herald*, July 25, 1977, p. A-1 (Associated Press accounts).
17. Quoted from Hyneman and Carey, *A Second Federalist*, 283–84.
18. *New York Times* v. *United States* (The Pentagon Papers Case), 403 U.S. 713 (1971).
19. *Beauharnais* v. *Illinois*, 343 U.S. 250 (1952).
20. *New York Times* v. *Sullivan*, 376 U.S. 254 (1964).
21. *Ashton* v. *Kentucky*, 384 U.S. 195 (1966).
22. *Terminiello* v. *City of Chicago*, 337 U.S. 1 (1949).
23. *Gertz* v. *Robert Welch, Inc.*, 418 U.S. 323 (1974); *Cox Broadcasting Corp.* v. *Cohn*, 420 U.S. 469 (1975).
24. *Time, Inc.* v. *Firestone*, 96 S. Ct. 958 (1976).
25. *Hess* v. *Indiana*, 414 U.S. 105 (1973).
26. *Bond* v. *Floyd*, 385 U.S. 116 (1966).
27. *Watts* v. *United States*, 394 U.S. 705 (1969).
28. *Stromberg* v. *California*, 283 U.S. 359 (1931); *West Virginia State Board of Education* v. *Barnette*, 319 U.S. 624 (1943).
29. *United States* v. *O'Brien*, 391 U.S. 367 (1968).
30. *Street* v. *New York*, 394 U.S. 576 (1969); *Smith* v. *Goguen*, 415 U.S. 566 (1974); *Spence* v. *Washington*, 418 U.S. 405 (1974).
31. *Van Slyke* v. *Texas*, 418 U.S. 907 (1974).
32. *Chaplinsky* v. *New Hampshire*, 315 U.S. 568 (1942).
33. *Rosenfeld* v. *New Jersey*, 408 U.S. 901 (1971), from the dissenting opinion of Justice Lewis F. Powell, Jr.
34. *Cohen* v. *California*, 403 U.S. 15 (1971).
35. *Rosenfeld* v. *New Jersey*, 408 U.S. 901 (1971); *Lewis* v. *New Orleans* and *Brown* v. *New Orleans*, 408 U.S. 913, 914 (1971); *Lewis* v. *New Orleans* [*Lewis II*] 415 U.S. 130 (1974).
36. *Papish* v. *Board of Curators of the University of Missouri*, 410 U.S. 667 (1973).
37. *Eaton* v. *City of Tulsa*, 415 U.S. 697 (1974).
38. *Jacobellis* v. *Ohio*, 378 U.S. 184 (1964).
39. *Ginzburg* v. *United States*, 383 U.S. 463 (1966), dissenting opinion of Justice Potter Stewart.
40. *Roth* v. *United States* and *Alberts* v. *California*, 354 U.S. 476 (1957).
41. *Stanley* v. *Georgia*, 394 U.S. 557 (1969).
42. *Miller* v. *California*, 413 U.S. 15 (1973). Cf. *A Book Named*

"John Cleland's Memoirs of a Woman of Pleasure [Fanny Hill]"
v. *Attorney General of Massachusetts*, 383 U.S. 413 (1966). The
novel *Fanny Hill* was 277 years old when the Court decided it
was not legally obscene in this 1966 decision.

43. *Jenkins* v. *Georgia*, 418 U.S. 153 (1974); *Hamling* v. *United
States*, 418 U.S. 87 (1974).
44. *Mapp* v. *Ohio*, 367 U.S. 643 (1961·); *Griswold* v. *Connecticut*,
381 U.S. 479 (1965). *See* pp. 50–56.
45. *Stanley* v. *Georgia*, 394 U.S. 557 (1969); *Paris Adult Theatre* v.
Slaton, 413 U.S. 49 (1973).
46. *John Doe* v. *Commonwealth's Attorney General for the City of
Richmond*, 96 S. Ct. 1489 and 2192; facts and opinion, District
Court, 403 F. Supp. 1199.
47. *Griswold* v. *Connecticut*, 381 U.S. 479 (1965); *Roe* v. *Wade*,
410 U.S. 113 (1973); *Doe* v. *Bolton*, 410 U.S. 179 (1973); among
other important cases cited in *Griswold* specific mention may be
given *Meyer* v. *Nebraska*, 262 U.S. 390 (1923); *Pierce* v. *Society
of Sisters*, 268 U.S. 510 (1925); *Skinner* v. *Oklahoma*, 316 U.S.
535 (1942); *NAACP* v. *Alabama*, 357 U.S. 449 (1958).
48. *Planned Parenthood of Cent. Missouri* v. *Danforth*, 96 S. Ct.
2831 (1976). *See also Bellotti* v. *Baird*, 96 S. Ct. 2857 (1976);
Singleton v. *Wulf*, 96 S. Ct. 2868 (1976).
49. *Healy* v. *James*, 408 U.S. 169 (1972); *Papish* v. *Board of Curators of the University of Missouri*, 410 U.S. 667 (1973).
50. *Sweezy* v. *New Hampshire*, 354 U.S. 234 (1957).
51. *Keyishian* v. *Board of Regents*, 385 U.S. 589 (1967).
52. *Tinker* v. *Des Moines School District*, 393 U.S. 504 (1968);
Epperson v. *Arkansas*, 393 U.S. 97 (1968).
53. *United States* v. *Cruikshank*, 92 U.S. 542 (1876).
54. *DeJonge* v. *Oregon*, 299 U.S. 353 (1937).
55. *California Motor Transport Co.* v. *Trucking Unlimited*, 404 U.S.
508 (1972).
56. *Cox* v. *Louisiana* [*Cox I*], 379 U.S. 536 (1965).
57. *Cox* v. *Louisiana* [*Cox II*], 379 U.S. 559 (1965).
58. *Reynolds* v. *United States*, 98 U.S. 145 (1879).
59. *See* Henry Wilder Foote, *The Religion of Thomas Jefferson*
(1947, repr. ed.; Boston: Beacon Press, 1960), 23–40; Willard L.
Sperry, *Religion in America* (1946, repr. ed.; Boston: Beacon
Press, 1963), append. B.
60. *Zorach* v. *Clauson*, 343 U.S. 306 (1952).
61. *Lemon* v. *Kurtzman*, 403 U.S. 602 (1971).

62. *Everson v. Board of Education,* 330 U.S. 1 (1947); *Zorach v. Clauson,* 343 U.S. 306 (1952); *Walz v. Tax Commission of New York,* 397 U.S. 664 (1970).

63. In addition to the cases cited in refs. 60–63, *see also* the following: *Illinois ex. rel. McCollum v. Board of Education,* 333 U.S. 203 (1948); *Abington School District v. Schempp,* 374 U.S. 203 (1963); *Engel v. Vitale,* 370 U.S. 421 (1962); *Board of Education v. Allen,* 392 U.S. 236 (1968); *Epperson v. Arkansas,* 393 U.S. 97 (1968); *Committee for Public Education v. Nyquist,* 413 U.S. 756 (1973).

64. *Wolman v. Walter,* 97 S. Ct. 2593 (1977).

65. *Roemer v. Maryland,* 96 S. Ct. 2337 (1976).

66. *McGown v. Maryland,* 366 U.S. 420 (1961).

67. *Cantwell v. Connecticut,* 310 U.S. 296 (1940); *Davis v. Beason,* 133 U.S. 333 (1890); *Jones v. Opelika,* 319 U.S. 103 (1943); *Niemotko v. Maryland,* 340 U.S. 268 (1951); *Wisconsin v. Yoder,* 406 U.S. 205 (1972); *United States v. Seeger,* 380 U.S. 163 (1965); *Gillette v. United States,* 401 U.S. 437 (1971); *Welsh v. United States,* 398 U.S. 333 (1970); *Clay v. United States,* 403 U.S. 698 (1971); *Fein v. Selective Service,* 405 U.S. 365 (1972); statute quoted is 50 App. U.S.C. 456 (j).

68. *West Virginia State Board of Education v. Barnette,* 319 U.S. 624 (1943).

69. *Wooley v. Maynard,* 97 S. Ct. 1428 (1977).

CHAPTER FOUR In the Dock: Rights of Criminal Procedure

1. Quoted from A. E. Dick Howard, *Magna Carta: Text and Commentary* (Charlottesville, Va.: University Press of Virginia, Magna Carta Commission of Virginia, 1964), 40, 43; quotations are from chapters 20, 39, and 40 of the original (1215 A.D.) version. I have modified Howard's translation by substituting "punished" for "amerced" and "dispossessed" for "disseised." Of the extensive literature on the Magna Carta *see especially* the following: W. S. McKechnie, *Magna Carta* (Glasgow: Maclehose, 1914; repr. ed., New York: Burt Franklin, 1958); Faith Thompson, *The First Century of Magna Carta* (University of Minnesota Press, 1925) and *Magna Carta: Its Role in the Making of the English Constitution 1300–1629* (University of Minnesota Press, 1948); J. C. Holt, *Magna Carta* (Cambridge University Press, 1965); A. E. Dick Howard, *The Road from Runnymede: Magna*

Carta and Constitutionalism in America (Charlottesville, Va.: University Press of Virginia, 1968).

2. Quoted from R. J. White, ed., *The Political Thought of Samuel Taylor Coleridge: A Selection* (London: Jonathan Cape, 1938), 235.

3. Quoted from Josh Billings [pseudonym of Henry Wheeler Shaw], *Complete Works of Josh Billings* (New York: G. W. Carleton & Co., 1876; repr. ed., Chicago & New York: M. A. Donohue & Co., n.d.), 228. I am indebted to Professor David B. Kesterson for this citation. *See* his study, *Josh Billings (Henry Wheeler Shaw)* (New York: Twayne Publishers, Inc., 1973).

4. Anonymous, "An Honest Confession May be Good for the Soul, but not for the FBI," in Hall, Kamisar, LaFave, Israel, eds., *Modern Criminal Procedure* (St. Paul, Minn.: West Publishing Co., 1969), 461–62.

5. *Miranda* v. *State of Arizona,* 384 U.S. 436 (1966).

6. Miranda's confession is reprinted in full in Alan H. Schechter, *Contemporary Constitutional Issues* (New York: McGraw-Hill Book Co., 1972), 97; *see also* Otis H. Stephens, Jr., *The Supreme Court and Confessions of Guilt* (Knoxville: University of Tennessee Press, 1973), *esp.* chaps. 6–7.

7. Stephens, *The Supreme Court and Confessions of Guilt,* 188–91.

8. *Doyle* v. *Ohio,* 96 S. Ct. 2240 (1976).

9. *Michigan* v. *Mosley,* 432 U.S. 96 (1975).

10. Sir John Fortescue, *De Laudibus Legum Angliae* (1468–1471; "In Praise of the Laws of England"), chap. 27 at 93. Quoted from Edward S. Corwin, *The "Higher Law" Background of American Constitutional Law* (Ithaca, N.Y.: Cornell University Press, Great Seal Books, 1955), 37n. Sir John Fortescue was Lord Chief Justice of the King's Bench under King Henry VI.

11. *See* Aleksandr I. Solzhenitsyn's several works, especially *The Gulag Archipelago,* trans. Thomas P. Whitney, 3 vols. (New York: Harper & Row, 1973–). *Cf.* S. Wolin and R. M. Slusser, eds., *The Soviet Secret Police* (New York: Praeger, 1957). André Bonnichon, *Law in Communist China* (The Hague, 1956) as quoted in Jerome Cohen, *The Criminal Process in the People's Republic of China 1949–1963* (Cambridge, Mass.: Harvard University Press, 1968), 368–72. Those overwrought about police brutality in the United States are directed especially to "The Interrogation," *Gulag Archipelago,* 1:93–143; *also,* Ludmilla Thorne, "Mother Courage: How Vladimir Bukovsky Was Saved,"

New York Times Magazine (Feb. 27, 1977), 38–40, 52–3; *Time Magazine,* 109 (Mar. 7, 1977), 10–12.

12. *Terminiello* v. *City of Chicago,* 337 U.S. 1 (1949), dissenting opinion of Justice Jackson.
13. *Whitney* v. *California,* 274 U.S. 357 (1927), concurring opinion of Justice Brandeis in which Justice Holmes joined.
14. Constitution, ART. I, SEC. 9, CL. 2 (*see* append. B); *Ex parte Watkins,* 28 U.S. [3 Pet.] 193 (1830).
15. *See* Thomas M. Cooley, *A Treatise on the Constitutional Limitations* (1868; repr. ed., New York: Da Capo Press, 1972), 342–45.
16. *Brown* v. *Allen,* 344 U.S. 443 (1953); *Fay* v. *Noia,* 372 U.S. 391 (1963); *Preiser* v. *Rodriguez,* 411 U.S. 475 (1973).
17. *Stone* v. *Powell* and *Wolff* v. *Rice,* 96 S. Ct. 3037 (1976).
18. *Mapp* v. *Ohio,* 367 U.S. 643 (1961), overruling *Wolf* v. *Colorado,* 388 U.S. 25 (1949). *Cf. Rochin* v. *Calif.,* 342 U.S. 165 (1952).
19. *United States* v. *Calandra,* 414 U.S. 338 (1974).
20. *United States* v. *Robinson,* 414 U.S. 218 (1973); *Giordenello* v. *United States,* 357 U.S. 480 (1958); *Gustafson* v. *Florida,* 94 S. Ct. 488 (1973); *Terry* v. *Ohio,* 392 U.S. 1 (1968); *Chimel* v. *California,* 395 U.S. 752 (1969).
21. *United States* v. *Janis,* 96 S. Ct. 3021 (1976). *Cf. Byars* v. *United States,* 273 U.S. 28 (1928); *Elkins* v. *United States,* 364 U.S. 206 (1960), for the "silver-platter" doctrine.
22. *Miranda* v. *Arizona,* 384 U.S. 439 (1966); *Escobedo* v. *Illinois,* 378 U.S. 748 (1964). *Cf. Harris* v. *New York,* 91 S. Ct. 643 (1971); *Oregon* v. *Hass,* 95 S. Ct. 1215 (1975); *Oregon* v. *Mathiason,* 97 S. Ct. 711 (1977).
23. *Giordenello* v. *United States,* 357 U.S. 480 (1958); *Beck* v. *Ohio,* 379 U.S. 89 (1965).
24. *Hurtado* v. *California,* 110 U.S. 516 (1884).
25. *Hurtado* v. *California,* 110 U.S. 516 (1884).
26. Cooley, *A Treatise on Constitutional Limitations,* 319 n; Joseph Storey, *Commentaries on the Constitution of the United States* (Boston, 1883), Sec. 1757. *Cf. Williams* v. *Florida,* 399 U.S. 78 at 92–96 (1970). ART. III, SEC. 2, CL. 3, reads: "The trial of all Crimes, except in Cases of Impeachment, shall be by jury. . . ."
27. *Gideon* v. *Wainwright,* 372 U.S. 335 (1963); *Duncan* v. *Louisiana,* 391 U.S. 145 (1968).
28. *Benton* v. *Maryland,* 395 U.S. 784 (1969).
29. *Ross* v. *Moffitt,* 417 U.S. 600 (1974).
30. *Kirby* v. *Illinois,* 404 U.S. 1055 (1972).

31. *Wilkerson* v. *Utah,* 99 U.S. 130 (1878); *In re Kemmler,* 136 U.S. 436 (1890); *Weems* v. *United States,* 217 U.S. 349 (1910); *Robinson* v. *California,* 370 U.S. 660 (1962).
32. *Furman* v. *Georgia,* 408 U.S. 238 (1972).
33. Quoted from Justice Brennan's dissent to the decisions in *Gregg, Jurek,* and *Profitt. See* Ref. 34 below, S. Ct. 2971 (1976). The internal quote is from Justice Tuttle's opinion in *Novak* v. *Beto,* 453 F. 2d 661, 672 (CA5 1971).
34. *Gregg* v. *Georgia,* 96 S. Ct. 2909 (1976). Other death penalty cases decided on the same day (July 2, 1976) were: *Jurek* v. *Texas,* 96 S. Ct. 2950; *Profitt* v. *Florida,* 96 S. Ct. 2960; *Woodson* v. *North Carolina,* 96 S. Ct. 2978; *Roberts* v. *Louisiana,* 96 S. Ct. 3001.
35. Source of historical data is Warren Weaver, Jr., "Death Penalty a 300-Year Issue in America," New York *Times,* July 3, 1976, p. 7.
36. *Time* Magazine, 109 (Jan. 24, 1977), 52.

CHAPTER FIVE The Civil Rights Revolution: A New Birth of Freedom?

1. Quoted from Charles C. Tansill, ed., *Documents Illustrative of the Formation of the Union of the American States,* 69th Congress, 1st Session, House Document No. 398 (Washington, D.C.: Government Printing Office, 1927), 22. *See* Appendix A.
2. "Gettysburg Address," November 19, 1863, quoted from Mortimer J. Adler and William Gorman, eds., *The American Testament* (New York: Praeger Publishers, 1975), 119.
3. "First Inaugural Address," March 4, 1861, quoted from Richard N. Current, ed., *The Political Thought of Abraham Lincoln* (Indianapolis, Ind.: Bobbs-Merrill Co., Inc., American Heritage Series, 1967), 175–76.
4. *Brown* v. *Board of Education* [*Brown I*], 347 U.S. 483 (1954); the other cases decided at the same time carry the same citation: *Briggs* v. *Elliott, Davis* v. *County School Board, Gebhart* v. *Belton;* also decided the same day was the case from the District of Columbia, *Bolling* v. *Sharpe,* 347 U.S. 497 (1954).
5. *Youngstown Sheet & Tube Co.* v. *Sawyer,* 343 U.S. 579 (1952). Truman seized the steel industry in the name of Charles Sawyer, his Secretary of Commerce.
6. *Plessy* v. *Ferguson,* 163 U.S. 537 (1896), a case affirming the

constitutionality of segregating passengers on railway cars. The first use of the "separate but equal" doctrine was in *Roberts* v. *City of Boston,* 59 Mass. 198 (1849).

7. This account is drawn mainly from William A. Harbaugh's excellent study, *Lawyer's Lawyer: The Life of John W. Davis* (New York: Oxford University Press, 1973), chap. 28; the Bickel quotation is given at *ibid.,* 516 and is cited from Alexander M. Bickel, *The Least Dangerous Branch: The Supreme Court at the Bar of Politics* (Indianapolis, Ind.: Bobbs-Merrill, 1962), 249; cf. Daniel M. Berman, *It Is So Ordered: The Supreme Court Rules on School Segregation* (New York: W. W. Norton Co., 1966); G. Theodore Mitau, *Decade of Decision: The Supreme Court and the Constitutional Revolution, 1954–1964* (New York: Charles Scribner's Sons, 1967); Francis M. Wilhoit, *The Politics of Massive Resistance* (New York: George Braziller, 1973); Charles V. Hamilton, *The Bench and the Ballot: Southern Federal Judges and Black Voters* (New York: Oxford University Press, 1973).

8. *Dred Scott* v. *Sandford,* 60 U.S. [19 How.] 393 (1857). In declaring the Missouri Compromise (Act of March 6, 1820, 3 STAT. 548, SEC. 8, proviso) unconstitutional by a seven-to-two majority, the Court held Congress's action not warranted as a regulation of territory belonging to the United States under ART. IV, SEC. 3, CL. 2 or permissible under terms of the Fifth Amendment of the Constitution. This was only the second time the Court had declared an act of Congress unconstitutional. Congress meanwhile had itself repealed the Missouri Compromise through adoption of the Kansas-Nebraska Act on May 25, 1854.

9. *Slaughter-House Cases,* 83 U.S. [16 Wall.] 36 (1873).

10. *Brown* v. *Board of Education of Topeka* [*Brown I*] 347 U.S. 483 (1954).

11. *Brown* v. *Board of Education of Topeka* [*Brown II*], 349 U.S. 294 (1955).

12. *Swann* v. *Charlotte-Mecklenburg Board of Education,* 402 U.S. 1 (1971) *Green* v. *County School Board,* 391 U.S. 430 (1968).

13. *Swann* v. *Charlotte-Mecklenburg Board of Education,* 402 U.S. 1 (1971).

14. *Keyes* v. *School District No. 1, Denver, Colorado,* 413 U.S. 189 (1973).

15. "*Milliken I,*" *Milliken* v. *Bradley,* 418 U.S. 717 (1974). For a detailed account of the *Keyes* and *Milliken* cases and a scathing critique of the whole desegregation effort of the Court *see* Lino

A. Graglia, *Disaster by Decree: The Supreme Court Decisions on Race and the Schools* (Ithaca and London: Cornell University Press, 1976), *esp.* chaps. 10 and 11; *see* p. 203. *See "Milliken II," Milliken* v. *Bradley*, 97 S. Ct. 2749 (1977).

16. *Runyon* v. *McCrary*, 96 S. Ct. 2586 (1976).
17. *Pasadena City Board of Education* v. *Spangler*, 96 S. Ct. 2697 (1976).
18. These provisions are retained in 42 U.S.C.
19. 18 U.S.C. Sec. 242, drawn from the 1866 and 1870 Acts as modified by the 1968 Civil Rights Act.
20. *Cf.* 18 U.S.C. Sec. 241 which is the basis of *United States* v. *Guest*, 383 U.S. 745 (1966). *See* pp. 209–210.
21. *Cf.* 42 U.S.C. Sec. 1983 and 1985 (3); *Monroe* v. *Pape*, 365 U.S. 167 (1961), *Collins* v. *Hardyman*, 341 U.S. 651 (1951), and *Griffin* v. *Breckenridge*, 403 U.S. 88 (1971).
22. James C. Davies, "The J-Curve of Rising and Declining Satisfactions as a Cause of Some Great Revolutions and a Contained Rebellion," in Hugh D. Graham and Ted Robert Gurr, eds., *Violence in America: Historical and Comparative Perspectives,* A Report to the National Commission of the Causes and Prevention of Violence, 2 vols. (Washington, D.C.: U.S. Government Printing Office, 1969), 2:567.
23. E. Merton Coulter, *The South During Reconstruction, 1865–1877* (Baton Rouge, La.: Louisiana State University Press, 1957), 169. *Cf.* 42 U.S.C. Sections 1981 and 1982; the latter Section is the basis of the Court's decision in *Jones* v. *Alfred H. Mayer Co.* (393 U.S. 409 [1968]), p. 211.
24. *Civil Rights Cases,* 109 U.S. 3 (1883).
25. This thumbnail sketch relies principally on the sources cited in refs. 22–24 as well as the following: Wilhoit, *Politics of Massive Resistance,* chap. 1; Samuel Eliot Morison and Henry Steele Commager, *The Growth of the American Republic,* 2 vols., 4th ed. (New York: Oxford University Press, 1950), 2: chap. 23; Richard B. Sherman, *The Republican Party and Black America: From McKinley to Hoover, 1896–1933* (Charlottesville, Va.: University Press of Virginia, 1973), chap. 7; the Nov. 20, 1922 NAACP advertisement in the New York *Times* is quoted from *ibid.,* 194. For a balanced and concise discussion see Morison and Commager, *Growth of the American Republic,* 2:1–55; bibliography is given in ibid., 829–34.
26. *See* August Meier and Elliott Rudwick, *CORE: A Study of the*

Civil Rights Movement, 1942–1968 (New York: Oxford University Press, 1973); Edward J. Bacciocco, Jr., *The New Left in America: Reform to Revolution, 1956 to 1970* (Stanford, Ca.: Hoover Institution Press, 1974); Joe R. Feagin and Harlan Hahn, *Ghetto Revolts: The Politics of Violence in American Cities* (New York: Macmillan Pub. Co., 1973).

27. *Contractors Association v. Secretary of Labor*, 404 U.S. 854, *certiorari denied* (1971); *Griggs v. Duke Power Co.*, 401 U.S. 424 (1971); *McDonnell Douglas Corp. v. Green*, 411 U.S. 792 (1973); cf. *Bitzer v. Matthews* and *Fitzpatrick v. Bitzer*, 96 S. Ct. 2666 (1976); *Washington v. Davis*, 96 S. Ct. 2040 (1976); *McDonald v. Santa Fe Transportation Co.*, 96 S. Ct. 2574 (1976).

28. *Reynolds v. Sims*, 377 U.S. 533 (1964).

29. *Kramer v. Union Free School District*, 395 U.S. 621 (1969).

30. *Guinn v. United States*, 238 U.S. 347 (1915).

31. *Lane v. Wilson*, 307 U.S. 268 (1939).

32. *Smith v. Allwright*, 321 U.S. 649 (1944).

33. *Davis v. Schnell*, 336 U.S. 933 (1949).

34. *Oregon v. Mitchell*, 400 U.S. 112 (1970).

35. *South Carolina v. Katzenbach*, 383 U.S. 301 (1966).

36. *Katzenbach v. Morgan*, 383 U.S. 641 (1966).

37. *Oregon v. Mitchell*, 400 U.S. 112 (1970).

38. *Harper v. Virginia Board of Elections*, 383 U.S. 663 (1966).

39. W. L. Riordan, *Plunkitt of Tammany Hall* (New York: McClure, Phillips, 1905), 38–9; Paul T. David and Ralph Eisenberg, *Devaluation of the Urban and Suburban Vote* (Charlottesville, Va.: University of Virginia Bureau of Public Administration, 1961).

40. *Colegrove v. Green*, 328 U.S. 549 (1946); *see* the discussion and relevant literature in C. Herman Pritchett, *The American Constitution* (3rd ed.; New York: McGraw-Hill Book Co., 1977), 60–67.

41. *Baker v. Carr*, 369 U.S. 186 (1962).

42. *Wesberry v. Sanders*, 376 U.S. 1 (1964).

43. *Reynolds v. Sims*, 377 U.S. 553 (1964).

44. *Hadley v. Junior College District*, 397 U.S. 50 (1970).

45. *Mahan v. Howell*, 410 U.S. 315 (1973); *see also Connor v. Finch*, 97 S. Ct. 1828 (1977).

46. *Kirkpatrick v. Preisler*, 394 U.S. 526 (1969); *White v. Weiser*, 412 U.S. 783 (1973).

47. *Gomillion v. Lightfoot*, 364 U.S. 339 (1960).

48. *Gaffney* v. *Cummings*, 412 U.S. 735 (1973); *Burns* v. *Richardson*, 384 U.S. 73 (1966); *Whitcomb* v. *Chavis*, 403 U.S. 124 (1971).
49. *White* v. *Regester*, 412 U.S. 755 (1973); *cf.* two recent decisions in this regard, *City of Richmond* v. *United States*, 422 U.S. 358 (1975); *Beer* v. *United States*, 96 S. Ct. 1357 (1976).
50. From among the numerous cases, *see Strauder* v. *West Virginia*, 100 U.S. 313 (1880); *Hernandez* v. *Texas*, 347 U.S. 475 (1954); *Alexander* v. *Louisiana*, 405 U.S. 625 (1972).
51. *Buchanan* v. *Warley*, 245 U.S. 60 (1971); *Shelley* v. *Kraemer*, 334 U.S. 1 (1948).
52. *Reitman* v. *Mulkey*, 387 U.S. 369 (1967).
53. *Gayle* v. *Browder*, 352 U.S. 904 (1956) overruling *Plessy* v. *Ferguson*, 164 U.S. 537 (1896); *Bailey* v. *Patterson*, 369 U.S. 31 (1962).
54. *Mayor and City Council of Baltimore* v. *Dawson*, 350 U.S. 877 (1955); *Evans* v. *Abney*, 396 U.S. 435 (1970); *Palmer* v. *Thompson*, 403 U.S. 217 (1971).
55. *Loving* v. *Virginia*, 388 U.S. 1 (1967); *McLaughlin* v. *Florida*, 379 U.S. 184 (1964).
56. Title II, 78 Stat. 243, 42 U.S.C. Sec. 2000a *et seq. See Hamm* v. *City of Rock Hill*, 379 U.S. 306 (1964).
57. *Civil Rights Cases*, 109 U.S. 3 (1883). *See* pp. 189–91.
58. *Terry* v. *Adams*, 345 U.S. 461 (1953).
59. *Ex parte Virginia*, 100 U.S. 339 (1880).
60. *United States* v. *Guest*, 383 U.S. 745 (1966).
61. *Griffin* v. *Breckenridge*, 403 U.S. 88 (1971).
62. *Jones* v. *Alfred H. Mayer Co.*, 392 U.S. 409 (1968).
63. *McDonald* v. *Santa Fe Transportation Co.*, 96 S. Ct. 2574 (1976). *See also Trans World Airlines, Inc.* v. *Hardison*, 97 S. Ct. 2264 (1977).
64. *Regents of the University of California* v. *Allan Bakke*, 97 S. Ct. 1098 (1977), *certiorari* granted; Alexander Bickel, *The Morality of Consent* (New Haven, Ct.: Yale University Press, 1975), 133.
65. *Strauder* v. *West Virginia*, 100 U.S. 303 (1880).
66. *Taylor* v. *Louisiana*, 419 U.S. 522 (1975) and *Peters* v. *Kiff*, 407 U.S. 493 (1972), respectively.
67. *Yick Wo* v. *Hopkins*, 118 U.S. 356 (1886).
68. *Milliken* v. *Bradley*, 418 U.S. 717 (1974). *See* the earlier discussion and citations at notes 1–17, pp. 171–86.

69. *Keyes* v. *School District No. 1,* 413 U.S. 189 at 200.
70. *Swann* v. *Charlotte-Mecklenburg Board of Education,* 402 U.S. 1 at 18; quoted in *Keyes* at 209.
71. *Green* v. *County School Board,* 391 U.S. 430 at 437–8; quoted in *Keyes* at 201 note 11.
72. *Palmer* v. *Thompson,* 403 U.S. 217 at 224 (1971) as quoted by Justice Powell in *Keyes* at 233–4.
73. Justice Powell concurring in part and dissenting in part in *Keyes* at 231–2 and quoting *Wright* v. *Council of the City of Emporia, Virginia,* 407 U.S. 451 (1972) at 462; internal quote from *Davis* v. *School Commissioners of Mobile Co.,* 402 U.S. 33 (1971) at 37.
74. *Keyes* at 224 note 10.
75. *Washington* v. *Davis,* 96 S. Ct. 2040 (1976). Justice White's majority opinion has the effect, in part, of rebutting Justice Powell's arguments in the latter's separate opinion to the *Keyes* decision, discussed above.
76. *Village of Arlington Heights* v. *Metropolitan Housing Development Corp.,* 97 S. Ct. 555 (1977). *See also Dayton Board of Education* v. *Brinkman,* 97 S. Ct. 2766 (1977).
77. *General Electric Co.* v. *Gilbert,* 97 S. Ct. 401 (1976).
78. *Washington* v. *Davis,* 96 S. Ct. 2040 at 2054 (1976); *see also Dothard* v. *Rawlinson,* 97 S. Ct. 2720 (1977) which reaffirmed the test of "discriminatory pattern" in cases brought under Civil Rights Act of 1964, Sec. 701, as sufficient to establish a *prima facie* case of sex-based discrimination.
79. *Green* v. *County School Board,* 391 U.S. 430 (1968); "*Milliken I,*" *Milliken* v. *Bradley,* 418 U.S. 717 (1974); "*Milliken II,*" *Milliken* v. *Bradley,* 97 S. Ct. 2749 (1977).
80. *Lindsley* v. *National Carbonic Gas Co.,* 220 U.S. 61 (1911).
81. Ibid.
82. *F. S. Royster Guano Co.* v. *Virginia,* 253 U.S. 412 (1920).
83. *San Antonio Independent School District* v. *Rodriguez,* 411 U.S. 1 (1973).
84. Robert J. Harris, *The Quest for Equality* (Baton Rouge, La.: Louisiana State University Press, 1960), 59.
85. Robert G. Dixon, Jr., "The Supreme Court and Equality: Legislative Classifications, Desegregation, and Reverse Discrimination," *Cornell Law Review,* 62 (March, 1977), 501.
86. *Korematsu* v. *United States,* 323 U.S. 214 (1944); *see* Dixon, "The Supreme Court and Equality," 504.

87. *Dunn* v. *Blumstein,* 405 U.S. 330 (1972), Chief Justice Burger dissenting.
88. Dixon, "The Supreme Court and Equality," 517.
89. *Vlandis* v. *Klein,* 412 U.S. 441 (1973).
90. *Dept. of Agriculture* v. *Murry,* 413 U.S. 508 (1973); *Cleveland Board of Education* v. *LaFleur,* 414 U.S. 632 (1974).
91. *Storer* v. *Brown,* 415 U.S. 724 (1974); *American Party of Texas* v. *White,* 415 U.S. 767 (1974); *Sosna* v. *Iowa,* 419 U.S. 393 (1975).
92. *Storer* at 759, Justice Brennan, dissenting.
93. Ibid. at 730, citing *Williams* v. *Rhodes,* 393 U.S. 23 (1968); and *Dunn* v. *Blumstein,* 405 U.S. 330 (1972).
94. Dixon, "The Supreme Court and Equality," 501; *see* the discussion ibid., 525–33.
95. *Craig* v. *Boren,* 97 S. Ct. 451 (1976) at 457.
96. *Califano* v. *Goldfarb,* 97 S. Ct. 1021 (1977). *See also Linmark Assoc., Inc.* v. *Township of Willingboro,* 97 S. Ct. 1614 (1977), a First Amendment case applying the "important governmental objective" test on the way to rejecting the township's contentions and finding a violation of protected commercial speech.
97. *Weinsberger* v. *Salfi,* 422 U.S. 749 (1975).
98. *Murgia* v. *Mass. Board of Retirement,* 96 S. Ct. 2562 (1976).
99. Dixon, "The Supreme Court and Equality," 524 n.

CONCLUSION Citizenship, Liberty, and the American Prospect

1. Quoted from Alexis de Tocqueville, *Democracy in America,* 2 vols., ed. J. P. Mayer, trans. George Lawrence (New York: Harper & Row, 1966; repr. ed., Garden City, N.Y.: Doubleday & Co., Anchor Books, 1969), 2:705.
2. Quoted from "Address at Sanitary Fair," April 18, 1864, as given in Ralph B. Winn, ed., *A Concise Lincoln Dictionary: Thoughts and Statements* (New York: Philosophical Library, 1959), 65–66.
3. Quoted from Letter of Taft to William Kent, June 29, 1909, Taft Letterbook, Series 8 [Secretary of War, Presidential, & Yale], Taft Papers, as given in Donald F. Anderson, *William Howard Taft: A Conservative's Conception of the Presidency* (Ithaca & London: Cornell University Press, 1973), 59. Taft, a Republican from Connecticut, was the twenty-seventh President of the United States from 1909 to 1913 and the tenth Chief Justice of the United States from 1921 to 1930.

4. *Knauer v. United States,* 328 U.S. 654 (1946); *Osborn v. Bank of the United States,* 22 U.S. [9 Wheat.] 737 (1824).

5. 8 *United States Code* 1481.

6. *Afroyim v. Rusk,* 387 U.S. 253 (1967). *Cf. Rogers v. Bellei,* 401 U.S. 815 (1971).

7. *Crowley v. Christensen,* 137 U.S. 86 (1890); *Jacobsen v. Massachusetts,* 197 U.S. 11 (1904). Cf. Raoul Berger, *Government By the Judiciary: the Transformation of the Fourteenth Amendment* (Cambridge, Mass.: Harvard University Press, 1977).

8. *Constitution,* ART. II, SEC. 1, CL. 8; ART VI, CL. 3.

9. Plato, *Crito* (51b-c), trans. Hugh Tredennick.

10. Winston Churchill, quoted from a speech in the House of Commons, November 11, 1947, as given in Dorothy Price and Dean Walley, eds., *Never Give In! The Challenging Words of Winston Churchill* (Kansas City, Mo.: Hallmark Editions, 1967), 49–50.

11. Maurice Cranston, "Destiny of Democracy," London *Times Literary Supplement,* June 4, 1976, p. 669.

12. Jean-Jacques Rousseau, *The Social Contract,* bk. I, chap. 7 (1762).

13. James Bryce, *The American Commonwealth,* 2 vols., New ed. (New York: Macmillan Co., 1921), vol. 2, chap. 84, p. 338.

Appendix A
THE DECLARATION OF INDEPENDENCE—1776*
In Congress, July 4, 1776
The Unanimous Declaration of the Thirteen United States of America

When in the Course of human events, it becomes necessary for one people to dissolve the political bands which have connected them with another, and to assume among the powers of the earth, the separate and equal station to which the Laws of Nature and of Nature's God entitle them, a decent respect to the opinions of mankind requires that they should declare the causes which impel them to the separation.—We hold these truths to be self-evident, that all men are created equal, that they are endowed by their Creator with certain unalienable Rights, that among these are Life, Liberty and the pursuit of Happiness.—That to secure these rights, Governments are instituted among Men, deriving their just powers from the consent of the governed,—That whenever any Form of Government becomes destructive of these ends, it is the Right of the People to alter or to abolish it, and to institute new Government, laying its foundation on such principles and organizing its powers in such form, as to them shall seem most likely to effect their Safety and Happiness. Prudence, indeed, will dictate that Governments long established should not be changed for light and transient causes; and accordingly all experience hath shown, that mankind are more disposed to suffer, while evils are sufferable, than to right themselves by abolishing the forms to which they are accustomed. But when a long train of abuses and usurpations, pursuing invariably the same Object evinces a design to reduce them under absolute Despotism, it is their right, it is their duty, to throw off such Government, and to provide new Guards for their future security.—Such has been the patient sufferance of these Colonies; and such is now the necessity which constrains them to alter their

---

* Printed from the facsimile of the engrossed copy of the original manuscript in the Library of Congress.

former Systems of Government. The history of the present King of Great Britain is a history of repeated injuries and usurpations, all having in direct object the establishment of an absolute Tyranny over these States. To prove this, let Facts be submitted to a candid world.—He has refused his Assent to Laws, the most wholesome and necessary for the public good.—He has forbidden his Governors to pass Laws of immediate and pressing importance, unless suspended in their operation till his Assent should be obtained; and when so suspended, he has utterly neglected to attend to them.—He has refused to pass other Laws for the accommodation of large districts of people, unless those people would relinquish the right of Representation in the Legislature, a right inestimable to them and formidable to tyrants only.—He has called together legislative bodies at places unusual, uncomfortable, and distant from the depository of their public Records, for the sole purpose of fatiguing them into compliance with his measures.—He has dissolved Representative Houses repeatedly, for opposing with manly firmness his invasions on the rights of the people.—He has refused for a long time, after such dissolutions, to cause others to be elected; whereby the Legislative powers, incapable of Annihilation, have returned to the People at large for their exercise; the State remaining in the mean time exposed to all the dangers of invasion from without, and convulsions within.—He has endeavoured to prevent the population of these States; for that purpose obstructing the Laws for Naturalization of Foreigners; refusing to pass others to encourage their migration hither, and raising the conditions of new Appropriations of Lands.—He has obstructed the Administration of Justice, by refusing his Assent to Laws for establishing Judiciary powers.—He has made Judges dependent on his Will alone, for the tenure of their offices, and the amount and payment of their salaries.—He has erected a multitude of New Offices, and sent hither swarms of Officers to harrass our people, and eat out their substance.—He has kept among us, in times of peace, Standing Armies, without the Consent of our legislatures.—He has affected to render the Military independent of and superior to the Civil power.—He has combined with others to subject us to a jurisdiction foreign to our constitution, and unacknowledged by our laws; giving his Assent to their Acts of pretended Legislation:—For quartering large bodies of armed troops among us:—For protecting them, by a mock Trial, from punishment for any Murders which they should commit on the Inhabitants of these States:—For imposing Taxes on us without our Consent:—For depriving us in many cases, of the benefits of Trial by Jury:—For transporting us beyond Seas to be tried for pretended offences: —For abolishing the free System of English Laws in a neighbouring Province, establishing therein an Arbitrary government, and enlarging its Boundaries so as to render it at once an example and fit instrument for introducing the same absolute rule into these Colonies:—For taking away our Charters, abolishing our most valuable Laws, and altering fundamentally the Forms of our Governments:—For suspending our own Legislatures, and declaring themselves invested with power to legislate for us in all cases whatsoever.—He has abdicated Government here, by declaring us out of his Protection and waging War against us.—He has plundered our seas, ravaged our Coasts, burnt our towns, and destroyed the lives of our people.—He is at this time transporting large Armies of foreign Mercenaries to compleat the works of death, desolation and tyranny, already begun with circumstances of Cruelty & perfidy scarcely paralleled in the most barbarous ages, and totally unworthy the Head of a civilized nation.—He has constrained our fellow Citizens taken Captive on the high Seas to bear Arms against their Country, to become the executioners of their friends and Brethren, or to fall themselves by their Hands.—He has excited domestic insurrections amongst us, and has endeavoured to bring on the inhabitants of our frontiers, the merciless Indian Savages, whose known rule of warfare, is an undistinguished destruction of all ages, sexes and conditions. In every stage of these Oppressions We have Petitioned for Redress in the most humble terms: Our repeated Petitions have been answered only by repeated injury. A Prince, whose character is thus marked by every act which may define a Tyrant, is unfit to be the ruler of a free people. Nor have We been wanting in attentions to our British brethren. We have warned them from time to time of attempts by their legislature to extend an unwarrantable jurisdiction over us. We have reminded them of the circumstances of our emigration and settlement here. We have appealed to their native justice and magnanimity, and we have conjured them by the ties of our common kindred to disavow these usurpations, which, would inevitably interrupt our connections and correspondence. They too have been deaf to the voice of justice and of consanguinity. We must, therefore, acquiesce in the necessity, which denounces our Separation, and hold them, as we hold the rest of mankind, Enemies in War, in Peace Friends.—

WE, THEREFORE, the REPRESENTATIVES of the UNITED STATES OF AMERICA, in General Congress, Assembled, appealing to the Supreme Judge of the world for the rectitude of our intentions, do, in the Name, and by Authority of the good People of these Colonies, solemnly publish and declare, That these United Colonies are, and of Right ought to be FREE AND INDEPENDENT STATES; that they are Absolved from all Allegiance to the British Crown, and that all political connection between them and the State of Great Britain, is and ought to be totally dissolved; and that as Free and Independent States, they have full Power to levy War, conclude Peace, contract Alliances, establish Commerce, and to do all other Acts and Things which Independent States may of right do.—And for the support of this Declaration, with a firm reliance on the protection of Divine Providence, we mutually pledge to each other our Lives, our Fortunes and our sacred Honor.

JOHN HANCOCK.

[Signatories omitted]

Source: Charles C. Tansill, ed., *Documents Illustrative of the Formation of the Union of the American States* (Washington, D.C.: Government Printing Office, 1927), 22–25.

Appendix B
The Constitution of the
United States of America

We the People of the United States, in Order to form a more perfect Union, establish Justice, insure domestic Tranquility, provide for the common defense, promote the general Welfare, and secure the Blessings of Liberty to ourselves and our Posterity, do ordain and establish this Constitution for the United States of America.

Article I

Section 1. All legislative Powers herein granted shall be vested in a Congress of the United States, which shall consist of a Senate and House of Representatives.

Section 2. The House of Representatives shall be composed of Members chosen every second Year by the People of the several States, and the Electors in each State shall have the Qualifications requisite for Electors of the most numerous Branch of the State Legislature.

No Person shall be a Representative who shall not have attained to the age of twenty five Years, and been seven Years a Citizen of the United States, and who shall not, when elected, be an Inhabitant of that State in which he shall be chosen.

Representatives and direct Taxes shall be apportioned among the several States which may be included within this Union, according to their respective Numbers, *which shall be determined by adding to the whole Number of free Persons, including those bound to Service for a Term of Years, and excluding Indians not taxed, three fifths of all other persons.*[1] The actual Enumeration shall be made within three Years after the first Meeting of the Congress of the United States, and within every subsequent Term of ten Years, in such Manner as they shall by Law direct. The Number of Representatives shall not exceed one for every thirty Thousand, but each State shall have at Least one Representative; and until such enumeration shall be made, the State of New Hampshire

---

[1] Superseded by the 14th Amendment. Throughout, italics are used to indicate passages altered by subsequent amendments.

shall be entitled to chuse three, Massachusetts eight, Rhode-Island and Providence Plantations one, Connecticut five, New-York six, New Jersey four, Pennsylvania eight, Delaware one, Maryland six, Virginia ten, North Carolina five, South Carolina five, and Georgia three.

When vacancies happen in the Representation from any State, the Executive Authority thereof shall issue Writs of Election to fill such Vacancies.

The House of Representatives shall chuse their Speaker and other Officers; and shall have the sole Power of Impeachment.

Section 3. The Senate of the United States shall be composed of two Senators from each State, chosen by the *Legislature thereof,*[2] for six Years; and each Senator shall have one Vote.

Immediately after they shall be assembled in Consequence of the first Election, they shall be divided as equally as may be into three Classes. The Seats of the Senators of the first Class shall be vacated at the Expiration of the second Year, of the second Class at the Expiration of the fourth Year, and of the third Class at the Expiration of the sixth Year, so that one third may be chosen every second Year; *and if Vacancies happen by Resignation, or otherwise, during the Recess of the Legislature of any State, the Executive thereof may make temporary Appointments until the next Meeting of the Legislature, which shall then fill such Vacancies.*[3]

No Person shall be a Senator who shall not have attained to the Age of thirty Years, and been nine Years a Citizen of the United States, and who shall not, when elected, be an Inhabitant of the State for which he shall be chosen.

The Vice President of the United States shall be President of the Senate, but shall have no Vote, unless they be equally divided.

The Senate shall chuse their other Officers, and also a President pro tempore, in the Absence of the Vice President, or when he shall exercise the Office of President of the United States.

The Senate shall have the sole Power to try all Impeachments. When sitting for that Purpose, they shall be on Oath or Affirmation. When the President of the United States is tried, the Chief Justice shall preside: And no Person shall be convicted without the Concurrence of two thirds of the Members present.

Judgment in Cases of Impeachment shall not extend further than to removal from Office, and disqualification to hold and enjoy any Office of Honor, Trust or Profit under the United States: but the Party convicted shall nevertheless be liable and subject to Indictment, Trial, Judgment and Punishment, according to Law.

---

[2] See 17th Amendment.
[3] See 17th Amendment.

Section 4. The Times, Places and Manner of holding Elections for Senators and Representatives, shall be prescribed in each State by the Legislature thereof; but the Congress may at any time by Law make or alter such Regulations, except as to the Places of chusing Senators.

The Congress shall assemble at least once in every Year, and such Meeting shall be on the first Monday in December, unless they shall by Law appoint a different Day.[4]

Section 5. Each House shall be the Judge of the Elections, Returns and Qualifications of its own Members, and a Majority of each shall constitute a Quorum to do Business; but a smaller Number may adjourn from day to day, and may be authorized to compel the Attendance of absent Members, in such Manner, and under such Penalties as each House may provide.

Each House may determine the Rules of its Proceedings, punish its Members for disorderly Behaviour, and, with the Concurrence of two thirds, expel a Member.

Each House shall keep a Journal of its Proceedings, and from time to time publish the same, excepting such Parts as may in their Judgment require Secrecy; and the Yeas and Nays of the Members of either House on any question shall, at the Desire of one fifth of those Present, be entered on the Journal.

Neither House, during the Session of Congress, shall, without the Consent of the other, adjourn for more than three days, nor to any other Place than that in which the two Houses shall be sitting.

Section 6. The Senators and Representatives shall receive a Compensation for their Services, to be ascertained by Law, and paid out of the Treasury of the United States. They shall in all Cases, except Treason, Felony and Breach of the Peace, be privileged from Arrest during their Attendance at the Session of their respective Houses, and in going to and returning from the same; and for any Speech or Debate in either House, they shall not be questioned in any other Place.

No Senator or Representative shall, during the Time for which he was elected, be appointed to any civil Office under the Authority of the United States, which shall have been created, or the Emoluments whereof shall have been increased during such time; and no Person holding any Office under the United States, shall be a Member of either House during his Continuance in Office.

Section 7. All Bills for raising Revenue shall originate in the House of Representatives; but the Senate may propose or concur with Amendments as on other Bills.

Every Bill which shall have passed the House of Representatives and the Senate, shall, before it become a Law, be presented to the President

---

[4] See 20th Amendment.

of the United States; If he approve he shall sign it, but if not he shall return it, with his Objections to that House in which it shall have originated, who shall enter the Objections at large on their Journal, and proceed to reconsider it. If after such Reconsideration two thirds of that House shall agree to pass the Bill, it shall be sent, together with the Objections, to the other House, by which it shall likewise be reconsidered, and if approved by two thirds of that House, it shall become a Law. But in all such Cases the Votes of both Houses shall be determined by Yeas and Nays, and the Names of the Persons voting for and against the Bill shall be entered on the Journal of each House respectively. If any Bill shall not be returned by the President within ten days (Sundays excepted) after it shall have been presented to him, the Same shall be a Law, in like Manner as if he had signed it, unless the Congress by their Adjournment prevent its Return, in which case it shall not be a Law.

Every Order, Resolution, or Vote to which the Concurrence of the Senate and House of Representatives may be necessary (except on a question of Adjournment) shall be presented to the President of the United States; and before the Same shall take Effect, shall be approved by him, or being disapproved by him, shall be repassed by two thirds of the Senate and House of Representatives, according to the Rules and Limitations prescribed in the Case of a Bill.

Section 8. The Congress shall have Power To lay and collect Taxes, Duties, Imposts and Excises, to pay the Debts and provide for the common Defence and general Welfare of the United States; but all Duties, Imposts and Excises shall be uniform throughout the United States;

To borrow Money on the credit of the United States;

To regulate Commerce with foreign Nations, and among the several States, and with the Indian Tribes;

To establish an uniform Rule of Naturalization, and uniform Laws on the subject of Bankruptcies throughout the United States;

To coin Money, regulate the Value thereof, and of foreign Coin, and fix the Standard of Weights and Measures;

To provide for the Punishment of counterfeiting the Securities and current Coin of the United States;

To establish Post Offices and post Roads;

To promote the Progress of Science and useful Arts, by securing for limited Times to Authors and Inventors the exclusive Right to their respective Writings and Discoveries;

To constitute Tribunals inferior to the Supreme Court;

To define and punish Piracies and Felonies committed on the high Seas, and Offences against the Law of Nations;

To declare War, grant Letters of Marque and Reprisal, and make Rules concerning Captures on Land and Water;

To raise and support Armies, but no Appropriation of Money to that Use shall be for a longer Term than two Years;

To provide and maintain a Navy;

To make Rules for the Government and Regulation of the land and naval Forces;

To provide for calling forth the Militia to execute the Laws of the Union, suppress Insurrections and repel Invasions;

To provide for organizing, arming, and disciplining, the Militia, and for governing such Part of them as may be employed in the Service of the United States, reserving to the States respectively, the Appointment of the Officers, and the Authority of training the Militia according to the discipline prescribed by Congress;

To exercise exclusive Legislation in all Cases whatsoever, over such District (not exceeding ten Miles square) as may, by Cession of particular States, and the Acceptance of Congress, become the Seat of the Government of the United States, and to exercise like Authority over all Places purchased by the Consent of the Legislature of the State in which the Same shall be, for the Erection of Forts, Magazines, Arsenals, dock-Yards, and other needful Buildings;—And

To make all Laws which shall be necessary and proper for carrying into Execution the foregoing Powers, and all other Powers vested by this Constitution in the Government of the United States, or in any Department or Officer thereof.

Section 9. The Migration or Importation of such Persons as any of the States now existing shall think proper to admit, shall not be prohibited by the Congress prior to the Year one thousand eight hundred and eight, but a Tax or duty may be imposed on such Importation, not exceeding ten dollars for each Person.

The Privilege of the Writ of Habeas Corpus shall not be suspended, unless when in Cases of Rebellion or Invasion the public Safety may require it.

No Bill of Attainder or ex post facto Law shall be passed.

No Capitation, or other direct, Tax shall be laid, unless in Proportion to the Census or Enumeration herein before directed to be taken.

No Tax or Duty shall be laid on Articles exported from any State.

No Preference shall be given by any Regulation of Commerce or Revenue to the Ports of one State over those of another: nor shall Vessels bound to, or from, one State, be obliged to enter, clear, or pay Duties in another.

No Money shall be drawn from the Treasury, but in Consequence of Appropriations made by Law; and a regular Statement and Account of the Receipts and Expenditures of all public Money shall be published from time to time.

No Title of Nobility shall be granted by the United States: And no

Person holding any Office of Profit or Trust under them, shall, without the Consent of the Congress, accept of any present, Emolument, Office, or Title, of any kind whatever, from any King, Prince, or foreign State.

Section 10. No State shall enter into any Treaty, Alliance, or Confederation; grant letters of Marque and Reprisal; coin Money; emit Bills of Credit; make any Thing but gold and silver Coin a Tender in Payment of Debts; pass any Bill of Attainder, ex post facto Law, or Law impairing the Obligation of Contracts, or grant any Title of Nobility.

No State shall, without the Consent of the Congress, lay any Imposts or Duties on Imports or Exports, except what may be absolutely necessary for executing its inspection Laws: and the net Produce of all Duties and Imposts, laid by any State on Imports or Exports, shall be for the Use of the Treasury of the United States; and all such Laws shall be subject to the Revision and Controul of the Congress.

No State shall, without the Consent of Congress, lay any Duty of Tonnage, keep Troops, or Ships of War in time of Peace, enter into any Agreement or Compact with another State, or with a foreign Power, or engage in War, unless actually invaded, or in such imminent Danger as will not admit of delay.

Article II

Section 1. The executive Power shall be vested in a President of the United States of America. He shall hold his Office during the Term of four Years, and, together with the Vice President, chosen for the same Term, be elected, as follows:

Each State shall appoint, in such Manner as the Legislature thereof may direct, a Number of Electors, equal to the whole Number of Senators and Representatives to which the State may be entitled in the Congress: but no Senator or Representative, or Person holding an Office of Trust or Profit under the United States, shall be appointed an Elector.

The Electors shall meet in their respective States, and vote by Ballot for two Persons, of whom one at least shall not be an Inhabitant of the same State with themselves. And they shall make a List of all the Persons voted for, and of the Number of Votes for each; which List they shall sign and certify, and transmit sealed to the Seat of the Government of the United States, directed to the President of the Senate. The President of the Senate shall, in the Presence of the Senate and House of Representatives, open all the Certificates, and the Votes shall then be counted. The Person having the greatest Number of Votes shall be the President, if such Number be a Majority of the whole Number of Electors appointed; and if there be more than one who have such Majority, and have an equal Number of Votes, then the House of Representatives shall immediately chuse by Ballot one of them for President; and if no Person have a Majority, then from the five highest on the List the said House shall in like Manner chuse the President. But in chusing the President, the Votes shall be taken by States, the Representation from each State having one Vote: A quorum for this Purpose shall consist of a Member or Members from two thirds of the States, and a Majority of all the States shall be necessary to a Choice. In every Case, after the Choice of the President, the Person having the greatest Number of Votes of the Electors shall be the Vice President. But if there should remain two or more who have equal Votes, the Senate shall chuse from them by Ballot the Vice President.[5]

The Congress may determine the Time of chusing the Electors, and the Day on which they shall give their Votes; which Day shall be the same throughout the United States.

No Person except a natural born Citizen, or a Citizen of the United States, at the time of the Adoption of this Constitution, shall be eligible to the Office of President; neither shall any Person be eligible to that Office who shall not have attained to the Age of thirty five Years, and been fourteen Years a Resident within the United States.

In Case of the Removal of the President from Office, or of his Death, Resignation, or Inability to discharge the Powers and Duties of the said Office, the Same shall devolve on the Vice President, and the Congress may by Law provide for the Case of Removal, Death, Resignation or Inability, both of the President and Vice President, declaring what Officer shall then act as President, and such Officer shall act accordingly, until the Disability be removed, or a President shall be elected.[6]

The President shall, at stated Times, receive for his Services, a Compensation which shall neither be encreased nor diminished during the Period for which he shall have been elected, and he shall not receive within that Period any other Emolument from the United States, or any of them.

Before he enter on the Execution of his Office, he shall take the following Oath or Affirmation:—"I do solemnly swear (or affirm) that I will faithfully execute the Office of President of the United States, and will to the best of my Ability, preserve, protect and defend the Constitution of the United States."

Section 2. The President shall be Commander in Chief of the Army and Navy of the United States, and of the Militia of the several States, when called into the actual Service of the United States; he may require the Opinion, in writing, of the principal Officer in each of the executive Departments, upon any Subject relating to the Duties of their respective Offices, and he shall have Power to grant Reprieves and Pardons for Offences against the United States, except in Cases of Impeachment.

---

[5] Superseded by the 12th Amendment.
[6] See 25th Amendment.

He shall have Power, by and with the Advice and Consent of the Senate, to make Treaties, provided two thirds of the Senators present concur; and he shall nominate, and by and with the Advice and Consent of the Senate, shall appoint Ambassadors, other public Ministers and Consuls, Judges of the supreme Court, and all other Officers of the United States, whose Appointments are not herein otherwise provided for, and which shall be established by Law: but the Congress may by Law vest the Appointment of such inferior officers, as they think proper, in the President alone, in the Courts of Law, or in the Heads of Departments.

The President shall have Power to fill up all Vacancies that may happen during the Recess of the Senate, by granting Commissions which shall expire at the End of their next Session.

Section 3.   He shall from time to time give to the Congress Information of the State of the Union, and recommend to their Consideration such Measures as he shall judge necessary and expedient; he may, on extraordinary Occasions, convene both Houses, or either of them, and in Case of Disagreement between them, with Respect to the Time of Adjournment, he may adjourn them to such Time as he shall think proper; he shall receive Ambassadors and other public Ministers; he shall take Care that the Laws be faithfully executed, and shall Commission all the Officers of the United States.

Section 4.   The President, Vice President, and all civil Officers of the United States, shall be removed from Office on Impeachment for, and Conviction of, Treason, Bribery, or other high Crimes and Misdemeanors.

Article III

Section 1.   The judicial Power of the United States, shall be vested in one supreme Court and in such inferior Courts as the Congress may from time to time ordain and establish. The Judges, both of the supreme and inferior Courts, shall hold their Offices during good Behaviour, and shall, at stated Times, receive for their Services, a Compensation, which shall not be diminished during their Continuance in Office.

Section 2.   The judicial Power shall extend to all Cases, in Law and Equity, arising under this Constitution, the Laws of the United States, and Treaties made, or which shall be made, under their Authority;—to all Cases affecting Ambassadors, other public Ministers and Consuls;—to all Cases of admiralty and maritime Jurisdiction;—to Controversies to which the United States shall be a Party—to Controversies between two or more States;—*between a State and Citizens of another State* [7];—between Citi-

---

[7] See 11th Amendment.

zens of different States;—between Citizens of the same State claiming Lands under Grants of different States, *and between a State or the Citizens thereof, and foreign States, Citizens, or Subjects.*[8]

In all Cases affecting Ambassadors, other public Ministers and Consuls, and those in which a State shall be Party, the supreme Court shall have original Jurisdiction. In all the other Cases before mentioned, the supreme Court shall have appellate Jurisdiction, both as to Law and Fact, with such Exceptions, and under such Regulations as the Congress shall make.

The Trial of all Crimes, except in Cases of Impeachment, shall be by Jury; and such Trial shall be held in the State where the said Crimes shall have been committed; but when not committed within any State, the Trial shall be at such Place or Places as the Congress may by Law have directed.

Section 3. Treason against the United States, shall consist only in levying War against them, or in adhering to their Enemies, giving them Aid and Comfort. No Person shall be convicted of Treason unless on the Testimony of two Witnesses to the same overt Act, or on Confession in open Court.

The Congress shall have Power to declare the Punishment of Treason, but no Attainder of Treason shall work Corruption of Blood, or Forfeiture except during the Life of the Person attainted.

Article IV

Section 1. Full Faith and Credit shall be given in each State to the public Acts, Records, and judicial Proceedings of every other State. And the Congress may by general Laws prescribe the Manner in which such Acts, Records, and Proceedings shall be proved, and the Effect thereof.

Section 2. The Citizens of each State shall be entitled to all Privileges and Immunities of Citizens in the several States.

A Person charged in any State with Treason, Felony, or other Crime, who shall flee from Justice, and be found in another State, shall on Demand of the executive Authority of the State from which he fled, be delivered up, to be removed to the State having Jurisdiction of the Crime.

No Person held to Service or Labour in one State, under the Laws thereof, escaping into another, shall, in Consequence of any Law or Regulation therein, be discharged from such Service or Labour, but shall be delivered up on Claim of the Party to whom such Service or Labour may be due.[9]

---

[8] See 11th Amendment.
[9] See 13th Amendment.

Section 3. New States may be admitted by the Congress into this Union; but no new State shall be formed or erected within the Jurisdiction of any other State; nor any State be formed by the Junction of two or more States, or Parts of States, without the Consent of the Legislatures of the States concerned as well as of the Congress.

The Congress shall have Power to dispose of and make all needful Rules and Regulations, respecting the Territory or other Property belonging to the United States; and nothing in this Constitution shall be so construed as to Prejudice any claims of the United States, or of any particular State.

Section 4. The United States shall guarantee to every State in this Union a Republican Form of Government, and shall protect each of them against Invasion; and on Application of the Legislature, or of the Executive (when the Legislature cannot be convened) against domestic Violence.

Article V

The Congress, whenever two thirds of both Houses shall deem it necessary, shall propose Amendments to this Constitution, or, on the Application of the Legislatures of two thirds of the several States, shall call a Convention for proposing Amendments, which, in either Case, shall be valid to all Intents and Purposes, as Part of this Constitution, when ratified by the Legislatures of three fourths of the several States, or by Conventions in three fourths thereof, as the one or the other Mode of Ratification may be proposed by the Congress; Provided that no Amendment which may be made prior to the Year One thousand eight hundred and eight shall in any Manner affect the first and fourth Clauses in the Ninth Section of the first Article; and that no State, without its Consent, shall be deprived of its equal Suffrage in the Senate.

Article VI

All Debts contracted and Engagements entered into, before Adoption of this Constitution, shall be as valid against the United States under this Constitution, as under the Confederation.

This Constitution, and the Laws of the United States which shall be made in Pursuance thereof; and all Treaties made, or which shall be made, under the Authority of the United States, shall be the supreme Law of the Land; and the Judges in every State shall be bound thereby, any Thing in the Constitution or Laws of any State to the Contrary notwithstanding.

The Senators and Representatives before mentioned, and the Members of the several State Legislatures, and all executive and judicial Officers, both of the United States and of the several States, shall be bound by Oath or Affirmation, to support this Constitution; but no religious Test shall ever be required as a Qualification to any Office or public Trust under the United States.

Article VII

The Ratification of the Conventions of nine States, shall be sufficient for the Establishment of this Constitution between the States so ratifying the Same.

Done in Convention by the Unanimous Consent of the States present the Seventeenth Day of September in the Year of our Lord one thousand seven hundred and eighty seven and of the Independence of the United States of America the Twelfth. In witness whereof We have hereunto subscribed our Names.

ARTICLES IN ADDITION TO, AND AMENDMENT OF, THE CONSTITUTION OF THE UNITED STATES OF AMERICA, PROPOSED BY CONGRESS, AND RATIFIED BY THE SEVERAL STATES, PURSUANT TO THE FIFTH ARTICLE OF THE ORIGINAL CONSTITUTION:

Amendment I

(Ratification of the first ten amendments was completed December 15, 1791.)

Congress shall make no law respecting an establishment of religion, or prohibiting the free exercise thereof; or abridging the freedom of speech, or of the press; or the right of the people peaceably to assemble, and to petition the Government for a redress of grievances.

Amendment II

A well regulated Militia, being necessary to the security of a free State, the right of the people to keep and bear Arms, shall not be infringed.

Amendment III

No Soldier shall, in time of peace be quartered in any house, without the consent of the Owner, nor in time of war, but in a manner to be prescribed by law.

Amendment IV

The right of the people to be secure in their persons, houses, papers, and effects, against unreasonable searches and seizures, shall not be violated, and no Warrants shall issue, but upon probable cause, supported by Oath or affirmation, and particularly describing the place to be searched, and the persons or things to be seized.

Amendment V

No person shall be held to answer for a capital, or otherwise infamous crime, unless on a presentment or indictment of a Grand Jury, except in cases arising in the land or naval forces, or in the Militia, when in actual service in time of War or public danger; nor shall any person be subject for the same offence to be twice put in jeopardy of life or limb; nor shall be compelled in any criminal case to be a witness against himself, nor be deprived of life, liberty, or property, without due process of law; nor shall private property be taken for public use, without just compensation.

Amendment VI

In all criminal prosecutions, the accused shall enjoy the right to a speedy and public trial, by an impartial jury of the State and district wherein the crime shall have been committed, which district shall have been previously ascertained by law, and to be informed of the nature and cause of the accusation; to be confronted with the witness against him; to have compulsory process for obtaining witnesses in his favor, and to have the Assistance of Counsel for his defence.

Amendment VII

In Suits at common law, where the value in controversy shall exceed twenty dollars, the right of trial by jury shall be preserved, and no fact tried by a jury, shall be otherwise reexamined in any Court of the United States, than according to the rules of the common law.

Amendment VIII

Excessive bail shall not be required, nor excessive fines imposed, nor cruel and unusual punishments inflicted.

Amendment IX

The enumeration in the Constitution, of certain rights, shall not be construed to deny or disparage others retained by the people.

Amendment X

The powers not delegated to the United States by the Constitution, nor prohibited by it to the States, are reserved to the States respectively, or to the people.

Amendment XI (1798)

The Judicial power of the United States shall not be construed to extend to any suit in law or equity, commenced or prosecuted against one of the United States by Citizens of another State, or by Citizens or Subjects of any Foreign States.

Amendment XII (1804)

The Electors shall meet in their respective states and vote by ballot for President and Vice-President, one of whom, at least, shall not be an inhabitant of the same state with themselves; they shall name in their ballots the person voted for as President, and in distinct ballots the person voted for as Vice-President, and they shall make distinct lists of all persons voted for as President, and of all persons voted for as Vice-President, and of the number of votes for each, which lists they shall sign and certify, and transmit sealed to the seat of the government of the United States, directed to the President of the Senate;—The President of the Senate shall, in the presence of Senate and House of Representatives, open all the certificates and the votes shall then be counted; —The person having the greatest number of votes for President, shall be the President, if such number be a majority of the whole number of Electors appointed; and if no person have such majority, then from the persons having the highest numbers not exceeding three on the list of those voted for as President, the House of Representatives shall choose immediately, by ballot, the President. But in choosing the President, the votes shall be taken by states, the representation from each state having one vote; a quorum for this purpose shall consist of a member or members from two-thirds of the states, and a majority of all the states shall be necessary to a choice. And if the House of Representatives shall not choose a President whenever the right of choice shall devolve upon them, *before the fourth day of March next following,*[10] then the Vice-President shall act as President, as in the case of the death or other constitutional disability of the President.—The person having the greatest number of votes as Vice-President shall be the Vice-President, if such number be a majority of the whole number of Electors appointed, and if no person

---

[10] Altered by the 20th Amendment.

have a majority, then from the two highest numbers on the list, the Senate shall choose the Vice-President; a quorum for the purpose shall consist of two-thirds of the whole number of Senators, and a majority of the whole number shall be necessary to a choice. But no person constitutionally ineligible to the office of President shall be eligible to that of Vice-President of the United States.

Amendment XIII (1865)

Section 1. Neither slavery nor involuntary servitude, except as a punishment for crime whereof the party shall have been duly convicted, shall exist within the United States, or any place subject to their jurisdiction.
Section 2. Congress shall have the power to enforce this article by appropriate legislation.

Amendment XIV (1868)

Section 1. All persons born or naturalized in the United States, and subject to the jurisdiction thereof, are citizens of the United States and of the State wherein they reside. No State shall make or enforce any law which shall abridge the privileges or immunities of citizens of the United States; nor shall any State deprive any person of life, liberty, or property, without due process of law; nor deny to any person within its jurisdiction the equal protection of the laws.
Section 2. Representatives shall be apportioned among the several States according to their respective numbers, counting the whole number of persons in each State, excluding Indians not taxed. But when the right to vote at any election for the choice of electors for President and Vice President of the United States, Representatives in Congress, the Executive and Judicial officers of a State, or the members of the Legislature thereof, is denied to any of the male inhabitants of such State, being twenty-one years of age, and citizens of the United States, or in any way abridged, except for participation in rebellion, or other crime, the basis of representation therein shall be reduced in the proportion which the number of such male citizens shall bear to the whole number of male citizens twenty-one years of age in such State.
Section 3. No person shall be a Senator or Representative in Congress, or elector of President and Vice President, or hold any office, civil or military, under the United States, or under any State, who, having previously taken an oath, as a member of Congress, or as an officer of the United States, or as a member of any State legislature, or as an executive or judicial officer of any State, to support the Constitution of the United States, shall have engaged in insurrection or rebellion against the same,

or given aid or comfort to the enemies thereof. But Congress may by a vote of two-thirds of each House, remove such disability.

Section 4. The validity of the public debt of the United States, authorized by law, including debts incurred for payment of pensions and bounties for services in suppressing insurrection or rebellion, shall not be questioned. But neither the United States nor any State shall assume or pay any debt or obligation incurred in aid of insurrection or rebellion against the United States, or any claim for the loss or emancipation of any slave; but all such debts, obligations, and claims shall be held illegal and void.

Section 5. The Congress shall have power to enforce, by appropriate legislation, the provisions of this article.

Amendment XV (1870)

Section 1. The right of citizens of the United States to vote shall not be denied or abridged by the United States or by any State on account of race, color, or previous condition of servitude.

Section 2. The Congress shall have power to enforce this article by appropriate legislation.

Amendment XVI (1913)

The Congress shall have power to lay and collect taxes on incomes, from whatever source derived, without apportionment among the several States, and without regard to any census or enumeration.

Amendment XVII (1913)

The Senate of the United States shall be composed of two Senators from each State, elected by the people thereof, for six years; and each Senator shall have one vote. The electors in each State shall have the qualifications requisite for electors of the most numerous branch of the State legislatures.

When vacancies happen in the representation of any State in the Senate, the executive authority of such State shall issue writs of election to fill such vacancies: Provided, That the legislature of any State may empower the executive thereof to make temporary appointments until the people fill the vacancies by election as the legislature may direct.

This amendment shall not be so construed as to affect the election or term of any Senator chosen before it becomes valid as part of the Constitution.

Amendment XVIII (1919)

Section 1. After one year from the ratification of this article the manufacture, sale, or transportation of intoxicating liquors within, the importation thereof into, or the exportation thereof from the United States and all territory subject to the jurisdiction thereof for beverage purposes is hereby prohibited.

Section 2. The Congress and the several States shall have concurrent power to enforce this article by appropriate legislation.

Section 3. This article shall be inoperative unless it shall have been ratified as an amendment to the Constitution by the legislatures of the several States, as provided in the Constitution, within seven years from the date of the submission hereof to the States by the Congress.[11]

Amendment XIX (1920)

The right of citizens of the United States to vote shall not be denied or abridged by the United States or by any State on account of sex.

Congress shall have power to enforce this article by appropriate legislation.

Amendment XX (1933)

Section 1. The terms of the President and Vice President shall end at noon on the 20th day of January, and the terms of Senators and Representatives at noon on the 3rd day of January, of the years in which such terms would have ended if this article had not been ratified; and the terms of their successors shall then begin.

Section 2. The Congress shall assemble at least once in every year, and such meeting shall begin at noon on the 3rd day of January, unless they shall by law appoint a different day.

Section 3. If, at the time fixed for the beginning of the term of the President, the President elect shall have died, the Vice President elect shall become President. If a President shall not have been chosen before the time fixed for the beginning of his term, or if the President elect shall have failed to qualify, then the Vice President elect shall act as President until a President shall have qualified; and the Congress may by law provide for the case wherein neither a President elect nor a Vice President elect shall have qualified, declaring who shall then act as President, or the manner in which one who is to act shall be selected, and

---

[11] Repealed by the 21st Amendment.

such person shall act accordingly until a President or Vice President shall have qualified.

Section 4. The Congress may by law provide for the case of the death of any of the persons from whom the House of Representatives may choose a President whenever the right of choice shall have devolved upon them, and for the case of the death of any of the persons from whom the Senate may choose a Vice President whenever the right of choice shall have devolved upon them.

Section 5. Sections 1 and 2 shall take effect on the 15th day of October following the ratification of this article.

Section 6. This article shall be inoperative unless it shall have been ratified as an amendment to the Constitution by the legislatures of three-fourths of the several States within seven years from the date of its submission.

Amendment XXI (1933)

Section 1. The eighteenth article of amendment to the Constitution of the United States is hereby repealed.

Section 2. The transportation or importation into any State, Territory, or possession of the United States for delivery or use therein of intoxicating liquors, in violation of the laws thereof, is hereby prohibited.

Section 3. This article shall be inoperative unless it shall have been ratified as an amendment to the Constitution by conventions in the several States, as provided in the Constitution, within seven years from the date of the submission hereof to the States by the Congress.

Amendment XXII (1951)

Section 1. No person shall be elected to the office of the President more than twice, and no person who has held the office of President, or acted as President for more than two years of a term to which some other person was elected President shall be elected to the office of President more than once. But this Article shall not apply to any person holding the office of President when this Article was proposed by the Congress, and shall not prevent any person who may be holding the office of President, or acting as President, during the term within which this Article becomes operative from holding the office of President or acting as President during the remainder of such term.

Section 2. This article shall be inoperative unless it shall have been ratified as an amendment to the Constitution by the legislatures of three-fourths of the several States within seven years from the date of its submission to the States by the Congress.

Amendment XXIII (1961)

Section 1. The District constituting the seat of Government of the United States shall appoint in such manner as the Congress may direct:

A number of electors of President and Vice President equal to the whole number of Senators and Representatives in Congress to which the District would be entitled if it were a State, but in no event more than the least populous State; they shall be in addition to those appointed by the States, but they shall be considered, for the purposes of the election of President and Vice President, to be electors appointed by a State; and they shall meet in the District and perform such duties as provided by the twelfth article of amendment.

Section 2. The Congress shall have power to enforce this article by appropriate legislation.

Amendment XXIV (1964)

Section 1. The right of citizens of the United States to vote in any primary or other election for President or Vice President, for electors for President or Vice President, or for Senator or Representative in Congress, shall not be denied or abridged by the United States or any state by reason of failure to pay any poll tax or other tax.

Section 2. The Congress shall have the power to enforce this article by appropriate legislation.

Amendment XXV (1967)

Section 1. In case of the removal of the President from office or of his death or resignation, the Vice President shall become President.

Section 2. Whenever there is a vacancy in the office of the Vice President, the President shall nominate a Vice President who shall take office upon confirmation by a majority vote of both Houses of Congress.

Section 3. Whenever the President transmits to the President pro tempore of the Senate and the Speaker of the House of Representatives his written declaration that he is unable to discharge the powers and duties of his office, and until he transmits to them a written declaration to the contrary, such powers and duties shall be discharged by the Vice President as Acting President.

Section 4. Whenever the Vice President and a majority of either the principal officers of the executive departments or of such other body as Congress may by law provide, transmit to the President pro tempore of the Senate and the Speaker of the House of Representatives their written declaration that the President is unable to discharge the powers and duties of his office, the Vice President shall immediately assume the powers and duties of the office as Acting President.

Thereafter, when the President transmits to the President pro tempore of the Senate and the Speaker of the House of Representatives his written declaration that no inability exists, he shall resume the powers and duties of his office unless the Vice President and a majority of either the principal officers of the executive departments or of such other body as Congress may by law provide, transmit within four days to the President pro tempore of the Senate and the Speaker of the House of Representatives their written declaration that the President is unable to discharge the powers and duties of his office. Thereupon Congress shall decide the issue, assembling within forty-eight hours for that purpose if not in session. If the Congress, within twenty-one days after receipt of the latter written declaration, or, if Congress is not in session, within twenty-one days after Congress is required to assemble, determines by two-thirds vote of both Houses that the President is unable to discharge the powers and duties of his office, the Vice President shall continue to discharge the same as Acting President; otherwise, the President shall resume the powers and duties of his office.

Amendment XXVI (1971)

Section 1.   The right of citizens of the United States, who are 18 years of age or older, to vote shall not be denied or abridged by the United States or any state on account of age.

Section 2.   The Congress shall have the power to enforce this article by appropriate legislation.

GLOSSARY*

Abolitionist. One who favored the abolition of American slavery in the period from the 1830s to the Civil War; an anti-slavery activist.

Absorption. A metaphorical term used by the Court beginning in the 1930s to describe the process of applying the protections contained in the Bill of Rights to the states by absorbing those rights into the due process clause of the Fourteenth Amendment. *See* Nationalization, Incorporation of the Bill of Rights; Selective Incorporation.

Adversary Proceeding. One having opposing, contesting parties; one in which the party seeking relief (plaintiff) has given legal warning to the other party (defendant), thereby affording the latter an opportunity to contest the issues.

Affirmative Action. The requirement of positive corrective measures to be formulated by employers to systematically remedy the effects of past racial or sex-based discrimination and to prevent its recurrence. Plans usually include an analysis of work-force utilization; specification of numerical goals (quotas) for adding minority persons to the work-force; a timetable for achieving such goals; explanation of methods to be used to eliminate discrimination and to increase the number of underrepresented classes of personnel; and specification of administrative responsibility to oversee the affirmative action program for the agency or organization. Such plans are required of all governmental agencies and all other recipients of public funds, including universities and contractors.

Anti-Federalists. In the first instance, those who opposed ratification of the Constitution of 1787 when initially proposed, its proponents and supporters, called themselves the "Anti-Federalists." The Anti-Federalists

---

* The abbreviation *q.v.* (*quod vide* = which see) is used in the text of this "Glossary" to refer the reader to other pertinent terms defined herein. In addition to unabridged dictionaries, the following sources are useful sources in defining technical legal and political terms: James A. Ballentine, *Law Dictionary With Pronunciations* (Rochester, N.Y.: Lawyer's Cooperative Pub. Co., 1948); Henry Campbell Black, *Black's Law Dictionary*, 4th ed. (St. Paul, Minn.: West Pub. Co., 1968); Jack C. Plano and Milton Greenberg, *The American Political Dictionary*, 4th ed. (Hinsdale, Ill.: Dryden Press, 1976).

included many illustrious Americans, including (to take Virginians alone) Patrick Henry, George Mason, James Monroe, and Richard Henry Lee. Belief that the new constitution meant too great a loss of the states' rights, or of individual liberty, or that it was too undemocratic supplied reasons for the Anti-Federalist stance. Once ratified, the old opponents of the Constitution later regrouped and eventually re-emerged with Thomas Jefferson their leader to become the Republican Party (that is, the present-day Democratic Party) by 1796, largely composed of agrarian frontiersmen. Thereafter the term "anti-Federalist" denoted Jeffersonian Republicans, or Democrats as they became by the 1820s. This was the origin of the American political party system. The Federalists (nearly extinct by 1816) are the distant forefathers of the Republicans of today; the Anti-Federalists of the 1790s, who became the Jeffersonian Republicans, are the forefathers of the modern Democrats.

Arraignment. An open-court hearing at which a person accused of a crime is formally told of the charges against him and given the opportunity to plead guilty or not guilty.

Bad Tendency Test. A court test in the area of freedom of speech and expression. A regulation must be justified as a means of preventing anyone from uttering or writing anything tending to be injurious to the public welfare, or tending to corrupt morals, incite a crime, or disturb the peace.

Bail. The release of a person from custody upon the assurance of two or more persons (or sometimes upon his own recognizance) that he shall appear at the appointed time to answer the charges against him; also, the bail bond itself, or instrument executed by an accused person together with one or more other persons who assure the court that the accused will appear to answer the charges.

Balancing or Weighing Test. A widely used court test applied to determine the constitutionality of abridging a guarantied right by weighing or balancing it against the general interests of society and the state in such a regulation.

Brandenburg Rule. Stated in *Brandenburg* v. Ohio, 395 U.S. 444 (1969) at 447: ". . . the principle that the constitutional guarantees of free speech and free press do not permit a State to forbid or proscribe advocacy of the use of force or of law violation except where such advocacy is directed to inciting or producing imminent lawless action and is likely to incite or produce such action."

Chilling Effect Test. A court test used to void regulations or statutes whose effect is to suppress or "chill" speech without sufficient reason, thereby unconstitutionally invading freedom of expression.

Clear And Present Danger. A court test in the area of freedom of speech and expression generally. A regulation restricting expression must be justified as a means necessary to avert some evident and immediate danger to society within the power of government to prevent.

Clear and Probable Danger. A modification of the clear and present danger test (*q.v.*) in the area of freedom of speech and expression. An invasion of free expression must be to avoid some grave evil to society, provided it can be shown that a substantial probability exists of the evil actually occurring.

Congressional Prescription. Something directed to be done as a positive duty under the law through congressional enactment or statute.

Court Proscription. Something made unlawful by a court order or mandate.

Court Tests. Various standards or rules ("tests") by which judges assess the legality and constitutionality of regulations and laws.

De Facto Segregation. Actual segregation of the races, not traceable to official policy or state action.

De Jure Segregation. Segregation that results from state action or policy.

Dictum, dicta. Singular and plural abbreviated forms of the Latin legal expression *obiter dictum*, "that which is said in passing." A dictum in a court opinion, accordingly, is a rule of law set forth in a case which is not vital to the decision. Such expressions do not become precedents.

Equal Protection. The doctrines arising from Court interpretation of the "Equal Protection of the Laws Clause" (Fourteenth Amendment) which apply to the states and of the analogous "strand" in the "due process of law" clause (Fifth Amendment) which apply to the federal government. As a rule, equal protection requires that governments treat persons similarly situated equally under the law; it prohibits invidious discrimination on the basis of race, creed, gender or national origin. Conversely, it requires governmental classifications to be rationally related to some legitimate state interest, and if such classifications are "suspect" (race-based, for example) or involve the abridgment of basic liberties ("fundamental interests" or "rights"), there must be a compelling state interest that can withstand strict scrutiny by the judiciary. This clause came to prominence especially after 1954 and the *Brown v. Board of Education* desegregation decision. Today it vies with the due process clauses as the textual source of most cases brought before the federal courts. More generally, the equal protection of the laws of a state is extended to persons within its jurisdiction as constitutionally required when its courts are open to them on the same conditions as to others for the security of their persons and property, the prevention and redress of wrongs, and the enforcement of contracts; when they are subjected to no restrictions in the acquisition of property, the enjoyment of personal liberty, and the pursuit of happiness, which do not generally affect others; when they are liable to no other or greater burdens and charges than such as are laid upon others; and when no different or greater punishment is enforced against them for a violation of the laws. *See* Due Process of Law, Procedural and Substantive.

Establishment Clause.   The first clause of the first statement in the First Amendment, guarantying freedom of religion: "Congress shall make no law respecting an establishment of religion, or respecting the free exercise thereof; . . ." The second clause is the Free Exercise Clause.

Ex Post Facto Law.   A term related to crimes and their punishment, not to civil matters. It means a statute that makes a crime of some act that was not a crime when done; or one which increases the punishment for a crime after the crime has been committed. The underlying principle is that persons have a right to fair warning of that conduct which will give rise to criminal penalties.

Exclusionary Rule.   Arising from the Fourth Amendment, the exclusionary rule generally means that evidence obtained by illegal search and seizure cannot be used in a criminal proceeding against the person who is the victim of the search and seizure. This is not a personal constitutional right but a court-created remedy designed to compel the police to respect the provisions of the Fourth Amendment. It dates from *Mapp v. Ohio*, 367 U.S. 643, (1961).

Expatriation.   The voluntary act of abandoning one's country, renouncing allegiance to it, and becoming the citizen or subject of another; abandonment of nationality and allegiance.

The Federalist.   Series of eighty-five essays or "papers" by Alexander Hamilton, John Jay, and James Madison published in 1787–88 in New York newspapers under the pseudonym "Publius" and written to persuade that state's ratification convention to approve the Constitution. It is the classic statement of American constitutional and political theory.

Felony.   A serious criminal offense, such as murder. More generally, any crime punished by imprisonment in a state penitentiary or by death is a felony. *See* Misdemeanor.

Fighting Words Test.   A court test that justifies regulation of expression, if the utterance of the proscribed language seems likely to directly inflict injury, or to provoke public disorder and endanger the peace. This test proscribes lewd, libelous, obscene, profane, or insulting speech.

Gerrymandering.   Manipulation of the arrangement of election district boundaries so as to give unfair advantage one political party or faction at the expense of another, which would command a majority were the boundaries fairly drawn. The objective is to gain partisan political advantage by spreading support for one's party over as many districts as possible. These boundary lines usually are drawn by the majority party in the state legislature.

Gertz Rule. Stated in *Gertz v. Robert Welch, Inc.*, 418 U.S. 323 (1974) at 347: ". . . the States may define for themselves the appropriate standard of liability for a publisher or broadcaster of defamatory falsehood injurious to a private individual." The Court qualified this rule by insisting that the state statutes require that some fault (such as negligence) be shown, if private libels are found. Moreover, damages may not be presumed but must be shown; and if punitive damages are awarded, the New York *Times* rule of "actual malice" must be proved. *See* New York Times Rule, for libels of public officials or public figures.

Gitlow Doctrine. Stated in *Gitlow v. New York*, 268 U.S. 652 (1925) at 666: "For present purposes we may and do assume that freedom of speech and of the press—which are protected by the First Amendment from abridgment by Congress—are among the fundamental personal rights and 'liberties' protected by the due process clause of the Fourteenth Amendment from impairment by the States." This dictum (*q.v.*) begins the explicit absorption, or selective incorporation, of the Bill of Rights into the Fourteenth Amendment, thus formally initiating nationalization.

Grand Jury. A body of from twelve to twenty-three citizens organized for the purpose of inquiring into the commission of crimes within the county in which they reside and to vote indictments (*q.v.*) against supposed offenders.

Guaranty. The protection of a right afforded by a law or a provision of the Constitution.

Higher Law. This term is a synonym for the phrase in the Declaration of Independence, "the Laws of Nature and of Nature's God. . . ." It refers to divine law and natural law which, in English and American jurisprudence, were generally understood to be the perfect sources of admittedly imperfect human law. The Constitution is, from this higher law perspective, conceived to be an expression of the "eternal, immutable laws of good and evil, to which the creator himself in all his dispensations conforms; and which he has enabled human reason to discover, so far as they are necessary for the conduct of human actions." Sir William Blackstone as quoted by Clinton Rossiter in Edward S. Corwin's, *The "Higher Law" Background of American Constitutional Law* (Ithaca, N.Y.: Cornell University Press, Great Seal Books, [repr. ed.] 1955), vi.

Incorporation of the Bill of Rights. Term for the process by which

Supreme Court decisions between 1925 and 1969 included ("incorporated") most of the principal individual liberties mentioned in the first eight amendments into the term "liberty" in the Fourteenth Amendment, thereby extending their protection so as to prohibit invasion by the states. The original Bill of Rights applied only to the federal government. *See* the nearly synonymous terms: Selective Incorporation, Absorption, and Nationalization of the Bill of Rights.

Indictment. An accusation founded on legal testimony of a direct and positive character, and the concurrence of at least twelve members of a grand jury that (upon the basis of evidence presented to them) the defendant is guilty.

Information. A written accusation of a crime preferred by a prosecutor without the intervention of a grand jury.

Intent Test. A court test in the area of racial discrimination (and perhaps other equal protection litigation) which requires plaintiffs to show that there was purposeful or intentional discrimination in a regulation (and not merely that its effect was to have adverse and "disproportionate impact" on a minority group) if a *prima facie* (*q.v.*) case is to be established and the burden of justifying the regulation as constitutional thereby shifted to the state. *Washington* v. *Davis*, 426 U.S. 229, 96 S. Ct. 2040 (1976). *See* the discussion in chapter 5.

Injunction. An order by a court restraining or prohibiting a person from doing a certain act which appears to be against equity or conscience.

Judicial Review. The doctrine that the judicial power of the United States includes the power to declare null and void (unconstitutional) acts of Congress, or of the state legislatures, which conflict with the Constitution. Argued in *The Federalist No. 78* by Hamilton, it was settled in law by John Marshall's opinion in *Marbury* v. *Madison* (1804). This is a unique development of American law, despite some tendencies in that direction by Sir Edward Coke in the early seventeenth century in England.

Jus Sanguinis. A Latin term meaning "right of blood relationship." By an act of Congress, citizenship is conferred to children born to U.S. citizens abroad, provided at least one of the parents is a citizen and has lived for a time in the United States prior to the birth of the child. *See* Jus Soli.

Jus Soli. A Latin term meaning "right of the soil." All persons born in the United States are, by that fact, American citizens under the principle of *jus soli*. The only exception is the children of those persons living here but not "subject to the jurisdiction" of the United States, such as foreign diplomats. Fourteenth Amendment. *See* Jus Sanguinis.

Justiciable. A justiciable controversy or question is one which it is within the scope of judicial power to resolve. There are several elements: there must be a real case involving actual grievances; the person bringing the complaint must have a stake in its outcome and standing (*q.v.*) to sue; the case must be ripe for judicial consideration, so that administrative relief and (perhaps) lower court determinations have previously been given; finally, the court appealed to must have jurisdiction. Certain questions are *not* justiciable because they are regarded as too "political." This means that they can only, or best, be resolved not by the judiciary but by the other, political and representative branches of the government—the legislative and executive branches—because popular consensus and public consent are crucial.

Ku Klux Klan. A political activist and terrorist organization which first appeared in the post-Civil-War South as a force to supply vigilante justice and enforce white supremacy. It was characterized by a costume of flowing robes and masks, torches, and burning crosses. To the credulous, the klansmen appeared to be spirits from another world. The original Klan was disbanded in 1871, but renegade imitative and criminal organizations sprang up subsequently. The "modern" Klan, still in existence, was organized in 1915 and is racist and xenophobic.

Law of the Land. A synonym for "due process of law." Contained in the *Magna Carta* (1215 A.D.), chap. 39. *See* headnote to chap. 4 of this book. Contained in the "Supremacy Clause" of the U.S. Constitution (Art. VI, Cl. 2.) *See* Due Process of Law; Supremacy Clause.

Least Restrictive Means. A court test that requires regulations restricting the exercise of protected liberties to do so as little as possible as a necessary means to the attainment of valid state objectives.

Libel. A malicious publication that tends to blacken the memory of a dead person or the reputation of a living one and to expose him to hatred, contempt, or ridicule.

Lynching. Inflicting punishment without legal trial by a mob or unauthorized persons; illegal infliction of punishment by a combination of persons for an alleged crime.

Mandamus. A Latin legal term meaning "we command." A Writ of Mandamus is a court order to some inferior court, official, or person requiring the performance of some particular duty therein specified, the duty deriving from the official station of the party to whom the order is directed, or by the operation of the law. A mandamus is a positive command and will not restrain action. *See* Injunction.

Manifest Destiny. The nineteenth century American belief that expansion of the nation's boundaries to the Pacific was divinely ordained and, hence, inevitable.

Misdemeanor. A crime that is not so serious as to be punishable by imprisonment in a state penitentiary or by death. *See* Felony.

Nationalization of the Bill of Rights. Term for the process of making the specific protections of the first eight amendments national in application so as to apply equally to the states as well as the federal government. *See* Incorporation.

New Substantive Due Process. Interpretation of the "due process of law" clauses (Fifth and Fourteenth Amendments) by the Court, especially since *Griswold* v. *Connecticut* (1965), as protecting personal privacy and a range of other rights not explicitly mentioned in the Constitution (such as the rights of travel, association, procreation, abortion) against governmental abridgment. *See* Substantive Due Process *and* Old Substantive Due Process.

New York Times Rule. Stated in *New York Times Co.* v. *Sullivan,* 376 U.S. 254 (1964) at 279–80: "The [First Amendment] constitutional guarantees require . . . a federal rule that prohibits a public official from recovering damages for a defamatory falsehood relating to his official conduct unless he proves that the statement was made with 'actual malice'—that is, with knowledge that it was false or with reckless disregard of whether it was false or not." By this rule, subsequent punishment for publication of apparently criminal (libelous) matter is severely attenuated, especially if one is a public official. *See* Prior Restraint; Gertz Rule; Sedition; Libel.

Old Substantive Due Process. Interpretation of the "due process of law" clauses (Fifth and Fourteenth Amendments) by the Court after 1890, and especially after *Lochner* v. *New York* (1905), to secure individual economic liberty against state intrusion and regulation. *See* Substantive Due Process *and* New Substantive Due Process.

Over-breadth. A court test of the constitutionality of regulations on the basis of their lack of specificity and narrowness in achieving an admittedly legitimate state purpose. Provisions that are too broad or sweeping are regularly voided.

Pentagon Papers. A 7000-page series of top-secret government documents dealing with the origins of U.S. involvement in the Vietnam War. Written by experts under the direction of Secretary of Defense Robert S. McNamara, they were published by the *New York Times* and other newspapers through the complicity of Dr. Daniel Ellsberg, one of their authors, without government authorization. This led to the decision in *New York Times* v. *U.S.,* 403 U.S. 713 (1971), upholding the doctrine of prior restraint (*q.v.*) and protection of the press by the Constitution in publishing stolen government documents of high security sensitivity.

Petit Jury. The trial jury. Normally composed of twelve persons, it is impaneled and sworn in a district court to try and determine by a unanimous verdict (usually) questions of fact in criminal and civil actions, on the basis of law and the evidence given them in open court.

Police Power. The whole range of governmental powers possessed by the states, except for the taxing power. It is the power of the states' governments to legislate and take other actions necessary to secure the lives, safety, health, morals, welfare, and property of itself and its people. This broad power is inherent in sovereignty and, under our Constitution, assured to the states by the Tenth Amendment's "Reserve Clause."

Preferred Position. The notion that the liberties protected by the Bill of Rights, and most especially those listed in the First Amendment, are "fundamental" in the American "scheme of ordered liberty." On Justice Cardozo's theory in *Palko* v. *Connecticut*, 302 U.S. 319 (1937), these preferred freedoms have been "absorbed" into the Fourteenth Amendment as protections against the states *because* of "the belief that neither liberty nor justice would exist if they were sacrificed." "Preferred position" was coined in *Murdock* v. *Pennsylvania*, 319 U.S. 105 (1943) at 115.

Preliminary Examination. A state hearing before a magistrate or judge of an inferior court (municipal court or justice court) in which a person arrested for a felony (*q.v.*) is given opportunity to test the prosecutor's case so that the judge can determine whether there is probable cause (*q.v.*) that a crime has been committed and that the arrestee committed it. In federal courts, the hearing is before a commissioner and bail may be set. Where an indictment has been returned, or where the crime is a misdemeanor (*q.v.*), there usually is no requirement of a preliminary hearing.

Presentment. The notice taken by a grand jury of an offense, on the basis of their own knowledge or observation, without any bill of indictment being laid before them by the prosecutor.

Prima Facie. A Latin legal term meaning "at first sight." A prima facie case is one that is persuasive and sufficient to prove the issue "at first sight," unless contradicted and overcome by other evidence.

Primary Effect Test. A court test in the area of freedom of religion which requires that the primary effect of state support of sectarian institutions be neutral, not religious. The Court formulated it this way in *Abington School Dist.* v. *Schempp*, 374 U.S. 203 (1963) at 222: "The test may be stated as follows: what [is] the . . . primary effect of the enactment? If [it] is the advancement or inhibition of religion then the enactment exceeds the scope of legislative power as circumscribed by the Constitution. That is to say that to withstand the strictures of the Establishment Clause [*q.v.*] there must be a . . . primary effect that neither advances nor inhibits religion."

Prior Restraint. Censorship before publication; suppression of matter before it is published. The "Doctrine of Prior Restraint" prohibits such censorship or suppression and was the early foundation of freedom of the press. Thus, Blackstone (1769) said: "The liberty of the press is indeed essential to the nature of a free state; but this consists in laying no *previous* restraints upon publications, and not in freedom from censure for criminal matter when published." Sir William Blackstone, *Commentaries on the Laws of England*, 4:151–52. *See* the discussion in chap. 3.

Probable Cause. In general, the term means a reasonable ground of suspicion, supported by circumstances sufficient to warrant a cautious man in believing that the party is guilty of the offense with which he is charged. Precise meaning depends upon context.

Procedural Due Process. The aspect of "due process of law" (Fifth and Fourteenth Amendments) which requires fairness in the manner or procedure by which governmental policies are applied. This has great importance today in all kinds of proceedings of governmental agencies, administrative, legislative, as well as judicial. *See* Substantive Due Process, with which it is to be contrasted.

Ratification. The process whereby the people gave approval to the Constitution of 1787, speaking through ratification conventions elected for the purpose. Article VII provided that the Constitution would go into effect (be ratified) when approved by nine of the original thirteen states. Amendments to the Constitution all have been proposed by Congress (upon two-thirds vote of a quorum of each house) and all but the Twenty-first Amendment (repealing prohibition as commanded by the Eighteenth Amendment) have been ratified by state legislatures rather than special conventions (*see* ART. V.) Since 1789, over 5000 amendments have been introduced into Congress but only thirty-one have been formally proposed, and twenty-six ratified by the requisite three-fourths of the states. One amendment, the Equal Rights Amendment, now is pending before the state legislatures and must be ratified by March 22, 1979, or die, since seven years was (as usual) allowed by Congress for the ratification process.

Reapportionment. Reallocation of legislative seats. *Congressional* reapportionment begins with the designation of the number of seats in the House of Representatives each state is to have on the basis of the constitutionally guarantied one Representative plus the additional number computed after the census is taken each ten years. Reapportionment of congressional seats under court decisions generally means that each district in the state must have about the same number of residents, the "one man one vote" principle. *Legislative* reapportionment relates to the state legislatures. There, court decisions mandate that both upper and lower houses of bicameral bodies be elected by legislative districts of nearly equal populations. *See* Redistricting.

Redistricting.   The redrawing of legislative and congressional election district lines so as to divide a state into nearly equal districts in terms of population. Greater tolerance for variation is extended to congressional districts than to legislative districts. Redistricting also has virtually eliminated multi-member districts in favor of single-member districts: almost all legislative districts now elect one representative or one senator, as the case may be. All congressional districts are single-member districts. *See* Reapportionment; Gerrymandering.

Reverse Discrimination.   Discrimination against the white majority of persons.

Sedition.   Attempting by word, deed, or writing to promote public disorder, riots, rebellion, or civil war; if overt acts, such sedition may be treason. The Sedition Act of 1798, enacted during the presidency of John Adams, made it an offense to libel the government and its officers. Four persons were prosecuted under it, but the law was so unpopular that it was soon repealed. After World War I, into the 1920s and 1930s, there were a number of prosecutions under federal espionage laws and state criminal syndicalism laws. During and after World War II, there were prosecutions under statutes aimed as persons and organizations believed to be plotting and conspiring both to advocate the overthrow of American government and actually to accomplish that purpose. *See* Brandenburg Rule.

Selective Incorporation.   The most acceptable term to denote the process whereby the various protections of the Bill of Rights have been assimilated to the due process clause of the Fourteenth Amendment and, thereby, given effect against infringements by the states. *See* Incorporation; Nationalization of the Bill of Rights; Absorption.

Silver Platter Doctrine.   The doctrine that evidence illegally obtained by *state* officers was admissible in federal court as evidence of a *federal* crime, provided there was no connivance with federal officers in obtaining it. It dates from *Byars* v. *U.S.*, 273 U.S. 28 (1928) and was supplanted by the Exclusionary Rule (*q.v.*) in 1961.

Slander.   Formerly either spoken or written defamation. Today it is speaking base or defamatory words of another person which tend to prejudice his reputation, office, trade, or means of making a living.

Speech-Plus *and* Symbolic Speech.   Aspects of the Freedom of Speech protected under the First Amendment and the Fourteenth Amendment. Speech-plus includes leafleting, picketing, parading, demonstrating, using sound trucks, engaging in door-to-door solicitation. Symbolic speech includes various forms of conduct with a communicative content, such as flag salutes, draft card burning, flag burning and other forms of flag desecration, wearing shirts and jackets with various symbols or words displayed on them.

Standing. The legal ability to sue in a court of law. In a federal court a person instituting a suit ("plaintiff") must meet several requirements: have a personal stake in the outcome of the controversy, one that warrants his request that a federal court assume jurisdiction, and one that justifies use of the court's remedies on his behalf. In addition, the plaintiff must show himself to be injured by the challenged action of the defendant, economically or in some other way.

Stare Decisis. A Latin legal term meaning "stand by the decision." In constitutional law, it is the doctrine that precedent controls subsequent similar cases as a general rule.

Strict Scrutiny Test. A court test in equal protection cases that reverses the normal presumption of a statute's validity and shifts the burden of proof to the state to show the validity of a regulation or statute. Strict scrutiny is applied where "fundamental rights" or "interests" of individuals are implicated by a statute's operation.

Substantive Due Process. The aspect of "due process of law" (Fifth and Fourteenth Amendments) which requires that the objectives or substance of governmental policies be legitimate and within constitutional bounds. From around 1890 until 1937 the term was used almost exclusively to denote freedom of contract and economic liberty generally (*see* Old Substantive Due Process). Since that time up to the present it has been gradually redefined by the Court to include a range of liberties not specifically mentioned in the Constitution, such as privacy and those inexplicit liberties alluded to by the Ninth Amendment (*see* New Substantive Due Process). Substantive due process is a major mode of contemporary "higher law" (*q.v.*) jurisprudence in American constitutional law, and court decisions.

Suffrage. The right to vote; a political right under control of the state.

Supremacy Clause. ART. VI, SEC. 2, U.S. Constitution: "This Constitution, and the Laws of the United States which shall be made in Pursuance thereof; and all Treaties made, or which shall be made, under the authority of the United States, shall be the supreme Law of the Land; and the Judges in every State shall be bound thereby, any Thing in the Constitution or Laws of any State to the Contrary notwithstanding." In addition to incorporating the principle of "Law of the Land" (*q.v.*), the importance of this clause is that it makes our federal system work by requiring state courts to enforce federal law and by establishing that, although the powers of the federal government are limited, they are supreme in the spheres of operation delegated to them. State laws that conflict with national laws are null and void by this principle.

True Bill. An indictment (*q.v.*). The words "True Bill," when written on an indictment and signed by the foreman of a grand jury, indicate that the requisite majority of the grand jury concur in indicting the person. A "No Bill" carries the contrary meaning; also, "Ignoramus" ("we do not know") sometimes is used instead of "No Bill."

TABLE OF CASES

United States v. Janis: 70, 150–152

Village of Arlington Heights v. Metropolitan Housing Development Corp.: 220–221
Vlandis v. Klein: 226

Washington v. Davis: 218–219, 220, 221, 222
Washington v. Texas: 71

West Coast Hotel Co. v. Parrish: 50–51
West Virginia State Board of Education v. Barnette: 127, 128
Whitney v. California: 47
Wolf v. Colorado: 70
Wolman v. Walter: 124
Wynehamer v. New York: 33

Yick Wo v. Hopkins: 220

SUBJECT INDEX

private actions, 207–213; *habeas corpus* writs and, 147; legislation in, 186–197; Supreme Court and, 213–228; voting rights, 187, 192, 193, 197–206

Civil Service Commission: 28

Civil War: 4, 179, 180

Civil War Amendments (Thirteen, Fourteen, and Fifteen): 179, 180, 193

Clark, Tom: 210

Clayton Act (1914): 36

Clear and present danger test: 45–46, 74, 75, 76, 119

Clear and probable danger test: 75–76; 94, 99

Coke, Sir Edward: 28–29, 30, 42, 47

Cold War: 98, 245

Coleridge, Samuel Taylor: 132, 140, 145

Commentaries (Blackstone): 22, 28, 29, 88

Commerce clause: 209

Commercial speech (freedom of): 80

Common law: *see* English common law

Communism: 4, 75; and politics of containment, 98

Communist Party: 98, 144

Communist Party members: 53–54, 76, 99, 236

Community, as judge: 111

Community Relations Service: 193

Compelling state interests: 68–71

Complaint: 153–155

Compulsory school attendance: 126

Concept of ordered liberty: 65

Confessions: 156–157; inadmissible, 138, 139; voluntary, 136, 139

Congress, U.S.: and civil rights, 175, 186–197, 200–201; powers, 32, 61, 78, 211; voting rights, 197–206

Congress of Racial Equality (CORE): 116–117, 195

Conscience, freedom of: 91, 95

Conscientious objection: 120, 126, 128

Consent, principle of: 157

Conspiracy: 117, 187, 209–210

Constitution, U.S.: amendments to, 4, 5, 22 (*see also* listings by number); Bill of Rights (*see* Bill of Rights); capital punishment, 164; checks and balances, 20; citizenship, 236; commerce clause, 209; concept of liberty in, 3; congressional apportionment, 204; congressional powers, 32, 61, 78, 211; English common law background, 29–30; ex post facto laws, 160–161; *habeas corpus*, 147; necessary and proper clause, 78, 201; preamble, 58, 63–64; privileges and immunities clause, 27, 33, 63, 241; purpose, 17, 61; ratification, 5, 6–7; supremacy clause, 30, 201; Supreme Court powers, 5, 17–19, 21; text, 277–295; treason, 96; trial by jury, 159

Constitutional history: 6, 22, 29

Constitutional rights: curbing of, 80; further development of, 49; waiving, 138, 152

Constitutions, state; absorption of Bill of Rights, 67–68; individual rights protected, 3–4, 15, 31, 64, 92; property rights, 31; *see also* States

Containment, doctrine of: 98

Contraception: 111, 113

Contract, freedom of: 35, 39, 51

Due process of law: common law background, 20–21, 62; discrimination and, 27; economic rights and, 61; law of the land and, 30; liberty and, 45, 46, 48, 52, 54, 56, 91, 161; new substantive, 49–63; procedural, 23–27, 39, 50; selective incorporation of Bill of Rights and, 26; and state police power, 34, 35, 36, 39, 45, 51–52, 63, 118, 161

Duncan, Gary: 64

Duty: of citizens, 237–239; civic, 240–241; of opposition, 238–239; to vote, 240

Dyer anti-lynching bill: 192

Economic liberty: 32–38, 39, 51, 61

Education: desegregation of, 180–186, 195; parochial schools, 124; private schools, 185; separate but equal, 176–177, 181; unitary systems, 181, 182

Eighth Amendment: cruel and unusual punishment, 71, 146, 161; evolving standards of decency, 162–163, 164; excessive bail, 71, 80–81, 146, 154

Eisenhower, Dwight D.: 174, 195

Electoral system: 197

Ellsberg, Daniel: 100

Emancipation Proclamation (1863): 179, 186

Eminent domain: 65, 70

Employment: affirmative action policies, 196–197; discrimination in, 212, 218–219

Enforcement Act of 1870: 187

Enforcement clauses: 186, 191, 200–201, 211

English common law: 6, 22, 28–32, 67, 88

Entrapment: 119

Equal Employment Opportunities Act (1972): 196

Equal Employment Opportunity Commission (EEOC): 196–197

Equal Pay Act (1964): 196

Equal protection of the laws: apportionment and, 204; assertion of rights under, 239; civil rights and, 177, 179–182, 199, 213, 219, 220; higher law and, 222–228; State action and, 208–209; substantive due process and, 27, 28, 53, 56

Eros: 106

Espionage Act (1917): 74

Establishment clause: 124

Evidence, admissible: 150, 151

Evolution, theory of: 124

Evolving standards of decency: 162–163; 164

Exclusionary rule: 69, 149–152

Ex post facto laws: 6, 160–161

Expression, freedom of: 72–73, 74, 76, 79, 92–115; background principles, 93; scope, 95, 111–115; unprotected expression, 95–111; *see also* Speech, freedom of; Press, freedom of

Fair Housing Act (1968): 220

Fanny Hill (Cleland): 110

Federal Bureau of Investigation (FBI): 138–139

Federalist, The: 5–6, 241

Feinburg Law: 115

Felony: 152, 153

Field, Stephen J.: 33

Fifteenth Amendment: enforcement clause, 186, 200–201; gerrymandering and, 205; voting rights, 187, 198–199, 205, 208

Fifth Amendment: double jeopardy, 65–66, 67, 70, 145,

Fifth Amendment (*cont.*)
160; due process, 20–21, 23, 26, 27, 28, 30, 39, 56, 70, 177, 218–219; grand jury indictment, 70, 80, 156; just compensation, 65, 70; right to travel, implied, 53–54; self-incrimination, 67, 70, 113, 138, 139, 145, 149, 152, 156, 160

Fighting words test: 76–77, 105

First Amendment: 83–128; academic freedom, 114–115; chilling effect test and, 77; establishment of religion, 69, 120, 122; exercise of religion, 67, 68, 69, 125–126; freedom of expression, 73, 74, 92–115; freedom of press, 44–46, 64, 67–69, 86–90, 92–95, 99–111; freedom of speech, 44–46, 64, 66–69, 80, 87, 89, 91, 92, 95, 103–105, 128; limits, 74, 89, 94, 96, 105, 107; obscenity and, 107, 110; peaceable assembly, 69, 115–119, 145; preferred position status, 56, 63, 68, 81, 128; protected by due process, 64, 66–69, 77, 87; right of petition, 69, 115–119; right to privacy, implied, 113; other rights, 58

First-tier (equal protection) test: 224

Ford, Gerald R.: 78, 96–97

Fortas, Abe: 210

Fortescue, Sir John: 140

Fourteenth Amendment: adoption, 176; apportionment, 204; citizenship, 237; conspiracy implied, 210; due process, 20–21, 23, 26, 30, 39, 51, 53, 86, 118, 161; enforcement clause, 186, 191, 201, 211; equal protection, 27, 28, 53, 56, 177, 179–182, 199, 209, 213, 219, 220, 222–228, 239; impairment by the States, 45, 64, 92, 222; intent of, 56, 59, 62, 118; liberties incorporated through due process, 66–67, 73, 87, 91, 104, 159, 160, 161, 222; liberty, 45, 46, 51, 55, 57, 58; limits in, 118, 154, 156; privileges and immunities, 241; property right, 52; selective incorporation of Bill of Rights, 29, 48, 56, 62–70, 80, 141; State authority and private action, 34, 191, 199; State authority and segregation, 175, 207–208

Fourth Amendment: probable cause, 153; right to privacy, 150; unreasonable search and seizure, 67, 69, 113, 145, 148–149, 151

Frame of Government (1682): 121

Frankfurter, Felix: 71, 175, 203, 208

Franklin, Benjamin: 3

Freedom of choice programs: 181

"Freedom rides": 195

Free exercise clause: 125–126

Fundamental rights: concept and definition, 48, 55; protections of, 57–59, 63, 64, 65, 113; public interests and, 76; scope of, 55, 63, 68, 74, 113; substantive due process and, 51–56; *see also* Individual rights

Gag order: 93–95

Garvey, Marcus: 193

George III, King: 3

Gerrymandering: 182, 205

Gertz, Elmer: 102

Giles, William Branch: 15

Gilmore, Gary Mark: 165

Ginzburg, Ralph: 106

Gitlow, Benjamin: 43, 44, 46

Marshall, John: 12, 32, 47, 147; on *habeas corpus*, 146; *Marbury*, 13–19, 21, 23

Marshall, Thurgood: 67, 111, 184, 219, 240; *Brown*, 171–176, 178; *Milliken*, 223

Marshall Plan: 98

Matthews, Stanley: 214

Meredith, James: 195

Middle-tier test: *see* Substantial relationship test

Military Service Act (1967): 126

Miller, Samuel F.: 37

Milton, John: 93

Minimum rationality test: 223

Minimum wage laws: 36

Miranda, Ernesto Arturo: 135–137

Miranda cards: 138, 152

Miscegenation: 54, 207

Misdemeanor: 152, 153

Missouri Compromise (1820): 18, 32, 179

Mohammed: Messenger of God (movie): 97

Monroe, James: 6

Moral certainty: 148

Morality of Consent (Bickel): 213

Multimember districts: 205–206

National Association for the Advancement of Colored People (NAACP): 165, 193, 240

National security: 99, 100

National Urban League: 193

Nativism: 192

Naturalization: 235–236

Natural law formula: 29, 62–63

Near, J. M.: 85–86, 87

Necessary and proper clause: 78, 201

New Deal: 37, 193

New York *Times*: 99–100, 192

New York *Times* rule: 101, 102, 103

Niagra Movement: 193

Nicholas, John: 84, 91–92

Ninth Amendment: existence of certain rights, 26, 57–58, 63, 113; other rights encompassed, 128; right to privacy, recognized, 54–55, 57, 63, 113

Nixon, Richard M.: 25–26, 78, 96, 100, 196, 239

Oath of allegiance: 104, 236, 237, 240

Obscenity: 105–111; case illustrations, 106–111, 149–150; defining, 108–111; freedom of speech and, 73, 76, 95, 105, 107; and illegal search and seizure, 149–150; and right to privacy, 111–112; State action and, 78, 89, 106

Obstruction of justice: 117–119

Olson, Floyd B.: 86

One man, one vote principle: 204

Organized crime: 152, 157

Orientals, discrimination against: 214, 220, 236

Over-breadth test: 77–78, 117

Paine, Thomas: 3

Parental rights: 52, 113, 185

Parochial school aid: 120, 124

Passports: 53

Patently offensive: 110–111

Peaceable assembly: *see* Assembly, freedom of

Peckham, Rufus W.: 56

Penn, William: 121

Pentagon Papers: 99–100

Peremptory challenge: 159

Pericles: 84, 91

Peripheral rights: 50; defined, 81, 128

Perry Local School District, Stark County, Ohio: 243–244
Personal rights: *see* Fundamental rights
Petit jury: 146, 155, 157–165; impanelling process, 159; racial discrimination, 206, 213
Petition, freedom of: 69, 115–119
Petition of Right (1628): 147
Pickering, John: 14
Picketing: 95, 117, 119
Plea: 155, 156
Plea-bargaining: 156–157
Pledge of Allegiance: 120, 126, 127
Plunkitt, George Washington: 202
Plymouth Colony: 158
Police interrogation: *see* Interrogation
Police power, of states: and capitalist free enterprise, 33, 35–36; defined, 71–73, 111; and freedom of the press, 87; and fundamental rights, 58; *Gitlow* case, 44; and segregation, 177; and Sunday closing laws, 125
Police states: 141, 144, 238
Political parties: 199
Politics (Aristotle): 20
Poll tax: 202
Polygamy: 126
Pornography: 106, 111
Powell, Lewis F.: 78; *Arlington Heights,* 220–221; *Keyes,* 216–218; on segregation, 183
Preferred position doctrine: 74, 92; *see also* Preferred rights
Preferred rights: 56, 63, 68, 92, 128
Pregnancy: 221–222
Preliminary hearing: 148, 153, 155

Presentment: 153, 156
Press, freedom of: as applied to States, 68–69; case illustrations, 86–92, 99–111; libel, 101–104; national security, 99–100; obscenity, 106–111; prior restraint and, 93–95; protections of, 44–45, 46, 64, 92
Pretrial publicity: 93
Previous restraint, doctrine: 88, 89, 90, 93
Primary elections: 199
Prior restraint doctrine: 88, 89, 93, 94, 100
Privacy, right of: 50; civil rights and, 185; derived Constitutional sources, 55, 62, 63, 113, 150; higher law application, 57–58; other rights related to, 54, 81, 112–113, 128; substantive due process and, 54, 111
Private action, in racial discrimination: 180, 185, 189, 191, 199, 207–213; case illustrations, 209–213
Privileges and immunities clause: 27, 33, 63, 241
Probable cause: 150, 153, 155, 156, 157
Procedural due process: 23–27, 39, 50
Procreation: 81, 113
Proof: *see* Burden of proof
Property rights: 31, 32, 52; case illustrations, 33–36; personal liberty and, 38, 48
Proscription and prescription, in voting rights cases: 200–202
Prurient interest: 108
Public accommodations: 207
Public demonstrations: *see* Demonstrations
Public facilities: 206
Public figure: 101–103

Public passages, obstructing: 117, 118
Punishment: 140, 164; cruel and unusual, 71, 146, 161; death penalty, 161–165

Quartering of soldiers: 69, 81

Race relations: 71, 78, 180
Racial discrimination: *see* Discrimination
Rankin, J. Lee: 175
Ray, James Earl: 96
Real, Manuel L.: 185
Reasonable classification doctrine: 175
Reasonable doubt: *see* Beyond a reasonable doubt
Reconstruction Era: 186, 188–190
Redistricting: 174, 202–206
Red scare: 98–99
Regulatory power, state: 33–34, 51
Rehnquist, William H.: 55, 78–79, 221
Roosevelt, Franklin D.: 37, 193
Religion: 120–127; establishment of, 69, 120, 122; exercise of, 67, 68, 69, 125–126
Report of the President's Commission on Law Enforcement and Administration of Criminal Justice (1967): 156–157
Reports and Institutes (Coke): 28
Reserve clause: 72
Reverse discrimination: 211, 212–213
Revolutionary Age: 43
Rights, assertion of: 239–240; *see also* Fundamental rights; Individual rights; Peripheral rights
Rousseau, Jean-Jacques: 244
Rule of law principle: 20

Runyon, Russell and Katheryne: 184
Russo, Anthony J.: 100

St. Augustine: 47
Sanford, Edward T.: 44, 45, 47
Santayana, Georges: 246
Saturday Press, The: 86, 87, 90
Search and seizure: *see* Unreasonable search and seizure
Search warrants: 149, 151
Second Amendment, keep and bear arms: 69
Second-tier test: *see* Strict scrutiny test
Sedition Act (1798): 15, 91, 97, 103
Sedition: 95–100; case illustrations, 99–100; McCarthy era, 98–99; politics of containment, 98
Seditious expression: 91–92, 93, 95, 103
Segregation: on buses, 173, 206; *de facto*, 184, 215; *de jure*, 184, 186, 215; in education, 173, 175, 176, 185, 214–218; in employment, 196, 212, 218; in housing, 206; and intent, 213–222; interdistrict and intradistrict patterns of, 184; "Jim Crow" system, 192; in North, 183, 216; in private acts, 207–213; separate but equal, 177, 206; States and, 177
Selective incorporation: 56, 64–70; dual standard in, 67–68
Self-incrimination: 67, 70, 138, 145, 149, 150, 152, 156
Sentencing: 162
Separate but equal doctrine: 173, 176, 177, 181, 206
Separation of Church and State: 121–122, 125
Separation of powers: 20

Seventh Amendment, jury trial in civil cases: 71, 80
Sex, and obscenity: 108
Sex discrimination: 196, 221–222, 225, 227
Sharecropping system: 191–192
Sherman Anti-Trust Act (1890): 36
Simants, Erwin Charles: 95
Sixth Amendment: confrontation of witnesses, 67, 71; right to counsel, 67, 70, 137, 160; trial by jury, 64–65, 70, 94, 159, 214
Silver platter doctrine: 151–152
Slavery: 4, 178–179, 191
Smith Act (1940): 75–76, 99
Socialist Party: 43
Social Security Act (1935): 227
Socrates: 241
Sodomy law: 112
Solzhenitsyn, Aleksandr: 144, 245
Southern Christian Leadership Conference (SCLC): 195
Southern Independent School Association: 184
Speech, freedom of: commercial speech, 80; due process and impairment by States, 44–45, 64, 66–69, 77, 87, 92, 117, 118; limits on, 74, 89, 94, 96, 105, 107; repression of, 145; scope of, 75, 95, 103, 114, 128; speech-plus, 95, 104–105
Speech-plus: 95, 104–105
Speedy Trial Act (1974): 154–155
Spinoza: 244
Standing question: 79, 204
Stare decisis doctrine: 21–23, 175
States: discrimination and, 177, 208; police power of, 33, 35–36, 38, 44, 45, 71–73, 87, 111, 125, 177; regulatory power, 33–34, 51; reserve clause as ap-

plied to, 72; results of absorption and selective incorporation as applied to, 62–63, 69–71; state action vs. private action, 207–213; *see also* Constitutions, state
Statute of Virginia for Religious Freedom (1779): 121, 122
Sterilization: 53
Stevens, John Paul: 73, 79, 80, 125, 222
Stewart, Potter: 38, 111, 200; *Ginzburg*, 106–107; *Gregg*, 162–163; *Jones*, 211; on Pentagon Papers, 100; *Runyon*, 185
Strict scrutiny test: 60, 224–226, 228
Strikes: 36
Strong rational basis test: 226–227
Stuart, Hugh: 94–95
Student Nonviolent Coordinating Committee (SNCC): 195
Substantive due process: antecedents, 30–32; case illustrations, 33–36, 50, 52–56; as economic liberty, 32–38; growth of, 27–28; higher law background, 28–30, 39, 49–50, 56–59; implications, 58–63; new, 48, 49–63; old, 32, 39, 48; personal rights and, 51–56
Substantial relationship test: 226–227
Substantive equal protection: 28, 222
Sunday closing laws: 120, 125
Supremacy clause: 30, 201
Supreme Court, U.S.: activism in, 48, 78–79; authoritarianism, 60; cases of (*see* Table of cases); civil rights and, 175; conservatism in, 80; decision-making, 27, 29, 30, 36–37, 47,

57, 110, 217; higher law and, 8, 38, 58, 61, 228; individual rights and, 79–80; judicial review, 14–19, 21, 22, 30, 38, 78, 225–228; judicial supremacy, 19; jurisdiction, 15, 78; powers of, 17–19, 175, 176; *stare decisis*, 21–23; tests and standards used (*see* Court standards and tests)

Symbolic speech: 95, 104–105

Taft, William Howard: 234
Taney, Roger B.: 32, 60, 179
Task Force on Disorders and Terrorism: 97
Taxation: of Church property, 123; State powers of, 72
Tenth Amendment, reserve clause: 72
Terrorism, domestic: 96–97
Tests, imposed by courts: *see* Court standards and tests
Theodosis I, Emperor: 121
Third Amendment, quartering of soldiers: 69, 81, 113
Thirteenth Amendment: abolishment of slavery, 191; enforcement clause, 186, 191; private acts of discrimination, implied, 208, 210–211
Thought, freedom of: 91, 92–115
Three-prong test: 122, 124
Time magazine: 174
Tocqueville, Alexis de: 234
Toleration Act (1649): 121
Traffic citations: 150
Transportation: 206
Travel, right to: 53–54, 81
Treason: 96
Trial by jury: fair and impartial, 70, 94, 148; right to, 63, 64–65, 67, 70, 214; speedy trial, 70, 159
Truman, Harry S.: 98, 171–172

Twelfth Amendment, presidential electoral system: 197
Tyranny: 244

Unanimous verdict: 158, 159
Unions: 36
Union of Soviet Socialist Republics (USSR): 144
Universal Negro Improvement Association: 193
Unreasonable search and seizure (exclusionary rule): 67, 69, 145, 148, 149–152; case illustrations, 149–152; "fruits" of, 150

Vagueness test: 77–78, 104, 111, 117
Venue: 157
Verdict: setting aside, 159; unanimous, 158, 159
Vinson, Fred M.: 171, 174
Violent protest: 96
Voting rights: blacks, 187, 193, 197–207; legislation, 197–206
Voting Rights Act (1965): 193, 200, 209

Waiver, of constitutional rights: 138, 152
Wallace, Muhammed: 97
Wall of separation: *see* Separation of Church and State
Warrants, issuing of: arrest, 146, 153; on basis of information, 153; by court, 153; indictment by grand jury, 153; search, 149, 151
Warren, Earl: 29, 57, 174, 201, 210; *Brown*, 60, 176–177, 178; Court under, 78, 79; *Miranda*, 137–138, 139; on segregation, 27, 28
Washington, George: 3

Watergate scandal: 25, 100, 196, 245

White, Byron R: 119, 214, 226; *Davis,* 219; *Duncan,* 64–65; *Gertz,* 102; *Roemer,* 125

White Primary: 199

White supremacy: 191

Why We Can't Wait (King): 47–48

Wiretaps: 150

Witnesses: confrontation of, 67, 70; rights in obtaining, 67, 70, 146

Writ of *habeas corpus: see Habeas corpus*

Writ of mandamus: 14, 16–17

"Yellow dog" contract clauses: 36

Yick Wo: 214

Young, Wilfred M.: 136

Zealotry: 243, 244

DATE DUE

FEB 0 1 1993		
MAR 1 6 1993		
APR 1 4 2003		

DEMCO 38-297